Reformation

Reformation

A World in Turmoil

ANDREW
ATHERSTONE

LION

Published by Lion Books
an imprint of
Lion Hudson plc
Wilkinson House, Jordan Hill Road,
Oxford OX2 8DR, England
www.lionhudson.com/lion

ISBN 978 0 7459 7015 8
e-ISBN 978 0 7459 7016 5

First edition 2011

A catalogue record for this book is available
from the British Library

Cover image © The Art Archive/Alamy

Printed and bound in the UK, May 2015, LH26

For my beloved children – John, Anna, and Kate

Contents

PROLOGUE

Seeking Salvation

The sixteenth-century Reformation was one of the most dramatic and significant series of events in the history of Christianity. It sent shock waves through the western world and changed the face of Europe forever. Its impact upon the church has sometimes been likened to a second Day of Pentecost, a crucial turning point and a moment of crisis. To some, this cataclysmic rupture in the fabric of Catholic Christendom was interpreted as the labour pains of Christianity reborn. As one historian has put it, "No other movement of religious protest or reform since antiquity has been so widespread or lasting in its effects, so deep and searching in its criticism of received wisdom, so destructive in what it abolished or so fertile in what it created."[1]

The Reformation was brought to birth in different locations and at different stages by a complex permutation of factors. In part it was driven by socio-economic developments, such as urbanization, rising literacy, the creation of wealth, and popular unrest. In part the motivations were political, concerning dynastic survival, patriotism, civic pride, and independence. However, at the most fundamental level the Reformation was a theological movement. It was dominated by questions about God and the church, about life and death, heaven and hell. It divided Europe into two religious camps. "Catholics" emphasized their loyalty to the historic teaching of the old church, as represented by ecumenical councils and the pope in Rome. "Evangelicals" (from the New Testament word *evangel,* meaning "good news") claimed to have rediscovered the Christian gospel which had lain hidden during the Middle Ages. Yet the terminology was inexact. Catholics insisted they were the true guardians of the gospel, while evangelicals maintained they were the true representatives of the apostolic church.

Among the vast array of theological arguments during the Reformation, the most crucial one was about salvation: "What must I do to be saved?" Or, to put it another way, "How can humanity enjoy a relationship with Almighty God? How can men and women be assured of a place in heaven?" The evangelical reformers answered these questions in a radically different way from their Catholic contemporaries. Having re-examined the Bible texts, they came to the conclusion that salvation was a free gift from God, received through faith alone in Jesus Christ. This theological rediscovery was the founding principle of the European Reformation and had massive implications for the Christian church. Tens of thousands lost their lives, and nations went to war, over the question "What must I do to be saved?" Catholics and evangelicals offered incompatible answers, but all were agreed on the eternal significance of this most important of questions.

This book tells the story of the sixteenth-century Reformation from its origins in the European Renaissance to its dénouement in the wars of religion. It is a tale of the clash of ideologies, of men and women driven to heroic feats and desperate measures, of families and communities forever divided, of armies routed and bishops burned, of quiet scholars and trenchant preachers, of fickle kings and anarchic prophets, of courageous faith and unlikely friendships. This is the account of Christianity in crisis as the people of Europe engaged in their common quest for eternal salvation.

1

The Dawn of a Golden Age

In many ways the Christian church in Europe at the start of the sixteenth century was flourishing. The vast majority of people across the continent enjoyed participating in its activities, contributed cheerfully to its ministry, and expressed confidence in its spiritual provisions. The ancient traditions and rituals of the church shaped the daily lives of men and women in every community, whether in a prince's palace or a peasant's cottage. From cradle to grave, the church offered spiritual nourishment to every individual via the sacraments, beginning with baptism and ending with extreme unction (anointing with oil at the point of death). Religious festivals, feasts, and holy days were celebrated with enthusiasm and gave a pattern to the year, recalling significant events in the life of Jesus Christ and the Virgin Mary, or the heroic deeds of the saints. Processions, pilgrimages, and "mystery plays" (dramas of Bible narratives) provided regular entertainment and communal participation. Countless thousands travelled to the Holy Land or to Europe's major shrines to prove their dedication to God, to fulfil a vow or to seek a blessing. Churches, chapels, and monasteries dominated the landscape. Devotees gave liberally to fund the ministry of the clergy, or to build new cathedrals, chantries, colleges, and schools. Listening to sermons was also a popular pastime and large crowds flocked to hear travelling evangelists. Christianity was deeply embedded in the European way of life. The medieval church was a remarkably durable, flexible, and energetic institution, which was widely expected to go from strength to strength.

One sign of vitality was the array of innovative renewal movements which blossomed in every generation. Far from being a static and monolithic organization, the church welcomed regional diversity and encouraged new expressions of Christianity. For example, the fifteenth century saw the rise to prominence of the Brethren of the Common Life, a confraternity founded in the Netherlands by Geert Groote. Their emphasis upon private prayer and personal holiness became known as *devotio moderna* ("modern devotion"), a form of piety popular among both laity and clergy. Its theology was best expressed in *The Imitation of Christ* (c. 1418) written by Brother Thomas, a monk from Kempen in Germany.

Another sign of revitalization was the resurgence of the papacy. It had recovered from the traumas of the Papal Schism when two rival popes vied for power between 1378 and 1417 in France and Italy. The divisions were slowly healed and in the 1450s Pope Nicholas V began an ambitious project to rebuild Rome as a glorious capital city for the reunited church. His vision for a rejuvenated Vatican, with St Peter's Basilica at its heart, was maintained by his successors.

The Catholic church was also linked inextricably with the most significant renewal movement of the fifteenth century, the intellectual and cultural revolution labelled "the Renaissance" ("the Rebirth"). First associated with a network of scholars, poets, philosophers, and artists in Italy, it flowed across the Alps into the rest of Europe. The Renaissance was marked by an explosion in knowledge, creativity, and discovery in fields as diverse as history, cosmology, architecture, linguistics, geography, technology, mathematics, and political theory. It was the age of polymaths such as Leonardo da Vinci and Niccolò Machiavelli.

In Rome, the papacy demonstrated its commitment to intellectual pursuit with the founding of the Vatican Library in 1475, the largest library in Europe. Leading Renaissance artists like Botticelli, Raphael, and Michelangelo received major papal commissions to decorate the Sistine Chapel and other buildings in the Vatican. Meanwhile in Poland, the astronomer Nicolaus Copernicus, canon of the cathedral at Frauenburg (Frombork), discovered the "heliocentric" order of the universe. He circulated his mathematical calculations to friends as early as 1514, though he held back from publishing them for thirty years because they appeared to challenge the "geocentric" worldview of the Bible.

While Copernicus explored the heavens, a "New World" was opening up to European adventurers across the oceans. The Genoese colonist, Cristoforo Colombo, traversed the Atlantic on behalf of Fernando and Isabel of Aragon and Castile, and his convoy sighted land in October 1492 at what is now the Bahamas. Conquistadors soon moved beyond the Caribbean into Mexico and Peru, encountering ancient American peoples such as the Incas and the Aztecs. The discovery of this vast new continent provided unparalleled opportunities for evangelism and acquisition, winning souls for God and gold for the Spanish treasury.

Meanwhile in 1497 Vasco de Gama sailed down the west coast of Africa and around the Cape of Good Hope, sponsored by King Manuel I of Portugal, pioneering lucrative trade routes to India, China, and Japan. In Africa itself, the powerful ruler of Kongo, Nzinga Nkuvu, accepted baptism at the hands of Portuguese missionaries and was renamed King João I. Although he grew disillusioned with Christianity, his son Mvemba Nzinga (King Afonso I from 1509) was a zealous convert and established Kongo as a strategic Catholic kingdom. Catholicism was quickly becoming a global religion.

BACK TO THE SOURCES

Renaissance scholars were eager to rediscover the wisdom of ancient civilizations, especially the Greco-Roman world. With the motto *ad fontes* ("back to the sources") they sought to reappropriate classical texts which had been forgotten in medieval Europe. Re-engagement with the writings of Plato, Cicero, Seneca, Galen, and others helped to stimulate contemporary advances in philosophy, law, and medicine. The study of Greek was especially in vogue as manuscripts from the decimated Byzantine empire, which fell to Islamic conquest in 1453, began to circulate in western Europe.

This network of scholars was known as the "humanists", from *studia humanitatis*, the classical university curriculum (not to be confused with modern secular humanists). They were optimistic about the potentiality and progress of the human race, as expressed in *De Hominis Dignitate* ("*On the Dignity of Man* "), an oration from 1486 by the Florentine philosopher Giovanni Pico della Mirandola: "O great and wonderful happiness of man. It is given to him to have that which he desires and to be that which he wills."[1]

The Renaissance humanists helped to renew the theology of the Catholic church in the fifteenth and early sixteenth centuries by challenging the dominance of the "scholastics". This philosophical movement was divided into rival "schools" – most notably the *via antiqua* ("old way") associated with Thomas Aquinas and Duns Scotus, and the *via moderna* ("new way") associated with William of Ockham. Yet the scholastics held in common a desire to fuse the philosophy of Aristotle with the teaching of the Bible, exemplified by Aquinas's *Summa Theologiae* in the 1260s. Humanists began to use the name Duns – or "dunce" – as a term of abuse for stupid and pedantic authors who were well schooled in philosophy but ignorant of authentic Christianity. For example, Erasmus of Rotterdam derided the scholastics in 1499 because they "merely envelop all in darkness" and "spend their lives in sheer hairsplitting and sophistical quibbling".[2] He rejoiced in the overthrow of Aquinas and the rediscovery of New Testament Christianity, and prophesied: "we may shortly behold the rise of a new kind of golden age."[3]

One humanist who put his linguistic training to good use was the fifteenth-century Italian scholar Lorenzo Valla, who served in the court of Alfonso the Magnanimous, king of Sicily and Naples. He researched the so-called *Donation of Constantine*, a document which purported to show that in the early fourth century, Emperor Constantine the Great had bestowed the entire western half of the Roman empire upon Pope Sylvester I and his successors. The *Donation* was often used by the papacy to defend its territorial power, but Valla proved that it was a later forgery.

Next he put the Bible itself under the spotlight. In his *Collatio Novi Testamenti* he probed the accuracy of the "Vulgate", St Jerome's fifth-century Latin translation of the Bible, the standard version in use throughout western Christendom. Valla compared it with three codices of the original Greek text and noticed some significant discrepancies. For example, Jesus proclaimed at the start of his ministry, "*Metanoeite*, for the kingdom of heaven is near" (Matthew 4:17), which Jerome translated as "Do penance" instead of "Repent". This had encouraged an emphasis in the medieval church upon outward religious ceremonial instead of an internal change of heart. Likewise the angel Gabriel greeted the Virgin Mary as *kecharitomene* (Luke 1:28), which Jerome translated as "full of grace" instead of "highly favoured". This allowed Mary to be viewed as a source of divine grace and encouraged the growth of popular devotion to Mary in the Middle Ages. Valla warned that scholastic theologians such as Aquinas had fallen into error by using Jerome's mistranslations. This accusation had the potential to shake the foundations of the church, but Valla's conclusions remained buried among his manuscripts for fifty years.

BIBLE SCHOLARSHIP

Christian engagement with the original text of the Bible leaped forward at the start of the sixteenth century. Hebrew was little studied, even within the universities, but since the 1480s Johannes Reuchlin (a leading German humanist) had been collaborating with Jewish scholars to learn the language and to standardize its form in print. In 1506 he published *The Rudiments of Hebrew* (both a grammar and a lexicon), which opened the doorway to a better understanding of the Old Testament in Christian Europe.

Meanwhile another group of humanists at Alcalá University in Spain were engaged in a landmark project to publish the entire Bible in its original languages, under the guidance of Cardinal Francisco Ximenes de Cisneros, Archbishop of Toledo. It was called the "Complutensian Polyglot Bible" because Alcalá was known in Latin as "Complutum", and was printed in six folio volumes with parallel columns of Hebrew, Aramaic, Greek, and Latin. The work was dedicated to Pope Leo X, and Ximenes expressed his hope that "the hitherto dormant study of Holy Scripture may now at last begin to revive". The cardinal observed that with access to the original text, the Bible student could "quench his thirst at the very fountainhead of the water that flows unto life everlasting and not have to content himself with rivulets alone".[4] Although the volumes were printed between 1514 and 1517, they were not officially published until 1522, which allowed Erasmus to steal ahead and win the plaudits as the first person to publish the Greek New Testament.

Erasmus was the leading humanist scholar in northern Europe, a prodigious polymath, born in the Netherlands but a ceaseless traveller among the *literati* of France, England, Italy, and Switzerland. His vast array of publications included manifestos on education and eloquence, collections of proverbs, devotional and doctrinal treatises, biting satire, and volumes on philology and classical studies. His love of antiquity and early Christianity was seen in his devotion to St Jerome, whose writings he set out to edit. Erasmus called Jerome "the supreme champion and expositor and ornament of our faith", with rhetorical ability which "not only far outstrips all Christian writers, but even seems to rival Cicero himself".[5] As part of his research into Jerome's Vulgate, Erasmus mastered Greek and also tried to learn Hebrew, but stopped because he was "put off by the strangeness of the language, and at the same time the shortness of life".[6]

During his hunt for Bible codices in numerous monastic libraries and archives, he stumbled across a manuscript copy of Valla's *Collatio Novi Testamenti* at Parc Abbey near Leuven in 1504 and published it the following year. A decade later, Erasmus was ready with his own edition of the Greek New Testament, published in Basel in February 1516, alongside a revised version of the Vulgate and his annotations on the text. It was dedicated to Pope Leo X, who welcomed this biblical scholarship as a blessing to the church, encouraging its author, "you will receive from God himself a worthy reward for all your labours, from us the commendation you deserve, and from all Christ's faithful people lasting renown".[7] The first two editions sold 3,000 copies. It was a cornerstone in the Erasmian campaign not just to revive classical scholarship, but to renew the Christian church.

The most widely read section of Erasmus's ground-breaking *Novum Testamentum* was his passionate preface, *The Paraclesis*, an exhortation for Christians to re-engage with the Bible and a critique of contemporary church practice. He declared it "shameful" that those who claimed to follow Jesus Christ knew so little of his teaching, unlike Jews and Muslims who were well versed in their holy books.[8] He lamented that the church paid more attention to pagan philosophers like Aristotle and Plato, or scholastic authors like Aquinas and Scotus, than to Christ and the apostles. Religious orders such as the Benedictines, Augustinians, and Franciscans revered the rules of St Benedict, St Augustine, and St Francis but seemed to hold them in greater honour than the instructions of Christ. Likewise, Erasmus mocked those who clung to religious relics rather than the Bible:

If anyone shows us the footprints of Christ, in what manner,
as Christians, do we prostrate ourselves, how we adore them!
But why do we not venerate instead the living and breathing
likeness of him in these books? If anyone displays the tunic
of Christ, to what corner of the earth shall we not hasten so
that we may kiss it? Yet were you to bring forth his entire
wardrobe, it would not manifest Christ more clearly and truly
than the Gospel writings.[9]

He urged his readers to covet the Bible: "let us embrace it, let us continually occupy ourselves with it, let us fondly kiss it, at length let us die in its embrace, let us be transformed in it".[10]

Erasmus's favourite phrase to encapsulate the Christian message was *philosophia Christi* ("the philosophy of Christ"), which he summarized as a concern for inner piety and moral lifestyle, rather than outward religious duty or dogma. He argued that the best Christians were not necessarily divinity professors in the university or monks in the cloister, but anyone who modelled virtue, "even if he should be a common labourer or weaver... Only a very few can be learned, but all can be Christian, all can be devout, and – I shall boldly add – all can be theologians".[11] Unlike Aristotelian philosophy, which required intricate knowledge of obscure academic literature, he believed that the Christian gospel could be easily understood by the learned and the unlearned alike. All that was required was "a pious and open mind, possessed above all with a pure and simple faith".[12] This led logically to Erasmus's most radical proposal, at the heart of *The Paraclesis*, that the Bible should be widely distributed in accessible translations. He proclaimed:

I would that even the lowliest women read the Gospels and
the Pauline Epistles. And I would that they were translated
into all languages so that they could be read and understood
not only by Scots and Irish but also by Turks and Saracens...

Would that, as a result, the farmer sing some portion of
them at his plough, the weaver should hum some parts of
them to the movement of his shuttle, the traveller lighten the
weariness of the journey with stories of this kind! Let all the
conversations of every Christian be drawn from this source.[13]

VERNACULAR BIBLES

When Erasmus appealed in *The Paraclesis* for the Bible to be
translated into every language and given to every Christian,
his opponents labelled him a "Wycliffite" and a "Hussite", after
two notorious sects. John Wycliffe, a Catholic priest at Oxford
University, argued in *The Truth of Holy Scripture* (1378) that all the
teaching of the church should be tested against the Bible, which
should be translated into the vernacular. With this encouragement
his followers produced an English translation from the Latin
Vulgate in 1384, and a second version in 1396, which was used in
secret by the Wycliffite (or "Lollard") movement throughout the
fifteenth century. His theology was also influential at Prague in
Bohemia among the disciples of Jan Hus and in 1415 both men were
condemned by the ecumenical Council of Constance (Konstanz) on
the Swiss-German border. Hus was burned at the stake, but Wycliffe
had already been dead for thirty years so his corpse was exhumed
and burned instead.

The threat of Lollardy persuaded the Archbishop of Canterbury to
forbid the translation of the Bible into English, a ban which remained
in force until the 1530s. However, many other European languages
had vernacular translations before the end of the fifteenth century. A
German translation of the whole Bible was first published in Strassburg
in 1466 and there had been nine versions by 1483. Translations were
also produced in Italian, Dutch, Czech, French, Catalan, Spanish,
and Portuguese before 1500. However, these were all made from the
Latin Vulgate. Erasmus proposed beginning with the original biblical

languages of Hebrew and Greek, and for translations to be available to every Christian, not just to the literary elite.

The publication of Bibles was made possible by one of the great technological breakthroughs of the fifteenth century, the mechanical movable-type printing press. It was pioneered by Johannes Gutenberg, a goldsmith at Mainz in Germany, who printed 180 copies of the "Gutenberg Bible" (the Latin Vulgate) in 1455. Within half a century there were sixty printing presses in Germany and approximately 150 in Italy, mostly producing standard Catholic literature. The machine was exported from Cologne to England by William Caxton, merchant and diplomat, in the mid 1470s. Printed books enabled the rapid dissemination of ideas and quickly replaced expensive handwritten manuscripts. In the early sixteenth century this new technology was eagerly harnessed for Reformation propaganda.

PIETY AND PROFANITY

Humanist scholars and preachers not only promoted biblical study, but used their literary and oratorical skills to demand a wider reformation of the Christian church. Despite the vibrancy and popularity of contemporary religion, they identified many areas which were in need of improvement. Their most frequent targets were scholasticism, superstition, and hypocrisy. Erasmus led the way with his *Enchiridion Militis Christiani* ("*Handbook of the Christian Soldier*"), first published in 1503. It was a manual on interior spirituality, with an emphasis on moral behaviour rather than outward religious observance. In the preface to the new 1518 edition he famously declared, "*Monachatus non est pietas*" ("Being a monk is not the same as piety").[14] Erasmus insisted that true Christianity was not about "being an assiduous churchgoer, prostrating yourself before the statues of the saints, lighting candles, and repeating a certain number of prayers... God is appeased only by invisible piety".[15] Unlike later reformers, he did not call for the abolition of pilgrimages or relics, but reminded his readers that this external devotion was less important than godly behaviour:

What is the use of being sprinkled with a few drops of holy
water as long as you do not wipe clean the inner defilement
of the soul? You venerate the saints, and you take pleasure in
touching their relics. But you disregard their greatest legacy,
the example of a blameless life.[16]

The same point was made by Konrad Mutianus Rufus, a leading German humanist, who denounced the common belief that religious performance would win divine reward, observing that "only the ignorant seek salvation in fasts".[17]

In one of the essays in his *Adages*, Erasmus unpacked this theme further. He complained that much contemporary Christianity was about outward show which cloaked all manner of sin. In particular, he assailed the hypocrisy of bishops who dressed in gleaming robes with jewel-encrusted mitres, yet look underneath "and you find nothing but a soldier, a trader, or finally a despot, and you will decide that all those splendid insignia were pure comedy".[18] Erasmus lamented that so many Christian leaders were trying to "live so as to out-heathen the heathens in their passion for heaping up wealth, their love of pleasure, their sumptuous living, their savagery in war, and almost all other vices".[19] He especially chastised the conflation of spiritual and temporal realms, denouncing those war-mongering popes and bishops who were "well armed with javelins and missiles, but absolutely unarmed with Holy Scripture".[20]

Many others shared Erasmus's assessment of the needs of the church and joined his appeal for spiritual renewal. In Saxony, for example, Duke Georg described the church as no longer the "bride of Christ" but "a stinking decayed corpse".[21] Meanwhile in England, William Melton (Chancellor of York) portrayed the clergy as indolent and ignorant, "a crop of oafish and boorish priests".[22] Soon afterwards his friend, John Colet (Dean of St Paul's Cathedral in London), launched a blistering attack on the corruption of the church at the opening of the Canterbury Convocation (a synod of clergy) in February 1512. His provocative sermon was based upon St Paul's exhortation in the New Testament, "Be not conformed to this world, but be reformed in the newness of your minds" (Romans 12:2). Colet lamented that the church had become a "foul and deformed" harlot.[23] He lambasted clerical ambition, sensuality, avarice, and worldliness, complaining that many priests were entangled in secular affairs while ignoring their spiritual duties. Among the remedies which the dean proposed were a clampdown on simony (the purchase of ecclesiastical offices), absenteeism, and sexual immorality, and improved standards for ordination candidates.

Just three months after Colet's sermon, the fifth Lateran Council was opened in May 1512, in the Basilica of St John Lateran, Rome's famous cathedral. This grand gathering of bishops and cardinals called together by Pope Julius II was primarily intended as a demonstration of papal authority, in reaction against King Louis XII of France's attempt to sponsor a council at Pisa. Nevertheless, some theologians hoped they would address the pressing need for ecclesiastical reform. At the inaugural session Egidio da Viterbo (General of the Augustinian order) exhorted the bishops to seek the help of the Holy Spirit so that the church would be "cleansed from every stain it has received and... restored to its ancient splendour and purity".[24]

The Lateran Council continued to meet for five years, until March 1517, and did issue some reform legislation concerning the discipline of clergy and the censorship of books, but these measures had little impact. It was a wasted opportunity. As the council was about to be dismissed, Giafrancesco Pico della Mirandola addressed an oration to the pope, urging him to take action:

These diseases and these wounds must be healed by you, Holy Father; otherwise, if you fail to heal these wounds, I fear that God himself, whose place on earth you take, will not apply a gentle cure, but with fire and sword will cut off those diseased members and destroy them; and I believe that he has already clearly given signs of his future remedy.[25]

These words were later seen as prophetic. Since the papacy did not appear capable of pioneering a reformation, the work would fall to others who would soon became Rome's most implacable enemies.

FOLLY AND WISDOM

In order to expose the weaknesses they perceived within the church, several humanists harnessed the genre of satire. It reached a far wider audience than any theological treatises could do. For example, in 1494 the German scholar Sebastian Brant published *Das Narrenschiff* (*"The Ship of Fools"*) in Basel, a long comic poem describing over a hundred contemporary vices. It was no coincidence that a ship was also a popular metaphor for the church.

Erasmus adopted a similar approach in *Moriae Encomium* (*"The Praise of Folly"*), published in Paris in 1511. Speaking through the voice of Folly (foolishness personified), he lampooned contemporary society, much as a court jester was able to speak unpalatable truths no one else dared to tell. He mocked the foibles of a wide selection of people, ranging from schoolmasters, lawyers, and soldiers to orators, magistrates, and princes. Yet some of Erasmus's most caustic statements were reserved for the Christian church, which he castigated at length.

Folly derided the "sea of superstition" surrounding popular piety, such as the worship of fictitious saints.[26] She denounced the hypocrisy of those who lit candles to the Virgin Mary yet cared nothing about "emulating her chastity of life, her modesty and love of heavenly things".[27] Similarly she rebuked ignorant pilgrims who neglected their wives and children in order to travel hundreds of miles to pay homage at the shrines in Jerusalem, Rome, or Santiago de Compostela in Spain. Next Folly targeted the scholastic theologians (such as the Thomists, Scotists, and Ockhamists), observing that "you'd extricate yourself faster from a labyrinth" than from their "subtle refinements" and "tortuous obscurities".[28] She also assailed the ubiquitous array of monastic orders, mocking their incomprehensible preaching, their petty rivalries, and their obsession with trivial issues such as the colour of their girdles or the breadth of their tonsures.

When addressing the highest echelons of the church, Folly was equally strident in her critique. Bishops were accused of neglecting pastoral responsibility for their flocks: "They don't even remember that the name Bishop, which means 'overseer', indicates work, care, and concern. Yet when it comes to netting their revenues into the bag they can play the overseer well enough."[29] Likewise cardinals were denounced for their avarice and their lack of desire to imitate the apostles.

When it came to the papacy, Folly showed no restraint. She drew a sharp contrast between the "pomp and pleasure" of the popes (the so-called "vicars of Christ") and the servant ministry of Christ himself.[30] She thought it ironic that the popes should boast of defending the church against its foes, when they were guilty of doing the worst damage:

As if indeed the deadliest enemies of the church were not these impious pontiffs who allow Christ to be forgotten through their silence, fetter him with their mercenary laws, misrepresent him with their forced interpretations of his teaching, and slay him with their noxious way of life![31]

This caustic humour struck a nerve and *The Praise of Folly* went through twenty editions in five years. It was translated into Czech, French, German, Italian, and English, and was the book which made Erasmus a household name throughout Europe.

Encouraged by the success of *The Praise of Folly*, Erasmus continued to give vent to his criticisms of the church in the form of satire. He may have been responsible for an anonymous tract, *Julius Exclusus*, published after the death in 1513 of Pope Julius II, the infamous "warrior pope" (although Richard Pace, an English humanist and diplomat, has also been suggested as the author).

It took the form of an imaginary dialogue between the deceased pontiff and St Peter at the gates of heaven. The pope arrived wearing his glorious papal tiara and followed by a retinue of soldiers who had been killed during his military campaigns, but St Peter was appalled:

> *You've brought twenty thousand men with you, but not one of the whole mob even looks like a Christian to me. They seem to be the worst dregs of humanity, all stinking of brothels, booze, and gunpowder. I'd say they were a gang of hired thugs... And the more closely I look at you yourself the less I can see any trace of an apostle. First of all, what monstrous new fashion is this, to wear the dress of a priest on top, while underneath it you're all bristling and clanking with blood-stained armour?*[32]

The apostle interrogated the pope about his ministry and was forced to conclude: "I won countless thousands of souls for Christ; you led as many to destruction. I was the first to teach Christ to pagan Rome; you have been a teacher of paganism in Christian Rome."[33] At first Julius threatened to excommunicate St Peter with a bull (a formal papal pronouncement), his usual method of bringing earthly princes into submission. When that strategy failed, he planned to muster an army to break down the gates of paradise, just as he had forced his way into many earthly cities during the Italian Wars.

Erasmus's subversive and iconoclastic attitude to Christian piety was evident in his popular *Colloquies*, first published in 1518, with many expanded editions throughout his life. They took the form of comic dialogues, originally designed to help schoolboys learn Latin, but Erasmus quickly realized that they were an excellent way to communicate his views on religious and moral questions to an adult audience. They formed a collection of over sixty irreverent vignettes of daily life, addressing a wide range of subjects such as courtship, marriage, warfare, education, nobility, vows, gluttony, money, and monasticism.

Several colloquies tackled the twin themes of superstition and external religion. For instance, "The Funeral" contrasts the final days of two dying men – one obsessed by pretentious ceremonial, the other meeting his end with dignified prayer and Bible-reading. "The Fish Diet", the longest colloquy, takes the form of a conversation between a butcher and a fishmonger about church decrees (like fasting) and Christian freedom. They refer to the ludicrous instance of a young nun who was raped because she refused to break the rule of silence by crying for help. In "The Shipwreck", Erasmus portrayed the panic on board a sinking boat as passengers and crew foolishly beseeched the saints to rescue them. This theme was elaborated further in his best-known colloquy, "A Pilgrimage for Religion's Sake", which mocks the gullibility of an imaginary visitor to England's major shrines at Walsingham in Norfolk and Canterbury in Kent. The benighted pilgrim paid devotion to milk from the breasts of the Virgin Mary and to precious rags on which St Thomas Becket had blown his nose, happily offering money for the privilege.

Many enjoyed Erasmus's irreverent wit. Yet others were scandalized and his writings were condemned by conservative theologians who began to doubt his orthodoxy. Nevertheless, Erasmus repeatedly insisted that he welcomed traditional dogma and devotion, if correctly taught and rightly applied. He had no desire to challenge Catholic theology but only to expose flagrant moral abuse or superstitious practice. For example, when Maarten van Dorp of Leuven University rebuked *The Praise of Folly*, Erasmus replied that he had only assailed "foolish or bad theologians who don't deserve the name" and that his attack upon the veneration of saints "always has some qualification" to show that he approved of the doctrine.[34] However, others who followed in Erasmus's wake were determined to push further than the Renaissance humanists had dared to go. New voices began to speak out, calling not just for improvement in Christian morals and education but for a deep reformation of the fundamental doctrines of the church.

2

Captive to the Word of God

In the summer of 1505 a young Saxon law student was travelling back to his university at Erfurt, in central Germany. His name was Martin Luder (or Luther), and he was destined to become one of the leading figures of the European Reformation. He was a capable student, with a promising legal career mapped out before him, but on that journey his life took a dramatic turn. Almost at his destination, he was caught in a violent thunderstorm near the village of Stotternheim and as the lightning flashed near he cried out in terror, "Help me, St Anne, and I will become a monk."[1] It was an impetuous vow, brought forth by the prospect of sudden death. According to medieval tradition, Anne was the mother of the Virgin Mary and her cult was popular in Germany, though as Luther later prosaically wrote: "I cannot find a word about her in the Bible."[2] His prayer was motivated by fright, but when he survived the thunderstorm Luther was determined to fulfil the vow. His father was angry that he should throw away his career prospects in such a rash manner, and his friends tried to dissuade him, yet he resisted their pleas. Instead of returning to his university studies, Luther entered Erfurt's Augustinian monastery.

Luther was a diligent convert to the ascetic way of life. He was admired for his piety and later recalled that he had been "a good monk and kept the rules of my order so strictly that I can say: if ever a monk got to heaven through monasticism, I should have been that man".[3] Yet his zeal in fasting and prayer was driven by an acute sense of his own sinfulness and human frailty. He was terrified by the prospect of death and of falling into the hands of a holy and wrathful God. After his ordination as a priest in April 1507, aged twenty-three, he trembled as he conducted his first mass, overawed at this encounter with "the majesty of God... I, ashes, dust, and full of sin, speak with the living, eternally true God."[4] Luther went through a period of deep spiritual turmoil, weighed down by extreme scrupulosity and a desire to placate God's anger. He later wrote:

> In the monastery I did not think about women, money, or possessions; instead my heart trembled and fidgeted about whether God would bestow his grace on me. For I had strayed from faith and could not but imagine that I had angered God, whom I in turn had to appease by doing good works.[5]

He spent many hours confessing his sins to a fellow priest in the sacrament of penance, but instead of receiving assurance of forgiveness this process only further increased his distress.

THE SACRAMENT OF PENANCE

The sacrament of penance was a key part of the spiritual discipline of the medieval church, centred on confession of sins to a priest. Following the teaching of Thomas Aquinas, the sacrament was formally defined by the Council of Florence in 1439 as consisting of four steps:

1. Contrition: heartfelt sorrow for having sinned and a determination not to sin again.
2. Confession: spoken admission to a priest of every sin committed (known as "auricular" confession).
3. Satisfaction: acts of reparation decreed by the priest, such as fasting, prayer, almsgiving and going on pilgrimage.

4. Absolution: forgiveness pronounced by the priest, often with the words "*Ego te absolvo a peccatis tuis*" ("I absolve you of your sins").

Later in the sixteenth century the Council of Trent made penance a condition of receiving communion and pronounced "anathema" (a curse to eternal damnation) on those who denied either its divine origin or its necessity for salvation.[6]

However, Martin Luther found little spiritual help in the sacrament. Sometimes he was troubled that his confession was incomplete because he had forgotten to mention every sin. On other occasions he would applaud himself, "What a fine confession you just made", and then need to return immediately to the confessional to admit his pride.[7] He recalled:

> *When I was a monk I tried with all diligence to live according to the rule, and I used to be contrite, to confess and sedulously perform my allotted penance. And yet my conscience could never give me certainty: I always doubted and said "You did not do that correctly. You were not contrite enough. You left that out of your confession." The more I tried to remedy an uncertain, weak and afflicted conscience with the traditions of men, the more each day I found it more uncertain, weaker, more troubled.[8]*

Luther was helped through these difficulties by his father confessor, Johannes von Staupitz, vicar-general of the Augustinians in Germany, whom he called "a messenger from heaven". Staupitz taught him that the word *poenitentia* in the Vulgate meant not just an act of penance, but heartfelt repentance, which begins with love for God. This revolutionized Luther's thinking and the way in which he read the Bible, as he later recalled: "formerly almost no word in the whole Scripture was more bitter to me than *poenitentia*... now no word sounds sweeter or more pleasant".[9] This new perspective also increased Luther's hostility toward the sacrament of penance which he complained had been "transformed into the most oppressive despotism". He decried auricular confession and satisfaction as "the chief workshops of greed and power".[10]

EVANGELICAL BREAKTHROUGH

As a young monk, Luther had his first encounter with the church in Rome, capital city of western Christendom. He was sent there on administrative business in late 1510 by the Augustinian order in Erfurt, and walked all the way from Germany to Italy across the Alps. During his month in Rome he celebrated mass daily at an altar in one of the city's numerous churches and rushed as a pilgrim from shrine to shrine to see the countless relics of early saints and martyrs.

Yet instead of being impressed by the holiness of Rome's Christians, he was shocked at the immorality and blasphemy he witnessed. The irreverence of fellow priests during the mass, and the number of prostitutes working among the Italian clergy, startled the pious young Saxon. He later remembered some saying openly in the streets, "If there is a hell, then Rome is built on it."[11] Luther also began to question some of the inherited traditions. Like many other pilgrims, he climbed the *Scala Sancta* ("holy stairs") at the Lateran Palace, said to be the steps on which Jesus stood during his passion in Jerusalem, which according to legend had been rescued from Palestine in the fourth century by St Helena. Luther knelt on each of the twenty-eight marble steps saying the *Pater Noster* in order to receive a "plenary indulgence", which he hoped would release the soul of his grandfather from purgatory. Yet when he reached the top of the staircase he was left wondering, "Who knows if it is really true?"[12]

Not long after his return from Rome, Luther was plucked from his Erfurt cloister to teach theology at the University of Wittenberg, recently founded by Friedrich the Wise (Elector of Saxony). His academic potential made him an attractive recruit for the faculty of this fledgling institution. In Wittenberg, Luther's primary responsibility was to lecture on the Bible alongside his spiritual mentor, Johannes von Staupitz, whom he succeeded as Professor of Biblical Theology in 1512. He began by expounding the Old Testament Psalms and over the next few years worked carefully through the New Testament letters to the Romans, Galatians, and Hebrews.

As a result of his biblical study, Luther made the greatest theological discovery of his life – the doctrine of "justification by faith alone". It transformed his understanding of salvation and of relationship with God, and brought the spiritual relief for which he longed. The dramatic breakthrough is sometimes called Luther's "Tower Experience", because he was in the tower of the Augustinian monastery at Wittenberg when the light dawned. The event is impossible to date precisely, perhaps as early as 1512 or as late as 1519.

In preparing for his university lectures, Luther frequently confronted the biblical phrase *iustitia dei* ("the righteousness of God"). He understood this expression to mean the "avenging anger" of God acting in justice to punish sinners, and the idea terrified him.[13] He was doubly distressed when he encountered the phrase not just in the Old Testament law but even in the New Testament epistles, and began to rail against God with "a savage and confounded conscience", as he later recalled: "I did not love – nay, I hated this just God who punishes sinners, and if not with silent blasphemy, at least with huge murmuring I was indignant against God."[14]

However, as Luther meditated upon St Paul's letter to the Romans and compared it with the writings of Augustine of Hippo (founding father of his Augustinian order), he made a connection between two of Paul's statements – "The righteousness of God is revealed in the gospel" and "The righteous will live by faith"

(Romans 1:17). This led Luther to the conclusion that God's righteousness was not something to be feared, but was a good gift which enabled sinners to be counted as righteous before God. The proper response was therefore not to flee from God's righteousness, but to receive it "by faith" and with gratitude.

Luther welcomed this great theological discovery as the remedy to his previous spiritual anguish. As an old man looking back thirty years later, he described it as a sudden conversion experience, like that of St Paul himself: "I felt myself straightway born afresh and to have entered through the open gates into paradise itself." Having previously hated the "righteousness" of God, he now began "to love and extol it as the sweetest word of all".[15]

"Justification by faith alone" was to become the keynote of Luther's teaching and the bedrock of the entire evangelical Reformation. This revolutionary doctrine had massive implications for the Christian life, not least because it meant that human merit and good works were no longer grounds for salvation. As Luther put it, righteousness "is not based on our works: it is founded on the promise of God, who does not lie".[16] He described it as "alien righteousness", not originating with sinful human beings but "imputed" or "credited" to their account by God.[17] Luther coined the slogan *simul iustus et peccator* to signify that the Christian was simultaneously a sinner and yet righteous in God's sight. As he explained in his lectures on Romans during 1515–16, the Christian is "always a sinner, always penitent, always righteous".[18]

THE INDULGENCE CONTROVERSY

In the midst of this personal theological crisis and process of evangelical discovery, Luther found himself suddenly thrust onto the world stage of ecclesiastical politics. The issue which ignited the furore was the controversy over "indulgences" in the autumn of 1517. These certificates of forgiveness cancelled the penalties for sin that had been imposed by the church. The papal bull *Salvator Noster* (1476) extended their scope to cover not just the living, but also the dead, so indulgences could be bought on behalf of deceased friends or family, to speed their progress through the agonies of purgatory (where Christians were said to suffer punishment for their sins before they reached heaven). In order to finance the completion of St Peter's Basilica in Rome, Pope Leo X promoted the widespread sale of indulgences across Europe, a lucrative trade.

Within Germany, the pope commissioned Archbishop Albrecht to oversee sales in the territories of Mainz and Magdeburg, and the two men made a secret agreement to split the profits. The archbishop welcomed indulgence salesmen, the most notorious of whom was Johannes Tetzel, a Dominican friar and popular preacher. Tetzel urged the local German populace to invest in indulgences to help their friends and family in purgatory, proclaiming:

> *So why are you standing about idly? Run, all of you, for the salvation of your souls... Do you not hear the voices of your dead parents and other people, screaming and saying: "Have pity on me, have pity on me... We are suffering severe punishments and pain, from which you could rescue us with a few alms, if only you would." Open your ears, because the father is calling to the son and the mother to the daughter.*[19]

One of Tetzel's memorable mottos was, "When the coin in the coffer rings, a soul from purgatory springs!"[20] He was even accused of preaching that it was possible to rape the Virgin Mary and escape God's punishment by buying an indulgence, though Tetzel denied he had ever made such a claim.

Unlike Archbishop Albrecht, Friedrich the Wise banned indulgence hawkers from entering his territories. Therefore Tetzel set up his sales booth just a few miles from Saxony in the town of Jüterbog, to entice men and women from Wittenberg across the border, with their hard-earned savings, in search of indulgences. From Luther's perspective this created a pressing pastoral crisis. He had attacked indulgences before in Wittenberg sermons, but it was no longer merely a debate about scholastic theology. Now he entered the fray as a pastor seeking to protect his parishioners from Tetzel's intrusions.

First Luther wrote to the Archbishop of Mainz, on 31 October 1517, urging him to muzzle the indulgence preachers in his dioceses and accusing him of neglecting his spiritual responsibilities:

Thus are those souls which have been committed to your care, dear Father, being led in the paths of death, and for them you will be required to render an account... Christ has nowhere commanded indulgences to be preached, only the gospel. So to what danger does a bishop expose himself, who instead of having the gospel proclaimed among the people, dooms it to silence, while the cry of indulgences resounds through the land?[21]

With this letter, Luther sent a list of ninety-five Latin "theses" (theological propositions) which he urged the archbishop to consider. The theses were a vociferous denunciation of the corruption of the church, focused especially upon the authority of the pope and the errors of the indulgence hawkers. Although they did not represent a decisive break with medieval theology, they included a series of sharp challenges to the *status quo*, such as the following:

When our Lord and Master Jesus Christ said, "Repent", he willed the entire life of believers to be one of repentance. (Thesis 1)

Those who believe that they can be certain of their salvation because they have indulgence letters will be eternally damned, together with their teachers. (Thesis 32)

Any truly repentant Christian has a right to full remission of
penalty and guilt, even without indulgence letters. (Thesis 36)

Christians are to be taught that he who gives to the poor
or lends to the needy does a better deed than he who buys
indulgences. (Thesis 43)

Christians are to be taught that if the pope knew the
exactions of the indulgence preachers, he would rather that
the basilica of St Peter were burned to ashes than built up
with the skin, flesh, and bones of his sheep. (Thesis 50)

According to one later account (an early biography by Philipp Melanchthon), Luther also publicized his theses to the world on the same day by nailing them to the door of the Castle Church in Wittenberg. Within a fortnight they had been translated into German and circulated around the empire. They were like dynamite and struck a chord with widespread anti-papal feeling, though Luther's brazen opinions also scandalized many.

Archbishop Albrecht did not deign to reply to the Wittenberg professor. He simply sent a copy of the Ninety-Five Theses to Rome, where they were scrutinized by the papal theologians. Initially it seemed to be a clash between two rival monastic orders – Luther (the Augustinian) versus Tetzel (the Dominican). This suspicion was confirmed when the earliest riposte to Luther came from one of Italy's leading Dominicans, Silvestro Mazzolini (nicknamed "Prierias"), who asserted that it was heresy to question the infallibility of the pope from whom even the Bible derived its authority. Yet soon the conflict took on international proportions, and the stakes were raised. In August 1518 a papal summons arrived in Wittenberg, commanding Luther to appear at the Vatican within sixty days to answer for his errors. Meanwhile, behind the scenes there were already plans to have him captured. The pope's legate (ambassador) in Germany was instructed to arrest the professor if he refused to recant. The Augustinians in Saxony were told to seize him and send him to Rome "bound hand and foot" in chains.[22]

ON TRIAL

Many expected Luther to be silenced by Rome and quickly forgotten – just another troublesome monk embroiled in an insignificant ecclesiastical dispute. His protests would have been nipped in the bud, had it not been for the precarious political situation in the Holy Roman Empire. The empire was a grouping of dozens of disparate principalities, provinces, and cities, centred on modern-day Germany. At its height it encompassed modern-day Austria, the Czech Republic, Switzerland, and the Low Countries, even stretching into parts of France, Italy, and Poland. Each territory within the empire fell under the jurisdiction of a local "prince" (perhaps a duke, or count, or bishop), seven of whom had the right to elect the emperor (*Kaiser*). Luther's local prince and protector, Friedrich the Wise, exercised political clout as elector of Saxony, so the pope was reluctant to alienate him.

In many ways, Friedrich was wedded to traditional piety. He owned a remarkable collection of relics, built up over a lifetime and displayed for earnest pilgrims at the Castle Church in Wittenberg once a year. The treasures included part of Jesus' swaddling clothes, thirteen fragments from his manger, a piece of gold brought by the Magi, a strand from Jesus' beard, a morsel of bread from the Last Supper, and a thorn from the crown of thorns. There was a twig from Moses' burning bush, four hairs from the Virgin Mary, and a tooth from St Jerome. The collection encompassed over 19,000 bones from Christian saints and martyrs, including St Chrysostom, St Augustine, and King Canute. Devout pilgrims who viewed the relics were granted indulgences calculated in total to reduce the time spent in purgatory by 1,902,202 years and 270 days.[23]

Nevertheless, Prince Friedrich was eager to assert the independence of Saxony from Italian jurisdiction. He was also concerned to protect the academic freedom of his university in Wittenberg. Friedrich therefore refused to allow Luther to be taken to Rome, insisting that as a German theologian he should be tried by a German court. Pope Leo X was reluctant to provoke the prince, because he hoped to influence Friedrich's vote in the imminent imperial election.

As a compromise solution, Luther was sent in October 1518 to the imperial parliament (*Reichstag* or "Diet") at Augsburg, in southern Germany. There he was interrogated in private over three days by the papal legate, Cardinal Cajetan, an Italian Dominican and devotee of Thomas Aquinas. Again and again the cardinal urged Luther to retract his views about indulgences and the authority of the pope, but he made no headway. The professor wrote to a friend in Wittenberg that Cajetan "will hear nothing from me except, 'I recant, I revoke, I confess that I erred', which I would not say."[24] He complained that the cardinal "produced not one syllable of Scripture" but had merely relied on the scholastic theologians.[25] Cajetan denounced Luther as a heretic and exhorted Prince Friedrich either to send him to Rome or chase him from Saxony. There were hints that Luther might be kidnapped by the pope's allies, so he made his way hurriedly home from Augsburg in fear for his life.

The next time Luther ventured away from the safety of Electoral Saxony was in June 1519 when he crossed the border into neighbouring Ducal Saxony (under the rule of Duke Georg the Bearded, cousin of Friedrich the Wise). A theological disputation was arranged at Leipzig between two rival university professors, Andreas von Karlstadt from Wittenberg and Johann Eck from Ingolstadt. Luther also made the journey as Karlstadt's adviser, eager to face Eck with whom he had already quarrelled in print. Eck's book attacking the Ninety-Five Theses was filled, complained

Luther, with "nothing but the foulest abuse… nothing less than the malice and envy of a maniac".[26] He had recently called Eck "that little glory-hungry beast".[27]

The debate lasted almost three weeks and Luther soon took centre stage. His key message was that Christian doctrine was not defined by the pope or church councils but by the Bible, which was "the infallible word of God" by which all teaching must be judged.[28] Eck insisted it was heresy to question allegiance to the pope, but Luther observed that the early church and the Greek church had never recognized the authority of Rome – it was therefore possible to challenge the pope and remain a faithful Christian. In private correspondence he had already begun to wonder whether the pope might be "the Antichrist himself… so miserably is Christ (that is, the truth) corrupted and crucified" by papal decrees.[29] As anticipated, the University of Leipzig awarded the victory to Eck, who wrote to the pope urging official action against Luther. Next the universities of Cologne and Leuven pronounced against him, and his books were burned in many towns across Europe.

BREATHING SPACE

Luther was a prodigious author and a ceaseless stream of writings poured from his pen. From 1517 until his death in 1546 he published on average one work every two weeks, many of them significant treatises. As the ecclesiastical authorities in Rome tried to decide how best to handle this obstreperous monk, he was given invaluable breathing space to think more deeply about the implications of his new theological principles. During the final months of 1520 Luther published three highly influential tracts, laying out his early Reformation agenda for the whole world to take note.

To the Christian Nobility of the German Nation was addressed to Emperor Charles V and the local princes and knights of the Holy Roman Empire. It was a political manifesto appealing directly to

German national pride in the face of Italian tyranny, and opened with the bold words, "The time for silence is past, and the time to speak has come."[30]

Luther argued that it was the duty of secular rulers to reform the church because the bishops had abdicated responsibility. He proclaimed that according to the Bible every Christian was a "priest", so there was no spiritual distinction between clergy and laity, or religious and secular: "all are truly priests, bishops, and popes… A cobbler, a smith, a peasant – each has the work and office of his trade, and yet they are all alike consecrated priests and bishops".[31] Therefore the church was not exempt from temporal jurisdiction, and even the pope was not above the emperor. The treatise went on to outline numerous urgent areas in which change was needed. It appealed for the reform of monasteries and universities, and the abolition of clerical celibacy, masses for the dead, indulgences, obligatory fasts, the canonization of saints, papal taxes, and pilgrimages to Rome.

Luther also launched a fierce assault upon the ecclesiastical authorities, assailing the Roman curia (the papal court) as "a swarm of parasites", guilty of avarice. He asserted that the cardinals were "most unversed in Christian things. They do not seek to save souls, but, like all the pope's henchmen, only their own power, profit, and prestige."[32] However, he reserved his fiercest invective for the pope himself: "Even the rule of the Antichrist could not be more scandalous… in Rome the devil himself is in charge."[33] This sentiment was to become typical of Luther's polemical writings. He quickly concluded that the Roman hierarchy was leading the people of Europe away from the evangelical gospel, and thus imperilling their eternal salvation. Therefore he was determined to fight the papacy tooth and nail.

Two months later, Luther developed these themes in *The Babylonian Captivity of the Church*, a full-scale attack upon the sacramental system. According to Catholic teaching there were seven sacraments (as outlined in Peter Lombard's *Sentences* in the twelfth century) – baptism, confirmation, penance, Eucharist, ordination, marriage, and extreme unction. Yet now Luther set about demolishing this entire ecclesiastical framework. He asserted that two conditions were necessary for a true sacrament – a divinely instituted visible symbol (such as water, or bread and wine), attached to the gospel promise of forgiveness of sins. On this basis there were only two true sacraments, baptism and the Eucharist, although Luther was initially willing to include penance as well.

Much of the treatise was given over to exposing contemporary abuses of the Eucharist, such as the withdrawal of wine from the laity. He attacked transubstantiation as "a monstrous word and a monstrous idea" and denounced the doctrine of mass sacrifice (that Jesus Christ is re-sacrificed by the priest on the altar in a re-enactment of his death at Calvary) as "by far the most wicked abuse of all", as it undermined the doctrine of grace.[34] With its sumptuous vestments, secret gestures, and intricate chants, the Eucharist had departed from the simplicity of the New Testament.

As usual, Luther laid the blame for these abuses at the door of the authorities in Rome: "Blindness, sheer blindness, reigns among the pontiffs... Being wolves, they masquerade as shepherds, and being Antichrists, they wish to be honoured as Christ." Christians should therefore throw off the yoke of the papacy because it had "extinguished faith, obscured the sacraments and oppressed the gospel; but its own laws, which are not only impious and sacrilegious, but even barbarous and foolish, it has decreed and multiplied without end. Behold, then, our miserable captivity."[35]

There was a deliberate change of tone in Luther's next treatise, entitled *The Freedom of the Christian*, in which he explored the relationship between grace and works in the life of a believer. He reiterated his revolutionary idea that "faith alone, without works, justifies, frees, and saves". Nevertheless, he insisted that Christians were not released from the obligation to do good works – indeed those who had experienced salvation would automatically serve their neighbours out of "spontaneous love" in obedience to God. He summed up this teaching in an apparent paradox: "A Christian is a perfectly free lord of all, subject to none. A Christian is a perfectly dutiful servant of all, subject to all."[36]

The Freedom of the Christian expressed the heart of Luther's Reformation message about salvation, and in an act of apparent conciliation he dedicated it to the pope "as a token of peace and good hope".[37] The treatise was accompanied by an open letter, deliberately ironic, in which Luther portrayed Leo X as an innocent man surrounded by evil advisers:

> *The Roman church, once the holiest of all, has become the*
> *most licentious den of thieves, the most shameless of all*
> *brothels, the kingdom of sin, death, and hell. It is so bad that*
> *even Antichrist himself, if he should come, could think of*
> *nothing to add to its wickedness. Meanwhile you, Leo, sit as*
> *a lamb in the midst of wolves and like Daniel in the midst of*
> *lions... How can you alone oppose these monsters?*[38]

Here I stand!

Pope Leo X was not placated by Luther's patronizing protestations of sympathy. From Rome he had already issued a papal bull on 15 June 1520 entitled *Exsurge Domine* ("Arise, O Lord") which condemned Luther's teaching as a "poisonous virus".[39] It listed forty specific errors and called upon the professor to appear in Rome within sixty days or face excommunication. The bull eventually arrived in Wittenberg in October and exactly sixty days later – on 10 December – Luther's supporters arranged a bonfire onto which volumes of scholastic theology were ceremonially cast. The writings of Eck were consumed by the flames, as were several editions of canon law, the legal foundation of the whole Roman ecclesiastical system. Luther himself mingled with the excited crowd and quietly placed a printed copy of the papal bull into the pyre with the words, "Because you have confounded the truth of God, today the Lord confounds you. Into the fire with you!"[40]

It was a declaration of war and there was now no turning back. The pope responded on 3 January 1521 with a second bull, *Decet Romanum Pontificem* ("It Befits the Roman Pontiff"), excommunicating not just Luther but his followers too. He denounced the reformer as "the slave of a depraved mind", guilty of leading a "pernicious and heretical sect".[41] By custom, Luther should now have been handed over to the secular authorities and executed.

Instead, Friedrich the Wise continued to insist that Luther deserved a proper hearing before a German court. The preacher was therefore summoned to appear before the next imperial Diet, meeting in the city of Worms, presided over by Charles V, the new Holy Roman emperor. Luther was promised safe passage, but knew that he might not escape Worms alive. Despite his fear, he told a friend:

> *If God does not want to preserve me, then my head is of slight importance compared with Christ, who was put to death in greatest ignominy – a stumbling block to all, and the ruin of many. No one's danger, no one's safety can be considered here. We must rather take care that we do not expose the gospel to the derision of the godless… because we do not dare confess what we have taught and are afraid to shed our blood for it.*[42]

Ominously, the emperor issued a decree commanding that Luther's writings be confiscated and burned, but the rebel was determined to face him. He insisted he would go to Worms "in spite of all the gates of hell" and told Prince Friedrich, "Had I then known that as many devils were lying in wait for me as there were tiles on the roofs, I should nevertheless have leaped into their midst with joy."[43]

Luther appeared before the emperor and German princes at the Diet on Wednesday, 17 April 1521. He was not to be allowed to debate, but only to answer two simple questions: firstly, "Are these your books?" and secondly, "Will you recant?" When the titles of his publications were read out, Luther freely admitted that he was the author. Yet over the second question he surprised the court by asking for more time to think, because it was a crucial matter "of faith and the salvation of souls, and because it concerns the divine Word".[44] The princes retorted that Luther had had plenty of time to consider his answer before arriving in Worms, but nonetheless he was granted one more day.

The next afternoon he returned to a crowded assembly where onlookers pressed together and there was no space for anyone to sit except the emperor himself. Would Luther retract his books? Instead of giving a simple "yes" or "no" answer, he drew distinctions between his various publications. Some of them addressed Christian morals "simply and evangelically" and were welcomed even by his foes. To retract these would be to condemn "the very truth upon which friends and enemies equally agree". Other books challenged the papacy and to withdraw these opinions would only bolster Rome's "wholly lawless and unrestrained kingdom of wickedness" which held Germany in bondage. A third group of books attacked individuals and Luther confessed that some might be too vitriolic in tone, but that was no reason to ban them.

Nevertheless, he proclaimed that if the court could expose his errors with proof from the Bible, then he would happily renounce them and be "the first to cast my books into the fire".[45] He concluded: "I must say that for me it is a joyful spectacle to see that passions and conflicts arise over the word of God. For that is how the word of God works! As the Lord Jesus said, 'I came to send not peace, but a sword.'"[46]

Luther's interrogator, Johann von der Ecken (chief secretary of the Archbishop of Trier), warned him not to pretend that he was wiser than all the teachers of the church and had a better knowledge of the Bible than they. He demanded that Luther recant without further equivocation, to which the professor replied:

Unless I am convinced by the testimony of the Scriptures or by clear reason (for I do not trust either in the pope or in councils alone, since it is well known that they have often erred and contradicted themselves), I am bound by the Scriptures I have quoted and my conscience is captive to the Word of God. I cannot and I will not retract anything, since it is neither safe nor right to go against conscience. May God help me! Amen.[47]

According to published versions of this speech, which circulated far and wide, Luther was said to have broken out from Latin into German with the words, "Here I stand. I can do no other."[48] When the questioning was over, he threw up his hands in triumph, exclaiming, "I have come through, I have come through!"[49] Yet some of the Spaniards in the court were heard to shout, "To the fire! To the fire!"[50]

The following day Emperor Charles delivered his verdict. Like his ancestors before him, he was determined to protect the Catholic faith and to root out heresy. He would honour his guarantee of safe-passage, but once Luther arrived back in Wittenberg he would face the wrath of the empire. The reformer set out for the long journey home in some trepidation, guarded by twenty horsemen. Yet when they reached Thuringia, the convoy was attacked in a forest outside Eisenach. Luther was kidnapped, and bundled away by men armed with swords and bows. He disappeared from sight, and some thought he had been murdered. Albrecht Dürer, the German painter, lamented in his diary: "O God, if Luther be dead who will proclaim the holy gospel so clearly to us?"[51]

Meanwhile, back in Worms the imperial Diet drew to a close. With the help of Cardinal Girolamo Aleandro (the papal nuncio),

Emperor Charles drew up a final edict, proclaiming that Luther was to be "held in detestation… as a limb severed from the Church of God, the author of a pernicious schism, a manifest and obstinate heretic". He was to be refused food and lodging, or any other practical assistance. His books were to be burned and "utterly destroyed". His friends and sympathizers were to be attacked and have their property seized. Luther himself was to be captured, wherever he was hiding, and sent to the emperor under tight security for proper punishment.[52] Yet Erasmus observed with prescience: "The burning of his books will perhaps banish Luther from our libraries; whether he can be plucked out of men's hearts, I am not so sure."[53]

Troubles brewing in Wittenberg

Rumours soon began to circulate that Luther had not been assassinated, but had colluded in a "kidnap" staged by friends of Friedrich the Wise. For his own safety, the reformer had been taken in secret to Wartburg Castle, near Eisenach. There he grew his hair (to cover his monk's tonsure) and a beard, dressed as a knight, and went under the pseudonym "Junker Jörg" ("Squire George"). While exiled in this benign prison, which he called "my wilderness", Luther continued to write at great speed.[54] He churned out new treatises on monastic vows, auricular confession, and the misuse of the mass, and also began to translate the Bible into German. Although sidelined from the action, Luther urged his allies to push forward with the Reformation campaign he had launched: "I have bruised the head of the serpent, why don't you try to stamp on its body?"[55]

However, back in Wittenberg all was not well. Devoid of Luther's firm leadership, the reform movement began to fragment. His chosen deputy was Philipp Melanchthon, a brilliant Greek scholar at the university, who in 1521 published his *Loci Communes* ("*Common Places*"), bringing some systematic order to the evangelical theology scattered chaotically through Luther's works. Luther went as far as to say of the *Loci Communes,* "Next to Holy Scripture there is no better book."[56] Yet Melanchthon was a young man with the temperament of a quiet scholar, not a leader, and was quickly pushed aside.

Instead, the initiative was seized by his older colleague, Professor Karlstadt, supported by a former Augustinian monk, Gabriel Zwilling. They sought to drive forward the Reformation further and faster than before. Karlstadt began to celebrate the mass without priestly vestments, and administered both bread and wine to the people, with a simplified liturgy. He attacked the use in worship of images, musical instruments, and Gregorian chant, which he maintained "separates the spirit from God".[57] To demonstrate his freedom from vows of celibacy, Karlstadt publicly celebrated his marriage in January 1522 to Anna von Mochau, a fifteen-year-old girl.

At the same period a group of self-proclaimed "prophets" arrived in Wittenberg from the nearby town of Zwickau, led by Nikolaus Storch, a local weaver. They claimed to receive dreams and visions directly from God and began to preach radical doctrines such as the abolition of infant baptism. Evangelical unity was beginning to fracture, and Luther wrote in distress from his hiding place: "I have been waiting for Satan to attack this sensitive spot – but he decided not to make use of the papists. Now he is making efforts in and among us evangelicals to produce the worst conceivable schism. May Christ quickly trample him under his feet."[58]

In this atmosphere of leaderless theological ferment, riots broke out in Wittenberg and opponents of reform were threatened with violence. Prince Friedrich and the city council feared that the situation would unravel into anarchy. As reports of these spiralling tensions reached Wartburg Castle, Luther could bear his enforced seclusion no longer. Dismissing concerns for his safety, he returned to Wittenberg in early March 1522, after almost a year's absence.

There he immediately set about restoring order in the city, with a series of punchy sermons preached on eight consecutive days in the City Church. They became known as the "Invocavit Sermons", because the first was delivered on Invocavit Sunday (the first Sunday in Lent). Luther's visual appearance symbolized his theological message. He entered the pulpit in traditional clerical dress, cleanly shaven, with the monk's tonsure returned to his scalp. His key theme was that reform should take place patiently, at a pace which would carry along as many people as possible. They should be carefully weaned from Catholic piety rather than "dragged away from it by the hair... We must first win the hearts of the people."[59]

Luther insisted that the right method of Reformation was not fractious agitation, but clear and careful teaching of the Christian gospel: "In short, I will preach it, teach it, write it, but I will constrain no man by force, for faith must come freely without compulsion." Furthermore, he cautioned the Wittenbergers not to "make liberty a law".[60] In the Christian life there were many matters of indifference (*adiaphora*), neither forbidden nor commanded – such as marriage, monastic obedience, and images of saints. Evangelicals must allow freedom in these areas, Luther insisted. In a remarkable statement, given his years of hardship, the reformer scolded his recalcitrant congregation: "of all my enemies who have opposed me up to this time none have brought me so much grief as you".[61]

The Invocavit Sermons re-established Luther's control over the religious life of Wittenberg, as the inhabitants fell into line. The Zwickau prophets were dismissed as fanatics and quickly silenced. Karlstadt was banned from preaching and left the city with his reputation in tatters. He settled briefly as pastor of nearby Orlamünde, where he continued to usher in his iconoclastic reforms, but Luther chased him away from there too. Not many years before, the two men had been close evangelical allies, but now Luther denounced Karlstadt as "our worst enemy", possessed by "a rebellious, murderous, seditious spirit".[62] In return, Karlstadt assailed Luther as a half-hearted reformer, who was really no better than the pope.

Luther had reclaimed power and would never again let it fall from his grasp. His popularity and prestige continued to increase at a great rate, as the figurehead of the evangelical movement in Germany. Yet even Luther's mighty leadership could not restrain the powerful centrifugal forces at work within the Reformation. Within Wittenberg dissent was silenced, but fragmentation soon exploded to the surface elsewhere.

3

The Sharpened Sickle of Judgment

Thomas Müntzer was one of Martin Luther's earliest disciples in Saxony. The former priest owed his conversion to his Wittenberg mentor, acknowledging that it was through Luther's teaching that he had been "brought to birth by the gospel".[1] Yet the two men became violent enemies when their visions for the Reformation began to diverge radically. Müntzer brought the evangelical movement in Germany to the brink of disaster, as he became embroiled in apocalyptic warfare which ended in the slaughter of thousands.

On Luther's recommendation Müntzer was appointed as a pastor in May 1520 at Zwickau, not far from Wittenberg, but before long he proved a disruptive influence. His message was aggressively anticlerical, demanding the expulsion of all Catholic priests. Soon his Lutheran allies grew alarmed at his vitriol and began to chastise him for preaching "nothing but slaughter and blood" and for his "frenzied attacks on all and sundry".[2] The Zwickau authorities lost patience with Müntzer's ceaseless agitation and threw him out after less than a year, so he turned his back on Germany and travelled to Prague, the capital of Bohemia.

It was a strange choice of venue, since he did not speak Czech, but perhaps he was attracted by the legacy of the Bohemian reformer, Jan Hus, who had been burned at the stake in Prague in 1415. There Müntzer issued his *Prague Manifesto* in November 1521, addressed to the Christians in the city, overflowing with vehement denunciations of the clergy. He spoke abusively of "pseudo-spiritual monks", "donkey-fart doctors of theology" and "hell-based parsons", calling them "servants of Beelzebub", hypocrites and seducers ordained by the devil and fit only for "the abyss of hell". He likened the church to "a madam in a whore-house" and chastised "the brothel of Rome".[3] Müntzer proclaimed: "God will pour forth his invincible wrath over such arrogant people, hardened like blocks of oak, callous to all good… they are a pack of devils… there is no people under the sun who are a greater enemy of the living word of God than they."[4] He believed that God spoke directly to human hearts by his Holy Spirit, rather than via the dead letter of Scripture, and warned that the clergy were leading people astray because they knew their Bibles but not the voice of God. The manifesto ended with chilling words:

> In our time God wants to separate the wheat from the chaff…
> All the villainy, even in the highest places, must come to
> light… The time of the harvest is at hand! Thus God himself
> has appointed me for his harvest. I have made my sickle sharp,
> for my thoughts are zealous for the truth and my lips, skin,
> hands, hair, soul, body and my life all damn the unbelievers.[5]

The reformer saw it as his role to purge the church of its godless leadership, just as Elijah exterminated the prophets of Baal in the Old Testament.

Unsurprisingly, such sentiments provoked the hostility of the Prague authorities. They put Müntzer under house arrest and then expelled him from their city in early December 1521. He returned to Germany as an itinerant preacher and served for a few months as chaplain at a Cistercian nunnery near Halle, but was again thrown out. With an undiminished sense of his divine vocation, Müntzer wrote once more with heightened apocalyptic imagery: "Let all the tares shoot up as much as they like; they will all have to come under the flail with the pure wheat; the living God is sharpening his sickle in me so that I will later be able to cut down the red poppies and the little blue flowers."[6]

The Satan of Allstedt

Having catastrophically failed in his attempts to reform both Zwickau and Prague, Müntzer was given a third opportunity to develop his revolutionary ideas in April 1523 when he was appointed pastor of Allstedt, a small town with about 600 inhabitants. Here he came under the protection of Duke Johann of Thuringia (younger brother of Luther's patron, Friedrich the Wise), who welcomed the Reformation cause. Müntzer immediately began to draw large crowds from miles around to his fiery preaching at St John's Church, sometimes with a congregation of 2,000 people on Sundays. The other pastor in Allstedt, Simon Haferitz at St Wigberti's Church, also threw his weight behind Müntzer's message and together they sought to establish a purified Christian community.

Some of the preachers' vitriol was directed against their local Catholic opponents. For example, when Count Ernst von Mansfeld began to restrict reformed preaching in his territories, Müntzer challenged him to come to Allstedt for disputation and promised: "I will deal with you a thousand times more drastically than Luther with the pope."[7] In March 1524, on Maundy Thursday, a gang of arsonists burned down the nearby chapel at Mallerbach, famous for its shrine to the Virgin Mary, with Müntzer's approval. Yet when the Saxon princes tried to placate the offended Catholics, the reformer turned upon them too. He was rumoured to have called Elector Friedrich an "old greybeard with as much wisdom in his head as I have in my backside". Meanwhile Haferitz proclaimed that "our princes are those very people who endowed these convents and churches, which are nothing but brothels and murder-pits".[8] As tensions mounted, there was a brief but dramatic stand-off between local citizens and Duke Johann's representatives in Allstedt in mid-June 1524. The town council rallied the inhabitants to defend the walls, even arming women with pitchforks in fear of assault.

A few weeks later, Müntzer was given an opportunity to defend his views before Duke Johann himself. The duke, with his son (Prince Johann Friedrich) and their entourage, stayed overnight in Allstedt Castle en route to their home at Weimar. The reformer was allowed to preach to the court, which included several government officials from Saxony, and soon published an extended version of his address for wide circulation, popularly called *Sermon to the Princes*.

It was an exposition of Daniel chapter 2, one of the best known apocalyptic passages in the Old Testament about God's wrath and the overthrow of nations. He warned that the Christian church was being "devastated by ravaging wolves" and "the great blubbering of the unsaved scribes". In a startling image, he portrayed the religious and secular authorities as "eels and snakes copulating together in a heap". As in his *Prague Manifesto*, Müntzer proclaimed that preachers who are not receptive to God's "inner word", received directly from the Holy Spirit, do not know how to say anything essential about God even though they may have "devoured a hundred thousand Bibles". In particular, he assailed Luther for rejecting dreams and visions as a source of divine revelation, mocking him as "Brother Fattened-swine and Brother Soft-life".[9] In the passionate conclusion to his sermon, Müntzer urged the princes of Saxony to take up their swords in the cause of the gospel, just as Joshua and Jehu had done in the Old Testament:

> *Drive his enemies away from the elect, for that is your appointed task. Beloved ones, do not offer us any stale posturing about how the power of God should do it without your application of the sword. Otherwise, may the sword rust away in its scabbard on you. May God grant this!*[10]

In justification of the Mallerbach arson attack, he celebrated the destruction of pagan idols and altars as a biblical imperative, and declared it right for godless leaders, especially priests and monks, to be killed. Returning to one of his favourite images, the preacher proclaimed: "The tares must be pulled out of the vineyard of God at the time of the harvest... The angels who sharpen their sickles for the cutting are the earnest servants of God who fulfil the zeal of divine wisdom."[11]

With refugees pouring into Allstedt from other parts of Saxony, fleeing religious persecution, the situation in the town became increasingly volatile. For example, in nearby Sangerhausen supporters of the Reformation were arrested by the command of Duke Georg of Saxony (Catholic cousin of Prince Friedrich and Prince Johann). Müntzer wrote to these beleaguered evangelicals, just a week after his *Sermon to the Princes*, urging them to stand firm in the midst of suffering and tyranny, and prophesying that "the time has come when a bloodbath will befall this obstinate world because of its unbelief".[12]

Many fled from Sangerhausen to Allstedt, and Müntzer threatened that the Catholic officials would be "throttled like mad dogs" if they dared attempt to capture them.[13] A few days later he preached about King Josiah's destruction of idolatrous worship (2 Kings 23) and urged his congregation to establish a Christian League as an act of self-defence against Catholic attacks. Stirred up by this sermon, many went straight from church to the Allstedt town hall to enlist in the league. Five hundred people joined up that first Sunday, including the entire town council.

With Müntzer's shift from radical preacher to political revolutionary, the authorities in Saxony were increasingly alarmed. Luther issued a *Letter to the Princes of Saxony concerning the Rebellious Spirit*, urging them to banish Müntzer in order to keep the peace. Luther asserted that his erstwhile disciple was inspired not by the Holy Spirit but by a demonic spirit since the fruit of his ministry was the burning of churches.

The Wittenberg reformer explained: "Our calling is to preach and to suffer, not to strike and defend ourselves with the fist. Christ and his apostles destroyed no churches and broke no images. They won hearts with the Word of God, then churches and images fell of themselves." He argued that iconoclasm dealt only with outward religion, whereas the way to liberate souls was to preach the gospel. Müntzer might claim Old Testament precedent for his actions, but Luther drew attention to the ominous implications of that logic: "Indeed, if we Christians justified our damaging of churches and our violence by Jewish examples, then it would follow that we are bound to put all non-Christians to death. For the Jews were as strictly bidden to put to death Canaanites and Amorites as they were to destroy images."[14] Elsewhere Luther called his opponent the "Satan of Allstedt".[15]

In response, Müntzer composed a rambling and abusive tract, his last major publication, entitled *A Highly Provoked Defence and Answer to the Spiritless, Soft-living Flesh at Wittenberg*. He chastised Luther as "Doctor Liar" and "Father Pussyfoot", an "arrogant fool" who was motivated by envy. He labelled his enemy the "ambassador of the devil", likening him to a rabid fox and "venomous little worm".[16]

At the end of July 1524, Müntzer was summoned to Weimar along with four other officials to explain the recent unrest in Allstedt, but insisted he was only guilty of teaching the Bible. His Saxon protectors were rapidly losing patience. They gave him a final warning – that he must disband the Christian League, cease from preaching provocative sermons, stop publishing tracts, and allow the prosecution of the Mallerbach arsonists. Yet Müntzer was not willing to be silenced. Rather than wait to be thrown out, he left of his own accord. One night in early August he abandoned Allstedt for good, leaving behind his wife and baby son. Climbing over the city wall, he fled the district under cover of darkness.

THE ETERNAL LEAGUE OF GOD

Müntzer surfaced next at Mühlhausen, a large imperial city in Thuringia of about 8,500 inhabitants, and quickly found himself in trouble again. The city was still officially Catholic, but since 1523 had experienced iconoclastic riots and civic unrest, stirred up by the anticlerical preaching of Heinrich Pfeiffer, a former monk. Pfeiffer welcomed Müntzer as a co-agitator for religious and political reform, and matters came to a head in September 1524. During several days of rioting there were attacks on religious houses in which altarpieces and reliquaries were smashed, and in a show of strength, the two preachers marched out into the countryside and back again with more than 200 followers, carrying a red cross and holding aloft a naked sword. Fearing for their safety, the two bürgermeisters (mayors) and several councillors fled from the city. Pfeiffer and Müntzer's supporters drew up a list of demands – known as the "Eleven Mühlhausen Articles" – insisting that the city council make decisions only according to the Bible.

Nevertheless, these radical reformers and their popular protest movement failed to gather sufficient support. The peasants living in the seventeen dependent villages around Mühlhausen were reluctant to rally to the cause. They chastised the city dwellers for their unchristian behaviour and were abused in return as "miserable bags of maggots".[17] The village of Bollstedt was burned to the ground one morning, perhaps in retaliation for their refusal to join the protests. In the city there was uproar. Luther had sent a preacher to denounce Müntzer and the two sides assailed each other with bitter invective. Meanwhile Pfeiffer's followers in St Nicholas parish paraded around the city behind a crucifix, instructing all true Christians to join them. The city council called up reinforcements expecting a fresh outbreak of violence, and tried to reassert its authority by demanding oaths of loyalty from all citizens. Since Müntzer and Pfeiffer were largely responsible for the crisis, by popular demand they were expelled from Mühlhausen.

The exile of the radicals was brief. In a volatile atmosphere, civic opinion quickly swung back in their favour. Pfeiffer was reinstated before Christmas, after campaigning for support among peasants in the local villages. A peasant band, ready for a fight, marched on the suburbs in Pfeiffer's support and were rewarded with a defiant sermon from their champion. Müntzer, meanwhile, had been on an evangelistic tour near Lake Constance, in the Austrian territories of Klettgau and Hegau. He returned to Mühlhausen in February 1525 and was reinstalled at St Mary's Church. As the reformers continued their work, friaries and convents were assaulted, images smashed and the mass abolished. The old city council which had been hostile to their ministry was now toppled and a new "Eternal Council" was elected in its place.

Having successfully established a Christian League in Allstedt, bringing together the faithful elect in a solemn covenant against their enemies, Müntzer now repeated the experiment. His first attempt was in early March, when 2,000 men were mustered in fields outside the city, parading with full arms and artillery. He rode among the soldiers on horseback, exhorting them: "Whosoever among you is prepared to stand by God's word even unto death, and testify on oath to it, let him raise a finger; those who will not, let them step aside." Yet he was silenced by the captain of the militia, Eberhard von Bodungen, who retorted that preaching belonged in church not the countryside and protested: "Dear citizens, have you not already had your fill of oaths by the basketful, enough to hang round your necks?"[18] However, before long, Müntzer achieved his goal. He established the "Eternal League of God", a band of fellow radicals, with the motto *verbum domini manet in aeternum* ("The word of the Lord stands forever"). The organization claimed to have a spiritual purpose but was also explicitly militaristic, with captain, ensign, sergeants, corporals, piper, drummer, quartermaster, and field-surgeon. Müntzer inspired them with his apocalyptic vision of the imminent Day of Judgment, when true

Christians would do battle against God's enemies. The preacher led many from the Eternal League to their deaths in the violence which was to come.

THE PEASANTS WAR

Periodic peasant uprisings were commonplace throughout medieval Europe, usually suppressed with great brutality. In 1525 insurrection swept through much of central and southern Germany, focused on the regions of Thuringia, Franconia, and Swabia. Parts of Switzerland and Austria were also embroiled in the violence as isolated outbursts swelled together to form the so-called "Peasants War". It was the largest popular revolution Europe had ever witnessed, involving perhaps 300,000 rebels.

In many locations the peasants issued manifestos, outlining their grievances against their overlords and their demands for restitution. Best known were the Twelve Articles, widely circulated by the peasant rebels in Memmingen, an imperial city in Upper Swabia. They were drawn up in February 1525 by Sebastian Lotzer (a local tanner) and Christoph Schappeler (one of the city's evangelical reformers), with numerous scriptural quotations. The first article called for free preaching of the gospel and the right of congregations to appoint their own pastors. The rest focused upon economic injustice, addressing themes like tithes and taxes, serfdom, and forced labour, and the ownership of local forests, meadows, and rivers. Using a farming analogy, the Memmingen peasants complained: "Those who should protect and defend us have clipped and sheared us."[19] They promised to retract any of their demands if they could be proved to be contrary to the Bible.

In the wrong hands, some of Martin Luther's theological rhetoric emanating from Wittenberg could be interpreted as a mandate for political revolution and physical violence. For example, he had notoriously written in 1520:

If we punish thieves with the gallows, robbers with the sword,
heretics with fire, why do we not defend ourselves all the more
with all weapons against these perpetrators of destruction,
these cardinals, these popes, this whole filth heap of the
Roman Sodom, who are unceasingly destroying the Church of
God, and wash our hands in their blood.[20]

Likewise in *The Babylonian Captivity of the Church* he had proclaimed: "I lift my voice simply on behalf of liberty and conscience, and I confidently cry: No law, whether of men or of angels, may rightfully be imposed upon Christians without their consent, for we are free of all laws."[21] His treatise on *Secular Authority* (1523) acknowledged that princes were agents of God's wrath to punish wickedness, but also called them "the greatest fools or the worst criminals on earth", ignorant about "the salvation of souls".[22] When preaching near Wittenberg the previous year he had exhorted the congregation to resist any ruler who went against the gospel and to say, "You are no longer a prince to me; I am no longer obligated to obey you."[23]

The German peasants now appealed to Luther for guidance, so in a vain attempt to prevent bloodshed he entered the fray with his *Admonition to Peace.* At first he addressed the princes, suggesting that their tyrannical behaviour was responsible for the unrest. Indeed, Luther's own prince and protector, Friedrich the Wise, then on his death bed, freely acknowledged: "We princes do to the poor people much that is not good."[24] Luther believed the Twelve Articles from Upper Swabia were fair and just, and that the peasants were being taxed "out of their very skins". The rebellion was therefore a sign of the judgment of God against the rulers and a clarion call to repentance: "You must become different men and yield to God's word... It is not the peasants, dear Lords, who are resisting you; it is God himself." Unless the princes changed their ways, the result would be "the ruin, destruction, and desolation of Germany by cruel murder and bloodshed". Luther urged them to "fear God and respect his wrath", warning that God could easily punish them with a far smaller peasant army: "He can make peasants out of stones and slay a hundred of you by one peasant, so that all your armour and your strength will be too weak to save you." He exhorted the princes to respond to the peasants with kindness and to seek peace, not violence, which would "start a fire that no one can extinguish".[25]

Next Luther addressed the peasants, rebuking them too. He warned that false teachers, "bloodthirsty prophets of murder", had been sent among them by Satan to lead them astray. The peasant army had no right to call themselves Christians because their programme of rebellion was contrary to the gospel:

> *Christians do not fight for themselves with sword and musket, but with the cross and with suffering, just as Christ, our leader, does not bear a sword, but hangs on the cross. Your victory, therefore, does not consist in conquering and reigning, or in the use of force, but in defeat and in weakness...*[26]

Luther argued that governing authorities had divine permission to wield the sword, but the people did not. He protested that the peasants were using the evangelical gospel as a cloak to disguise their wickedness. In concluding his *Admonition to Peace*, he complained that both the princes and the peasants understood questions of justice in worldly terms. Therefore if any died in the conflict they would be eternally condemned as unbelievers. As a practical plan, the Wittenberg professor called for representatives to be chosen from the nobility and the city councils to arbitrate and settle the dispute amicably. He pleaded: "Why do you insist on filling the land with blood and robbery, widows and orphans? Oh, the devil has wicked plans!"[27]

Luther's *Admonition* came too late. Before it could be published violence erupted throughout Germany. Castles were plundered, monasteries sacked, and churches desecrated. Brigades of peasants terrorized their landlords and rulers in a campaign of looting, arson, and murder. In some districts, entire towns were put under siege as the uprising quickly spread. Shocked at the scale of the violence, Luther published a devastating treatise, *Against the Robbing and Murdering Hordes of Peasants*.

Gone was the moderation and peace-making of his *Admonition*. He now called upon the princes to fight fire with fire by unleashing their wrath against the peasant armies: "let everyone who can, smite, slay, and stab, secretly or openly, remembering that nothing can be more poisonous, hurtful, or devilish than a rebel." He likened the peasants to a mad dog which must be killed to stop it biting. They were doing Satan's work but trying to cover up their treachery by calling themselves Christians: "Thus they become the worst blasphemers of God and slanderers of his holy name… I think there is not a devil left in hell; they have all gone into the peasants. Their raving has gone beyond all measure." Luther proclaimed that it was the duty of the rulers to destroy the peasants without waiting for a judicial verdict, because they had a God-given responsibility to uphold justice:

> *He is within his rights, since the peasants are not contending any longer for the gospel, but have become faithless, perjured, disobedient, rebellious murderers, robbers, and blasphemers, whom even a heathen ruler has the right and authority to punish… This is not a time to sleep. And there is no place for patience or mercy. This is the time of the sword, not the day of grace.*

Germany's leading reformer promised that anyone who died fighting on the side of the princes would be a martyr in God's eyes, while each peasant who perished would become "an eternal firebrand of hell".[28] When the rebels were slaughtered without mercy, he was forced to deny that he had given a mandate for massacre. Yet he later confessed that his preaching had multiplied the killings: "In the rebellion, I struck all the peasants. All their blood is on my neck. But I know it from our Lord God that he commanded me to speak."[29]

THE SWORD OF GIDEON

As the violence spread, the religious radicals in Mühlhausen eagerly joined the conflagration, sensing that the Day of the Lord was close at hand. Müntzer's apocalyptic preaching provided explicit theological motivation. At the end of April 1525, he wrote to his faithful supporters in Allstedt exhorting them to action. Signing himself "a servant of God against the godless", and quoting freely from the Bible, he urged them to take up arms against God's enemies: "The time has come, the evil-doers are running like scared dogs!... Pay no attention to the cries of the godless. They will entreat you ever so warmly, they will whimper and wheedle like children. Show no pity... We cannot slumber any longer." In particular, Müntzer encouraged the people of Allstedt to overthrow the godless authorities:

> Go to it, go to it, while the fire is hot! Don't let your sword grow
> cold, don't let it hang down limply! Hammer away ding-dong
> on the anvils of Nimrod [the princes and rulers], cast down
> their tower to the ground! As long as they live it is impossible
> for you to rid yourselves of the fear of men. One cannot say
> anything to you about God as long as they rule over you. Go to
> it, go to it, while it is day! God goes before you; follow, follow![30]

This remarkable letter was one of Müntzer's most notorious productions. Shortly after the prophet's capture the following month, Luther published it in *A Shocking History and God's Judgment on Thomas Müntzer*, as further evidence of his former disciple's depravity. Elsewhere he described Müntzer as "that archdevil who rules at Mühlhausen, and does nothing except stir up robbery, murder, and bloodshed".[31]

The Mühlhausen prophets were soon on the march under the banner of their Eternal League. They joined forces with insurrectionists from Görmar and Eichsfeld, ransacking dozens of castles and convents, and plundering their wealth. The main rebel army was camped at Frankenhausen, where thousands of peasants flocked from the surrounding district, and Müntzer guaranteed to supply reinforcements. On 29 April he promised: "everyone, everyone, as many as we have, wants to come to you, marching through all the country-side".[32] Yet the Eternal League was too absorbed in its own campaign of pillage. Their allies at Frankenhausen were overawed by the military might of the local Catholic princes, Duke Georg of Saxony and Count Ernst von Mansfeld (whose fortress was at nearby Heldrungen). The rebels pleaded again for help without delay, "in order to save innocent Christian blood from the devilish jaws of the wolf".[33] Yet still Müntzer hesitated, a fatal mistake. He only arrived in Frankenhausen on 12 May, and with merely 300 men, while Pfeiffer and the rest of the Eternal League returned to their homes. By this time the initiative had been lost.

The rebels had hoped to stimulate a widespread uprising throughout Thuringia, but their support evaporated and they were left as an easy target for the Catholic troops. Müntzer issued increasingly desperate appeals for help from the towns of Ehrich, Walkenried, and Erfurt, but no reinforcements materialized. He wondered whether the people of Erfurt had lost courage because "the Lutheran gruel-sloppers have softened you up with their grubby soft-heartedness".[34] Although the peasants were hopelessly outnumbered, Müntzer continued to chastise their oppressors. On his arrival at the camp he wrote an open letter to Ernst von Mansfeld (later published in Luther's *Shocking History*) which called upon the count "to abandon your tyrannical raging... and to provoke the wrath of God no longer":

You it was who began the martyring of Christians; you it was
who denounced the holy Christian faith as villainy; you it
was who dared to eradicate the Christians. Just tell us, you
miserable, wretched sack of worms, who made you a prince
over the people whom God redeemed with his dear blood?

Müntzer challenged the count to appear before a peasant tribunal
at Frankenhausen, or otherwise be "hunted down and wiped out".
The letter was signed "Thomas Müntzer with the sword of Gideon"
– an allusion to the Old Testament judge who defeated the mighty
Midianite army with a small contingent of only 300 men, the size of
Müntzer's band.[35] At the same time he also wrote to Ernst's brother,
Count Albrecht von Mansfeld (a Lutheran), reminding him that
according to the prophet Ezekiel, "God instructs all the birds of the
heavens to consume the flesh of the princes."[36] As expected, Count
Ernst failed to answer the summons to the peasant tribunal, so three
of his servants were publicly executed by the rebels instead, with
Müntzer's approval.

The peasant army was encamped on a hill outside Frankenhausen,
where they were engaged on 15 May by Duke Georg's infantry
alongside cavalry sent from Hesse and Brunswick. Müntzer continued
to prophesy victory, but the rebels knew they faced certain slaughter
so now pretended that their intentions were peaceful: "We are not
here to harm anyone… We are not here to shed blood, either… we
have no desire to harm you."[37] In reply, the princes hinted that mercy
might be possible, but only if they surrendered unconditionally
and handed over Müntzer and his immediate followers alive. When
the artillery fired at the rebels and the cavalry charged, there was
pandemonium on the hillside. As the peasants fled in panic, many
were crushed to death in the stampede. Six hundred were taken
prisoner, but six thousand were killed that afternoon. Thuringia's
peasant rebellion had been brutally and bloodily stamped out in just
a few hours.

Some stragglers managed to escape from the battlefield, including Müntzer himself. He hid in the bedroom of a home in Frankenhausen, cowering under the bedclothes pretending to be ill, but was soon discovered by a search party. Taken to Heldrungen Castle and tortured on the rack, he agreed to sign a "Recantation", repenting of his insurrectionist preaching and asking to be reconciled to the Catholic church before he died. A few days later, the remaining rebels at Mühlhausen were also defeated and Pfeiffer was captured as he attempted to flee. These two discredited prophets, Müntzer and Pfeiffer, were brought to Duke Georg's army headquarters at Görmar. There they were beheaded, on 27 May, and their heads and bodies stuck on pike-staffs as a warning to all.

RUPTURE WITH ERASMUS

In the midst of the Peasants War, as rebels and rulers clashed on battlefields across Germany, Luther continued his vast array of other activities. One source of scurrilous humour to his enemies was his intimate relationship with Katherine von Bora, whom he had helped to escape to Wittenberg from her convent in the Catholic territories of Duke Georg of Saxony. The Augustinian monk and Cistercian nun were married in June 1525 and produced six children over the next few years. Meanwhile, on the international scene, this period also saw the final end of Luther's fragile relationship with Erasmus.

The Dutch humanist and the Saxon reformer had much in common. For many years they had both spoken out stridently against the corruptions of the church, especially monastic abuses and scholastic errors. Erasmus's writings, not least his critical edition of the New Testament, had helped to stimulate the Lutheran movement in its early days. Some hoped that Erasmus and Luther might combine forces as powerful advocates of a European-wide Reformation. Yet the two men remained deeply suspicious of one another. As early as March 1517, before Luther rose to fame with his

Ninety-Five Theses, he wrote privately: "I am reading our Erasmus but daily I dislike him more and more... he does not advance the cause of Christ and the grace of God sufficiently... Human things weigh more with him than the divine."[38] The Wittenberg preacher began to notice several significant areas of doctrinal divergence with his humanist ally. For example, Erasmus had a higher view of human potential than Luther would allow, as if the Bible could be understood "by study or innate intelligence" rather than an "infusion of the Spirit".[39] In contrast, Luther insisted, "The truth is mightier than eloquence, the Spirit greater than genius, faith more than education."[40] Likewise he criticized the Rotterdam scholar for being more concerned about Christian unity and tranquillity than the gospel. He came to the stark conclusion that Erasmian teaching was "completely incongruous with a knowledge of Christ" and "far from the knowledge of grace, since in all his writings he is not concerned for the cross but for peace".[41]

Erasmus claimed to be sympathetic to the Reformation cause, but was alarmed at the vitriol which pervaded Luther's tracts and the discord they generated in the church. He wrote to distance himself from the constant flow of vehement language emanating from Saxony:

> *Even now it is impossible to root out from men's minds the most groundless suspicion that your work is written with assistance from me and that I am, as they call it, a standard-bearer of this new movement... As for me, I keep myself uncommitted, as far as I can, in hopes of being able to do more for the revival of good literature. And I think one gets further by courtesy and moderation than by clamour. That was how Christ brought the world under his sway.*[42]

While chastising Luther's aggressive tone, at the same time Erasmus sought to protect him from the violence of his Catholic enemies.

Again, the peace of the church was the humanist's first priority. He would prefer Luther to be corrected gently than suppressed by force, as he explained to Archbishop Albrecht of Mainz:

I should be sorry to see him overwhelmed by some villainous faction; if he is wrong, I would rather he were set right than destroyed... Men in whom gentleness was most to be expected seem to thirst for nothing but human blood, and are all agape for nothing so much as to seize Luther and destroy him. This is to play the butcher, not the theologian.[43]

He likewise warned Cardinal Campeggio against the papal policy of persecution: "it must at least be more civilized to cure him than to snuff him out".[44]

Erasmus's deliberate neutrality brought him opprobrium from both sides. Some Catholics thought him complicit in Luther's teaching, and Cardinal Aleandro called him "the source of all this evil... the cornerstone of this heresy".[45] Pope Adrian VI urged him to protect his reputation by using his intellectual gifts and literary skill to destroy Lutheranism, but still the scholar remained reluctant. Nor would he side with the reformers, who therefore accused him of hypocrisy and cowardice. Although Erasmus had severely criticized Rome, he was unwilling to abandon the church of his birth:

Those who appear to support Luther have done all they possibly can to lure me into his camp... Christ I recognize, Luther I know not; the church of Rome I recognize, and think it does not disagree with the Catholic church. From that church death shall not tear me asunder, unless the church is sundered openly from Christ.[46]

By the spring of 1524, Luther had given up all hope of winning Erasmus for evangelicalism. He assailed the humanist's timidity and dismissively told him that the great Reformation cause had "long since outgrown your littleness".[47]

Under pressure from all sides, Erasmus was eventually persuaded to launch a public attack on Luther's theology. In September 1524 he published *The Freedom of the Will*, a doctrinal treatise criticizing Luther's view of God's sovereignty and grace. Luther replied in December 1525 with *The Bondage of the Will*, thanking his opponent for going straight to the heart of the theological dispute between them, rather than dealing with surface issues like the papacy, purgatory, indulgences, and similar "trifles".[48] Yet he dismissed the humanist arguments as trash wrapped up in elegant prose, "like refuse or ordure being carried in gold and silver vases".[49] The slanging match rumbled on until the end of 1527 and Erasmus issued a lengthy riposte in two parts, entitled *Hyperaspistes* ("*Protective Shield*"), almost ten times as long as his original diatribe. When all was said and done, despite his many criticisms of Catholicism, Erasmus was not willing to follow the reformers and break with Rome. He concluded:

> *I have never been an apostate from the Catholic Church. I know that in this Church, which you call the Papist Church, there are many who displease me, but such I see also in your Church. One bears more easily the evils to which one is accustomed.*[50]

He was to end his days within the Roman communion.

This clash between Erasmus and Luther exposed the deep divisions between humanism and evangelicalism, between Renaissance and Reform. The prospect that these two movements might be harnessed together in a pan-European coalition was to remain an idle dream. Despite many superficial similarities, and some overlap of personnel, they were fundamentally out of step in their understanding of the gospel message. The chasm could not be breached. In years to come, Luther's *Table Talk* (a record of his conversations while eating with friends) was peppered with abuse of his Dutch nemesis. He derided Erasmus as an "eel", a "croaking toad", a "snake" and "a double-dealing man". He went as far as to say, "I hate Erasmus from the bottom of my heart" and "I consider Erasmus to be the greatest enemy Christ has had these thousand years past."[51] Many observers believed there was a causal link between humanist scholarship and evangelical Reformation, and some Franciscan monks in Cologne began to circulate the aphorism "Erasmus laid the egg which Luther hatched". Yet Erasmus was under no such illusion and proclaimed, "I laid a poultry egg, Luther hatched a very different bird."[52]

4

A Warrior for Christ

"I will not have the papists call me Lutheran, for I did not learn Christ's teaching from Luther but from the very word of God."[1] So proclaimed Huldrych Zwingli, a young pastor in the German-speaking city of Zürich, where the Swiss Reformation began in the early 1520s. The evangelical movements in Switzerland and Saxony had much in common, though they took a different shape. Zwingli and Luther were born within seven weeks of each other, and they shared a common language (in different dialects) and a common passion to rebuild the biblical foundations of the church. Yet Zwingli always fiercely maintained his independence from Wittenberg. He insisted that he had come to his own conclusions about the Christian gospel by reading the letters of St Paul, not the treatises of Luther.

Zwingli began his career as a Catholic priest in the small canton of Glarus from 1506, where he was well known as a papal partisan and enjoyed a "pension" from Pope Julius II worth fifty gulden a year. The Swiss Confederation (a fragile alliance between thirteen independent cantons) was a pawn in the power struggle between France, the Holy Roman Empire, and the papacy during the Italian Wars of the early sixteenth century. Many cantons rented out their soldiers as mercenaries to the highest bidder, but Zwingli's sympathies lay with the armies of the pope, as evident in one of his earliest writings, *The Ox*, an allegorical poem. The noble ox stood for Switzerland, being enticed into a foolish alliance with the leopard (France) or the lion (the Holy Roman Empire) in their battles with the fox (Venice). Yet the pope was portrayed as a good shepherd to whom loyalty was due. When Swiss mercenaries helped to capture the city of Pavia near Milan, Zwingli celebrated their defence of the pope's dominions as "a matter of national honour".[2] He experienced warfare at first hand, marching alongside recruits from Glarus as their chaplain and field-preacher. He was present at the bloody battle of Novara in June 1513, when Swiss troops encircled and destroyed the French forces of Louis XII, leading to the restoration of Maximilian Sforza as Duke of Milan. Two years later he witnessed the slaughter of 10,000 Swiss mercenaries in the battle of Marignano, destroyed by the combined fury of France and Venice. Soon Zwingli began to abhor armed conflict and in his copy of Erasmus's *Adages* he underlined the sentence "*Dulce bellum inexpertis*" ("War is only sweet to the inexperienced"). Ironically, he was later to lose his life on a Swiss battlefield in a civil war he helped to provoke.

In November 1516 the young priest moved from Glarus to the village of Einsiedeln, in the neighbouring canton of Schwyz, dominated by an ancient Benedictine abbey. It was a famous centre of pilgrimage, attracting pious visitors from around Europe to its shrine to the Virgin Mary, which was said to possess miraculous healing powers. Here Zwingli withdrew from his political entanglements and focused instead upon scholarship and preaching. He was drawn into the humanist circle surrounding Erasmus, then based in Basel, and acquired a copy of the ground-breaking *Novum Testamentum* as soon as it was published. He began to learn Greek so that he could study the New Testament in its original language and copied out the letters of St Paul by hand, seeking to come to grips with their implications and remember them by heart. He also immersed himself in the early church fathers, especially Augustine, Ambrose, Jerome, and Chrysostom. As with his new humanist friends, Zwingli became increasingly critical of the ceremonial excesses of contemporary Catholicism, though he did not immediately see it as contradictory to biblical Christianity. As late as 1517 he participated in a pilgrimage to Aachen in Germany, with its giant Carolingian cathedral and numerous shrines.

Zwingli's growing reputation as a humanist scholar and a persuasive preacher, alongside his hostility to mercenary service, made him attractive to the authorities at Zürich – one of the largest and most influential cities in the Swiss Confederation. At the age of thirty-four, he was invited to take up the role of "people's priest" at the *Grossmünster* (Great Minster), Zürich's famous collegiate church, where his particular responsibility was to preach. In his first sermon on New Year's Day 1519, he announced his intention to work systematically through Matthew's Gospel, a radical departure from traditional homilies based upon the liturgical year, legendary saints or medieval dogma. As a keen humanist, he was determined to expound the plain meaning of the biblical text, without reference to scholastic interpretations.

After Matthew's Gospel he preached through the Acts of the Apostles, 1 and 2 Timothy, 1 and 2 Peter, Galatians, Hebrews, and Luke. Zwingli's teaching was increasingly dominated by Scripture, but like his hero, Erasmus, he was still firmly within the Roman communion. As a priest he regularly said mass, heard confessions, and took part in other traditional rituals. In April 1521, at the same period when Luther was making his courageous stand before the imperial Diet at Worms, Zwingli was elected to a canonry at Zürich's Great Minster and seemed embedded within Catholicism. Yet soon he came forward as a wholehearted pioneer of evangelical reform.

DEFIANT FREEDOM

The Reformation question exploded to life in Zürich at the start of Lent 1522 over the issue of fasting. By long-standing tradition, enforced by church regulations, all Christians were obliged to abstain from choice foods (such as meat, milk, butter, cheese, and eggs) during the forty days before Easter. However, one evening a dozen friends gathered in the house of a Zürich printer, Christoph Froschauer, where they cut two smoked sausages into small pieces and ate together. It was a deliberate defiance of the ecclesiastical rules and a provocative declaration of their Christian freedom. Two priests even joined in this rebellious meal. Zwingli was also present, and watched without eating, though he raised no objections.

When the city council began to investigate these crimes, Zwingli came out publicly on the side of the law-breakers, in a sermon entitled *The Choice and Freedom of Foods*, published as a short pamphlet by Froschauer. He argued from the New Testament that fasting was a human tradition, not a divine injunction, and therefore was a question for the conscience of the individual Christian, not a matter on which the authorities should legislate. He proclaimed: "If you like to fast, do it; if you don't like meat, don't eat it, but do not touch a Christian's freedom." When his opponents claimed Thomas Aquinas as their authority, Zwingli mocked the idea that "one single mendicant monk had been given the power to dictate to all Christian people".[3] The city council concluded, as an interim decision, that fast violators would be punished, but that the law would soon be reformed if the traditionalists could not justify their fasts on the basis of Scripture.

After Easter the debate moved swiftly on to the veneration of saints. Some of Zwingli's more radical supporters began to disrupt worship services and interrupt sermons, in an attempt to force the issue. Zwingli himself challenged a monk from Avignon, Franz Lambert, who visited Zürich and preached in the *Fraumünster* (Mary Minster) on the veneration of the Virgin Mary and the saints. Zwingli cried out in the middle of the monk's discourse, "Brother, this is where you err!"[4] As a result the city council commanded that the monks stop preaching scholastic sermons and instead imitate Zwingli's method of proclaiming the gospel from the Bible. The people's priest laid out his own views in *A Sermon on the Eternally Pure Maid Mary*, praising her as the "Mother of God", a perpetual virgin and a model Christian.

Yet he denounced the idea that she should be adored or that she had any role to play as a mediator of salvation. Instead he exhorted his congregation: "if you wish to specially honour Mary, then follow her purity, innocence and firm faith!"[5]

Another source of tension was the enforced celibacy of the clergy. The ministers of Zürich and the surrounding area petitioned the Bishop of Konstanz in July 1522 to abolish the practice, in an address which was soon translated into German and circulated throughout Switzerland. Again they appealed for Christian liberty, and for the church to follow the word of God not human tradition: "Chastity is a gift from God bestowed upon a few... Christ left everyone free."[6] They looked to the secular authorities to give legal protection to clerical wives and children. This was a pressing practical concern. Although canon law had forbidden clerical marriage for several centuries, many priests were known to raise families with their "housekeepers", a sin which the bishops agreed to overlook on payment of a fee. For example, in the diocese of Konstanz there were said to be 1,500 children of priests and the diocesan coffers swelled with the fines. The Zürich petitioners argued that many bishops in the early church had been married and that to enforce celibacy upon a virile young priest would turn him into a "dangerous animal", likely to fall into sexual immorality.[7] When the bishop rejected their appeal, they took matters into their own hands. Zwingli himself was married in secret to a young widow, Anna Reinhart, although they did not enjoy a public wedding until two years later when she was six months pregnant.

One of the underlying questions in all these disputes about fasting, saints, and celibacy was the principle of authority. Who was entitled to decide the issues? Was it the bishop? Or the scholars? Or the city council? Zwingli affirmed again and again that the Christian's only authority was the Bible, as he explained in his treatise, *The Clarity and Certainty of the Word of God*, based on a sermon he delivered at the Dominican convent at Oetenbach. In August 1522 he cut his final ties with the ecclesiastical authorities in *Apologeticus Archeteles*

("*The First and Final Defence*"), repudiating the right of the bishop to be the judge in spiritual matters and asserting scriptural authority. Zwingli's only aim, he insisted, was to lead people away from corrupt traditions to the Christ of the Bible.

Faced by these growing religious tensions, the city council in Zürich called a public debate on 29 January 1523 to settle the question. All the local clergy were obliged to attend and invitations were sent out to other Swiss city-states and to the Bishop of Konstanz. Unlike an academic disputation, the arguments were to be heard in German, not Latin. Most importantly, it was to be judged not by bishops or scholars, but by the city council on the basis of Scripture. In preparation, Zwingli issued Sixty-Seven Theses (not unlike Luther's Ninety-Five Theses) laying out his programme for reform. They opened with a forthright summary of his evangelical message:

1. *All who say that the gospel is invalid without the confirmation of the church err and slander God.*
2. *The sum and substance of the gospel is that our Lord Christ Jesus, the true Son of God, has made known to us the will of his heavenly Father, and has with his sinlessness released us from death and reconciled us to God.*
3. *Hence Christ is the only way to salvation for all who ever were, are, and shall be.*
4. *He who seeks or shows another way errs, and, indeed, he is a murderer of souls and a thief.*
5. *Hence all who consider other teachings equal to or higher than the gospel err, and do not know what the gospel is.*

Zwingli's theses went on to address an array of practical implications, such as the mass, fasting, clerical celibacy, excommunication, the death penalty, penance, purgatory, and priesthood. He attacked wealthy ecclesiastics who amassed riches in Christ's name for their "avarice and arrogance", and rejected monks' cowls and priests' vestments as a form of "gross hypocrisy and iniquity". In prophetic fashion, he warned that unless those in authority quickly humbled themselves before the cross of Christ, "perdition is upon them and the axe is laid to the root of the tree".[8]

The Zürich disputation attracted a large crowd, with 600 participants crammed into the town hall. The bishop's delegation was led by Johannes Fabri, who insisted that a small Swiss city was incompetent to decide religious questions better suited to an ecumenical council, an international assembly, or a major university like Paris, Cologne, or Leuven. Yet Zwingli replied that the Zürichers were a gathering of Christians with open Bibles, who did not need specially trained theologians to tell them what to believe:

> God does not ask us what popes, bishops and councils have ordered, or what is praiseworthy old custom, but how his will, his word and his commands are to be followed... We have the infallible and impartial judge, Holy Writ, in Hebrew, Greek and Latin...[9]

By lunchtime, the city council had already reached its verdict in Zwingli's favour. Since no one had been able to refute his Sixty-Seven Theses, he would be allowed to keep preaching. Furthermore, all other clergy were instructed to imitate his example by teaching "nothing but what can be proved by the holy gospel and the pure holy Scriptures".[10] It was a triumphant victory. Zwingli now had a firm foothold in Zürich and with a mandate from the city council he could push ahead with more far-reaching reforms.

THE DESTRUCTION OF IDOLS

Throughout 1523 the focus of agitation in Zürich was the reformation of public worship. Zwingli continued to insist that "the Bible must be your master", as outlined in his *Exposition of the Sixty-Seven Theses*, the most comprehensive explanation of his theology in German.[11] He appealed for radical revision to the Eucharistic liturgy in use at the *Grossmünster*, rejecting outright the theologies of transubstantiation and mass sacrifice, and denounced the veneration of images. He mourned Zürich's superstitious attitude to saints, which he blamed on the "fairy-tale preaching" of Catholic theologians, whom he abused as "lying, greedy maggots".[12] Encouraged by such sentiment, some Zwinglians began to take matters into their own hands by "cleansing" local churches. Painted icons, statues, and stained-glass windows were smashed and burned. Leo Jud, one of Zwingli's closest allies, called publicly for the destruction of these "idols".[13] Meanwhile two evangelicals pulled down a giant wooden crucifix on private property at Stadelhofen, just outside the city walls, and were thrown into the Wellenberg gaol for their vandalism.

Faced by growing anarchy, the Zürich city council decided to hold a second public disputation over three days at the end of October 1523. Invitations were widely distributed, to laymen as well as clergy, three local dioceses, the University of Basel, and the twelve other cantons in the Swiss Confederation. However, the bishops and the other states (except Schaffhausen) refused to send representatives, so it remained mostly a Zürich affair. Some 900 people were present, including 350 ministers. The reformed viewpoint was presented by Zwingli and Jud, who argued against pictures of Christ and the sacrificial nature of the mass. The Catholic party was led by Konrad Hofmann (an elderly canon at the *Grossmünster*), who defended these two aspects of traditional piety. Yet once again the underlying question was not the validity of images but the authority of the city council to judge the matter. Hofmann did not think they had the right to do so, but neither did Zwingli's more radical allies like Konrad Grebel and Simon Stumpf. The Catholics wanted the church authorities to be the judge. The radicals believed the Spirit of God had already given a judgment in

Scripture. Yet Zwingli was content to leave the verdict in the hands of the civic authorities.

At the disputation the council adopted the cautious suggestion of Komtur Schmid, from the village of Küsnacht near Zürich. He argued that the abolition of images would stir up strife because the people had not been properly taught the evangelical gospel. Therefore pastors should first be commanded to preach frequently on the subject, then congregations would realize that icons were futile, and eventually these decorations could be removed without a murmur. The council agreed, as a temporary measure, to maintain the *status quo*. There was to be no reformation of the mass and no further destruction of images, a policy which Zwingli was willing to accept for the time being, much to the infuriation of his radical supporters.

At the request of the council he wrote a brief summary of Reformation teaching on these topics, *A Short Christian Introduction*, for distribution to the clergy in Zürich and the surrounding district. It included a warning that Christian liberty did not mean freedom to disobey the secular authorities. Those who rejected the decrees of the government were among the "most dangerous enemies of God's teaching".[14] In an earlier treatise on *Divine and Human Righteousness*, directed against the evangelical radicals, he urged that Christians must obey civil laws and not take authority into their own hands in their rush to create a utopian community.

The actions of the city council might have been slow, but they were in a definite Reformation direction. In January 1524 Canon Hofmann and four of his Catholic supporters appeared before a panel of a dozen councilmen and theologians, to present their complaints against Zwingli's innovations. Yet they were simply told to obey the government's decrees, under threat of deportation. As a result Hofmann left Zürich, signalling the defeat of the local Catholic opposition.

Now the council acted with greater speed, urged forward by Zwingli's *Proposal Concerning Images and the Mass*. In June they commanded that all images, statues, paintings, and crucifixes be removed from churches in the city, in response to the teaching of Scripture. Rural congregations, which were more conservative, were encouraged to destroy their images as soon as a majority of the parish agreed. In some locations the destruction was completed, in an orderly manner, by carpenters and stonemasons. Elsewhere it was the action of iconophobic mobs. In a later treatise, *Reply to Valentin Compar* (1525), Zwingli argued that it was better to donate money to the poor than to waste it on icons and statues. Some claimed that paintings were "the poor man's Bible", but the preacher insisted that they did more spiritual harm than good.

These reforms began to drive a wedge between Zürich and the other twelve states in the Swiss Confederation. Zürich was accused of disturbing the peace, sowing discord, spreading anti-Catholic propaganda, and harbouring rebels. There were demands for it to be expelled from the confederation and troubles were multiplied when local iconoclasts began to trespass into Catholic cantons. Klaus Hottinger had been banished from Zürich, but in March 1524 he was captured, tortured, and executed in Lucerne; he is remembered as the first evangelical martyr of the Swiss Reformation. The following month the five "Inner States" of the confederation (Lucerne, Uri, Schwyz, Unterwalden, and Zug) pledged to stand together upon

> the ancient true and right Christian faith, and likewise to root out this Lutheran, Zwinglian, Hussite, erroneous and faulty teaching from all our territories and jurisdictions and, as far as we can and our power enables us, to attack, punish and suppress it.[15]

When the Carthusian monastery at Ittingen was looted and burned in July 1524, in an alarming echo of the peasant rebellions in southern Germany, the ringleaders were quickly arrested by the Zürich authorities. Yet the Catholic cantons pressed the matter further, demanding punishment. Against Zwingli's firm warnings, the city council reluctantly agreed to hand over the chief culprits, who were sent to Baden and interrogated under torture. Three were executed, not just as rebels but as heretics. Their deaths were greeted with consternation in Zürich as martyrdoms and a miscarriage of justice. With feelings running high, there were rumours of imminent civil war within the Swiss Confederation.

NO TURNING BACK

Within the confines of Zürich, Zwingli's position was increasingly secure and he sought to push the Reformation forward into new areas. The city council had hesitated to abolish the mass, but finally did so a few days before Easter 1525 – symbolizing the final breach with the Church of Rome. They authorized a new reformed communion liturgy in German, drafted by Zwingli, which transformed the way the service was celebrated. It now took the form of a simple meal, with the congregation sitting around a table. Silver chalices and patens were replaced by wooden cups and plates, with plain bread rolls and a jug of wine. Eucharistic vestments made way for black gowns. There was no organ music or chanting, and other traditional rituals were abolished in the drive for simplicity and clarity. Instead of daily mass in Zürich's many churches and chapels, the reformed Lord's Supper was now celebrated just four times a year, at Christmas, Easter, Pentecost, and early September.

Marriage laws in Zürich were also reformed in line with Old Testament regulations (Leviticus 18). Adultery was punishable by excommunication, but because marriage was no longer considered an indissoluble sacrament, divorce was permitted in the case of sexual infidelity. Jurisdiction over moral questions was removed permanently from the Bishop of Konstanz and granted to Zürich's Court of Domestic Relations, to which Zwingli acted as a consultant. Meanwhile the many monasteries and convents in Zürich were rapidly dissolved. Abbess Katharina von Zimmern of the *Fraumünster* was pensioned off, and the property and endowment transferred to the city. The Selnau convent became a hospital, while other monastic resources were redirected into welfare and education programmes. A new Poor Law sought to eradicate the prevalent practice of monks begging on the streets. These reforms demonstrated Zwingli's desire to bring not just liturgy and piety, but the whole of society, under the word of God.

One of Zwingli's chief aims was to reform the *Grossmünster* into a centre for biblical and theological training. In June 1525 he launched the *Prophezei*, a seminary for ministers, attached to the minster grammar school. The name was taken from 1 Corinthians 14, where the apostle Paul instructs the early Christians to eagerly desire "the gift of prophecy" – which Zwingli understood as the ability to teach the Bible. Every morning of the week, except Sundays and Fridays, the clergy and canons of Zürich, with the senior students of the grammar school and any visiting scholars, gathered together in the *Grossmünster*. There they studied an Old Testament text which was read three times, in the original Hebrew, in Latin (from the Vulgate translation), and in Greek (from the Septuagint translation). The passage was expounded twice, first in Latin, the language of the academy (usually by Zwingli) and then in German, the language of the people (usually by Jud). All ministers in the city were required to attend, but there was also an open invitation to the general public, and discussion was encouraged. In parallel with this detailed Old Testament study, the New Testament was taught every afternoon in the *Fraumünster* by Zwingli and his friend, Oswald Myconius. The seminary attracted a strong faculty – led first by Jakob Ceporinus and then by Konrad Pellikan, a former Franciscan monk and the first Christian to publish a Hebrew grammar.

The *Prophezei* helped to equip all the preachers in Zürich in evangelical methods of interpretation and exposition, while also training up the younger generation. The deployment of Bible teachers lay at the heart of Zwingli's Reformation programme. It also emphasized that his priorities in Christian ministry were distinct from his Catholic and radical opponents. In *The Shepherd* (1524) he drew a sharp contrast between "false shepherds" (unreformed priests) and "true shepherds" (reformed pastors). In *The Ministry* (1525) he distinguished the reformed pastor who is immersed in the Bible from the radical itinerant who misinterprets the text and misleads the congregation. The *Prophezei* stimulated the publication of numerous Bible commentaries, enabling Zürich preachers to circulate their ideas to a wider readership. Zwingli published his exegeses of Isaiah and Jeremiah, while other Old Testament studies were put together from student notes of his expositions. His New Testament exegeses were published after his death, edited by Jud. The influential *Zürich Bible* (1529) also originated in the *Prophezei*, the first complete translation of the Scriptures into German, five years before Luther finished his Old Testament in Wittenberg.

LAMBS TO THE SLAUGHTER

Although reforms in Zürich were gathering pace, division was increasingly apparent among Zwingli's followers. His radical allies agitated for faster change and soon became disillusioned with his leadership. The two most prominent radicals, Konrad Grebel and Felix Mantz, both broke with their former mentor around the time of Zürich's second disputation in October 1523. They spoke out against him as a vacillator who still stood halfway between purity and corruption. In particular, they criticized Zwingli for only turning from Catholic error when the city council gave permission. According to the radicals, God had unequivocally declared in Scripture what was required of the church, so Christians must put God's commands into action regardless of government decrees. Zwingli was described as a "false prophet" because of his concessions to the politicians.[16] Among the specific points at issue were the paying of tithes and interest, the swearing of oaths, the ownership of private property, and the exercise of church discipline. Grebel complained to his brother-in-law, the Basel scholar Joachim von Watt (nicknamed "Vadian"), that in Zürich the word of God had been "overthrown, set back, and bound by its most learned heralds".[17] He called Zwingli a "wretched prattler" and "arch-scribe".[18] Hitting back in his treatise, *Those Who Give Cause for Tumult* (1524), Zwingli accused the radicals of misreading the Bible and of acting without love for their neighbours.

In their attempts to establish an ideal Christian community, based on the model of the early church in the book of Acts, the radicals rejected the baptism of infants. They argued that the New Testament laid out a clear sequence for Christians to follow – preaching, repentance, faith, baptism – so only adult believers should be baptised. Zwingli often called them "pseudo-baptists" (false-baptists) or "cata-baptists" (anti-baptists). The epithet which stuck was "Anabaptists" (rebaptists), though the radicals rejected the name. Zwingli warned that by overthrowing the traditional practice of baptism, they would destabilize the city, yet the radicals insisted they were peace-lovers not insurrectionists. In an act of defiance, parents in the villages of Wytikon and Zollikon near Zürich refused to bring their new-born infants to church for baptism, and the Zollikon font was smashed. When private dialogue failed to resolve the issues, the Zürich city council called for a third public disputation in January 1525, at which Grebel and Mantz were invited to defend their views on the basis of Scripture. Once again, Zwingli dominated the event and the verdict went in his favour. The council commanded that anyone neglecting to baptize their children within eight days of birth would be deported from Zürich. Grebel and Mantz were also ordered to stop preaching and to disband their unauthorized meetings.

Nevertheless, the radicals chose to defy the government decrees. As with the apostle Paul, they proclaimed that they would not depart from the word of God even if an angel came down from heaven and commanded them to desist. On 21 January, just four days after the disputation, there was a secret gathering at Mantz's mother's house. Here Grebel baptized a former Catholic priest, Jörg Cajacob (nicknamed "Blaurock" because he often wore a blue coat), and Blaurock then proceeded to baptize fifteen other adult believers. Soon an Anabaptist community was founded in the region of Zollikon and within weeks it was reported that eighty adults had been baptized. Through their missionary zeal, their ideas quickly spread throughout the canton and to the neighbouring territories of Basel, Schaffhausen, and St Gallen. Converts were often baptized by immersion in local rivers, sometimes in large crowds. This new network of radical Christians became known as "the Swiss Brethren". They fully expected opposition, as Grebel observed: "True believing Christians are sheep among wolves, sheep for the slaughter. They must be baptised in anguish and tribulation, persecution, suffering, and death."[19]

Further disputations and dialogues failed to settle the baptism question. Zwingli declared that he saw nothing among the Anabaptists except "obstinacy and perversity" and "a measureless thirst for fame". Yet Blaurock called him "a heretic, a murderer, a thief, the true Antichrist who had misinterpreted the Bible worse than the pope".[20] In an act of provocation, one group of radicals paraded through the streets of the city like Old Testament prophets, crying, "Woe, woe to you, O Zürich" and warning that divine judgment would fall within forty days if the people did not repent. They denounced Zwingli as the "old dragon", a metaphor for Satan himself.[21]

In growing frustration the city council decided that more severe measures were necessary. Grebel went into hiding, but in October 1525 he and Blaurock were captured in a field at Grüningen, while preparing for an Anabaptist service, and locked up in the local castle. At first Mantz evaded the authorities but was arrested three weeks later and incarcerated with his friends. All were transferred to prison in Zürich, along with other members of the Anabaptist network. In March 1526 the government decreed that anyone who continued to perform baptisms "shall without appeal be put to death by drowning", a form of punishment deliberately chosen to mock Anabaptist practice.[22] On the same day, the three leaders were sentenced to life imprisonment, but they managed to escape through an open window after only a fortnight. They fled from Zürich and immediately continued their itinerant ministry of evangelism in the surrounding cantons. Grebel went to preach in Maienfeld, but died of the plague that summer. Mantz and Blaurock were recaptured in a forest near Grüningen in December.

During his months on the run, Mantz had broken his oath not to baptize, so the Zürich government carried out its fierce threat of execution. On Saturday 5 January 1527, he was taken from Zürich's Wellenberg prison to the River Limmat, testifying to the crowds en route that he was about to die for the truth. He was rowed by boat to a fish hut that was anchored in the middle of the river, where his arms and legs were bound as he sang confidently, "*In manus tuas, Domine, commendo spiritum meum*" ("Into your hands, O Lord, I commend my spirit", Psalm 31:5). Then the executioner pushed Mantz into the cold waters as his friends watched from the riverbank.

Blaurock was preserved from death because he had refrained from baptizing. Instead the authorities stripped him to the waist and beat him with rods from the Limmat River to the Niederdorf Gate, until the blood flowed down his back. He was expelled from the city and warned that he too would be drowned if he dared to return. As he left Zürich, Blaurock shook the dust from his clothes and his shoes, just as Jesus Christ had instructed his apostles to do when a city rejected the gospel message. He preached as an itinerant evangelist in Berne, Biel, and Appenzell, but was banished from these places too, so abandoned Switzerland and never returned. Instead Blaurock went to help a secret Anabaptist congregation in the Austrian Tyrol, whose pastor had been burned at the stake, but after a few months he was captured. The Austrian authorities tortured the preacher, wanting him to divulge information on Anabaptist activities in the region, and then burned him on 6 September 1529 near Klausen.

IN SEARCH OF ALLIES

The rapid progress of the Reformation in Zürich revealed deepening divisions within the Swiss Confederation, along confessional lines. This was made obvious by the Baden Disputation of May 1526 – sometimes called the "Swiss Diet of Worms".[23] Johann Eck, Luther's articulate opponent at the Leipzig Disputation in 1519, offered to tackle Zwingli too. He invited the Zürich reformer to debate theology at Baden in front of representatives from all the cantons in the confederation. Zwingli refused, because he was not confident of a fair hearing, nor that the promise of safe passage would be honoured (after all, three Zwinglians had been executed in Baden not long before).

However, Zürich did send representatives, despite Zwingli's boycott, and the Reformation party was led by Johannes Oecolampadius from Basel and Berchtold Haller from Berne. After a month of debate, Zwingli was finally condemned as a heretic. His writings and his preaching were banned throughout Switzerland. The confederation reaffirmed that only the church authorities had permission to interpret the Bible and that no one must interfere with traditional Catholic worship. Yet this declaration was by no means unanimous. Of the thirteen Swiss cantons, three refused to vote against Zürich – Berne, Basel, and Schaffhausen. This was a sure sign that the Reformation cause pioneered by Zwingli was beginning to spread.

Berne, the largest state in the confederation, broke decisively from the Catholic cantons soon after the Baden debate. It held its own disputation in January 1528 to consider Ten Theses drawn up by Haller, covering contentious issues like saints, images, celibacy, and the mass. The Catholic cantons refused to attend and the chief Catholic spokesman, Konrad Treger (an Augustinian monk from Freiburg), walked out after only five days, so the Reformation party was left triumphant. Zwingli led a large delegation from Zürich and dominated the proceedings. After listening to the arguments, the Berne government issued a mandate for reform, beginning with the abolition of images and the mass. It sought to imitate Zürich, complete with its own school of preaching modelled on the *Prophezei*.

A year later Basel followed suit. For several years it had tried to straddle the Catholic–Reform divide, allowing the celebration of the mass and the Lord's Supper side by side. Yet faced with iconoclastic riots, the city council finally agreed to ban the mass and order the destruction of images. This shift in policy forced the elderly Erasmus to leave Basel, but Oecolampadius rejoiced in this "cleansing" of churches: "It was a very sad sight, believe me, to superstitious people. They might well have wept tears of blood. Thus was vengeance wreaked on the images. The mass disappeared unlamented."[24] By September 1529 the city council of Schaffhausen, Zürich's nearest neighbour, had also legislated in favour of reform.

With Switzerland irrevocably divided along confessional lines, the confederation began to disintegrate. The competing cantons formed hasty alliances, sometimes with foreign allies, for the sake of self-preservation. Zürich, Konstanz, Berne, and St Gallen bound themselves together in the *Christliche Burgrecht* (Christian Civic Union), to defend the Reformation, and were soon joined by Basel, Schaffhausen, Biel, Strassburg, and Mülhausen (in Alsace). On the Catholic side the Five States, led by Lucerne, signed a treaty with Archduke Ferdinand of Austria to form the *Christliche Vereinigung* (Christian Alliance), promising "to abide by the old, true Christian faith".[25] As a show of strength, they executed the Zürich-born preacher, Jakob Kaiser, in Schwyz.

Armed conflict was inevitable and Zwingli was one of those agitating for war, in the belief that it was the best way to protect the Reformation in Switzerland. Unlike the Anabaptist pacifists, he was eager to advocate the use of the sword to enable the preaching of the gospel:

> *be firm and do not be afraid of war. For this peace which some are so strenuously pressing upon us means war, not peace. And the war upon which I am insisting is not war, but peace. I am not out for anyone's blood… Unless this takes place neither the truths of the gospel nor its ministers among us will be safe.*[26]

The government in Berne argued that "faith cannot be brought in by spears and halberds",[27] but Zwingli threatened to resign if the Christian Civic Union refused to engage the Catholic cantons.

The result was a bloodless battle at Kappel, on the border with Zug, in June 1529 where the armies of Zürich and Berne (numbering about 30,000 men) faced a much smaller force from the Five States (about 9,000 men). The Catholics had been abandoned by their Austrian allies, who were engaged in a war of their own against the Ottoman armies of Sultan Suleiman I. So a victory for the Christian Civic Union seemed certain and Zwingli wanted to press home the advantage to secure the Reformation cause throughout Switzerland. Yet the city councils of Berne and Zürich agreed to negotiate. Before a shot was fired the Catholic cantons signed the Kappel peace treaty, promising to dissolve their Christian Alliance with Austria. Zwingli's demands for unhindered preaching, war reparations, abolition of the mercenary system, and compensation for Kaiser's children, were never met. It was a major setback for his plans to reach the whole of Switzerland with the evangelical gospel, and signalled his growing alienation from the civic authorities in Zürich.

The Marburg colloquy

Some were still hopeful that all the evangelical states of Europe could be united in a common alliance against the forces of the pope and the Holy Roman emperor. This was as much a political necessity as a theological ideal. In Germany, the Gotha-Torgau treaty of 1526 brought together the two most influential evangelical princes, Landgrave Philipp of Hesse and Elector Johann of Saxony (Luther's prince), in a defensive pact against their Catholic neighbours. Yet they dreamed of a more ambitious union, binding together the Reformation across Germany and Switzerland. The cause was particularly pressing after the imperial Diet at Speyer in April 1529, which banned religious innovation, enforced the Edict of Worms, and passed censures upon Lutherans, Zwinglians, and Anabaptists. A coalition of six evangelical princes and fourteen imperial free cities had rejected these decrees, insisting that "in matters of God's honour and the salvation of souls" each estate "must stand for itself before God".[28] Their formal "protestation" against the decision of the Diet gave rise to the name "Protestant" (later a synonym for "evangelical"), but their pleas were ignored by the Catholic majority.

In an attempt to forge evangelical unity, Prince Philipp invited the leading reformers from across Germany and Switzerland to meet at Marburg in early October 1529. It had been obvious for several years that the teachings of Zwingli and Luther were increasingly divergent, especially concerning the Lord's Supper, and their treatises were filled with sharp censures against each other. For example, in his *Confession Concerning Christ's Supper* (1528), Luther proclaimed: "I regard Zwingli as un-Christian, with all his teaching, for he holds and teaches no part of the Christian faith rightly. He is seven times worse than when he was a papist."[29] Nevertheless, Philipp knew that agreement between these two men would go a long way to securing the stability of the Reformation movement.

Zwingli went to Marburg with some optimism, joined by Oecolampadius from Basel and Martin Bucer from Strassburg. The Lutheran delegation included Luther, Melanchthon, and Justus Jonas from Wittenberg, alongside Stephan Agricola from Augsburg and Andreas Osiander from Nuremberg. Under pressure to reach a public agreement, they issued Fifteen Articles outlining their common convictions on themes including the Trinity, original sin, redemption, faith, preaching, baptism, good works, private confession, political authority, and church tradition. There was much that the Swiss and German evangelicals held in common.

Yet the fifteenth article highlighted the chasm between them, concerning the presence of Christ in the Lord's Supper, on which neither side was willing to give ground. Although both reformers were agreed on the principle of *sola scriptura* – that the Bible was their authority – they could not agree how to interpret the sacred text. Much ink was spilt over the words of Jesus from the Last Supper as he broke bread with his disciples, "*Hoc est corpus meum*" ("This is my body", Matthew 26:26). Luther took these words literally and defiantly chalked them upon the negotiating table at Marburg, but Zwingli interpreted them figuratively. According to the Swiss reformer, Jesus meant "This *signifies* my body". After all, at the Last Supper, Jesus was *at* the table not *on* the table. He argued that it was absurd to take all Jesus' statements literally, like "I am the door" (John 10:9). Another controversial text was St Stephen's proclamation that Jesus was "standing at the right hand of God" (Acts 7:56). Zwingli took these words literally, arguing that Jesus' resurrection body was in heaven and therefore could not also be on the communion table. Yet here Luther maintained a figurative interpretation, insisting that Jesus' resurrection body could be omnipresent. He observed: "I do not accept mathematical dimensions as applicable to holy Scripture, because God is greater than all the mathematicians."[30] Zwingli believed that Luther was still bound to scholastic exegesis and that his teaching led to the worship of the Eucharistic elements. He loved to quote, "The Spirit alone gives life, the flesh counts for nothing" (John 6:63). Yet Luther believed that Zwingli's denial of the real presence of Christ was blasphemous and devilish. He would rather share fellowship with Rome than with Zürich: "Before I would have mere wine with the fanatics, I would rather receive sheer blood with the pope."[31]

Zwingli believed the Marburg debate had ended in a Swiss victory. He called Melanchthon "uncommonly slippery" and denounced Luther's "countless inconsistencies, absurdities and follies... The truth prevailed so manifestly that if ever a man was beaten in this world, it was Luther – for all his impudence and obstinacy – and everyone witnessed it, too."[32] For his part, Luther concluded that the Swiss reformers had been "blinded" by God and were not even Christians.[33] He observed that "they may indeed have our charity, but cannot by us be considered as brothers and members of Christ".[34] The parting of the two sides was acrimonious, and they refused to shake hands. As a unifying initiative, the Marburg Colloquy was an abject failure. When Zwingli and Luther returned home, they proceeded to interpret the Fifteen Articles in contradictory fashions, though the public debate did bring a lull to their public controversy.

Despite the Marburg debacle, Prince Philipp of Hesse continued his attempts to bring evangelicals together in theological and military alliance. Within Germany the Lutheran princes submitted a doctrinal statement to the imperial Diet at Augsburg in June 1530, outlining their theological position in twenty-eight articles. This "Augsburg Confession" was drafted by Melanchthon and became the official summary of Lutheran dogma. It was followed in February 1531 by the formation of the Schmalkaldic League, a pact between the evangelical princes and cities of Germany in defence against potential attack by Emperor Charles V. They agreed to welcome fellow Reformation states to the League, but only those who would sign the Augsburg Confession, thus deliberately excluding the Swiss.

DEAD AND DISMEMBERED

Back in Switzerland, the city of Zürich continued to seek viable political alliances. Approaches to Venice and Milan got nowhere. Zwingli sent a confessional statement to Paris (later published as *The Exposition of the Christian Faith*) hoping to woo King François I, but negotiations with the French proved fruitless because they did not want to alienate the Five States. After lengthy discussions, a "Christian Understanding" was agreed between Zürich, Basel, Strassburg, and Hesse in November 1530, promising mutual aid against Catholic attack, but it bore little fruit.

Meanwhile the Christian Civic Union was brought to the point of collapse. The reformed cantons could not agree among themselves how to relate to the Catholic cantons. Despite the Kappel peace treaty of 1529, the Five States continued to resist the Reformation and would not allow unfettered evangelical preaching. In Zürich, Zwingli and Jud advocated military conflict as the only solution. Yet Basel, Berne, and Schaffhausen were more cautious. They agreed only to a food blockade of the Five States during the summer of 1531, seeking to starve their enemies into submission, but it was a total failure.

As the reformed cities quarrelled, the Catholics seized the initiative and declared war. Zürich was caught off guard and in a state of disarray. A rapidly recruited force of 3,500 men, including many pastors who had prayed for war, was engaged in a skirmish near Kappel on 11 October by a Five States army twice the size. In less than an hour of chaotic combat, the reformed troops were disastrously defeated. Many fled. Some were drowned in the Mühlbach River as they ran away, weighed down by their armour. Others were hacked to pieces. Five hundred Zürichers were killed, including about twenty-five clergymen, while the Catholics lost a hundred men.

Lying on the battlefield, mortally wounded, was Huldrych Zwingli himself. He had ridden out with the troops, not as a chaplain but as an armed combatant. As the Catholic soldiers looted the corpses at nightfall they recognized the face of the dying preacher by torchlight. First he was offered the ministrations of a priest to say his final confession, but Zwingli shook his head. Then he was struck dead with a sword. The following day many came to gloat over Zwingli's corpse and curse it. They considered cutting it into five pieces and sending one portion to each of the Five States. Instead, his body was dismembered and burned, and the ashes were mixed with pigs' offal as a sign of contempt. Zwingli was just forty-seven years old.

A fortnight later the Five States attacked again and Zürich was forced to sue for peace. The Christian Civic Union was dissolved and many districts were re-Catholicized. Zwingli's dream of the entire Swiss Confederation reformed under the word of God lay in tatters. When the news reached Wittenberg, Luther was unmoved. He saw Zwingli's early death as "a judgment of God" upon his doctrinal errors. Luther believed his Swiss rival had reaped the reward he deserved, according to Christ's promise that "all who draw the sword will perish by the sword" (Matthew 26:52).[35]

As Zürich licked its wounds, there was a backlash in the city against Zwingli and his reformed pastors. Some blamed the disaster on his warmongering and political meddling. Sensing the public mood, the city council promised only to appoint peace-loving clergy in future and to exclude them from all political decisions. In December 1531 they chose Heinrich Bullinger as Zwingli's successor, who announced that the clergy would withdraw from council committees, though he maintained the right to speak about political questions from the pulpit.

With Zwingli's reputation at its lowest ebb, some of his erstwhile followers were even questioning his orthodoxy. Was the reformer's violent death a sign of God's condemnation of his teaching? Bullinger, however, remained faithful to the memory of his former mentor. He observed that several godly leaders in the Bible, like Zechariah,

Stephen, and James, had been brutally killed. Zwingli may have been defeated and dismembered in battle, but his reformed faith would ultimately prove triumphant, Bullinger prophesied. Likewise Myconius came to his friend's defence in a hagiography published in 1532. Bullinger went on to lead the church in Zürich for more than forty years but always insisted he was merely continuing the work begun by the city's first and greatest reformer.

5

Pacifists and Polygamists

Both Martin Luther in Saxony and Huldrych Zwingli in Zürich clashed with religious radicals, whom Luther called *Schwärmer* ("fanatics"). Some were evangelicals, willing to affirm the principles of *sola scriptura* and *sola fide*, but frustrated that the Reformation was making such slow progress. They agitated for a deeper and more decisive reform programme which took seriously the full implications of New Testament Christianity. Others were mystical prophets, apocalyptic revolutionaries or ecstatic anarchists, who believed that the voice of the Holy Spirit took precedence over the Bible. Numerous radical communities sprang up independently across Europe during the 1520s and 1530s, operating outside the official structures of the local church (whether Catholic or evangelical). They had little in common with each other, except a rejection of infant baptism and a subversive challenge to the ecclesiastical and political *status quo*. Their doctrines were diverse and often incompatible, but all were labelled "Anabaptists". They were ruthlessly persecuted by the governing authorities wherever they were discovered.

THE SWISS BRETHREN

With Konrad Grebel dead from the plague, Felix Mantz drowned by the Zürich authorities in the Limmat River, and Jörg Blaurock banished to Austria, leadership of the Swiss Brethren fell to Michael

Sattler, a former Catholic monk. As prior of a Benedictine abbey in the Black Forest region of southern Germany, he had begun to study the New Testament and was won over to the Reformation cause. In 1525 he joined the Anabaptists in Zürich but was expelled when the city council sought to repress the movement. Soon he was back in Germany, preaching in partnership with Wilhelm Reublin near Horb and Rottenburg, on the edge of the Black Forest. Many were converted and joined secret Anabaptist congregations.

In February 1527 there was a clandestine conference of Anabaptist pastors in the village of Schleitheim, near Schaffhausen, on the German–Swiss border. Here the Swiss Brethren agreed to seven key theological principles known as the "Schleitheim Confession", drafted by Sattler. It was a foundational document for their evangelical movement. It took for granted central Christian doctrines such as the grace of God, the redemption of sinners through faith in Jesus Christ, and the authority of the Bible, and instead focused upon questions of church order and discipline, which were the key points of disagreement among the reformers. They distanced themselves not just from medieval Catholicism, but also from Zwinglianism and Lutheranism.

One of the distinctive aspects of the Confession was its belief that there was a stark polarity between the Christian community and the non-Christian world. Unlike the "magisterial" reformers (so-called because they were happy to collaborate with the secular magistrates), the Anabaptists taught a doctrine of separation from unbelievers, which in practice meant that the Swiss Brethren cut ties with all non-Anabaptists. They refused to swear oaths or serve as magistrates, and were committed to non-violence because Jesus told his followers not to resist evil but to turn the other cheek (Matthew 5:39). They acknowledged that secular authorities were ordained by God to use the sword to punish evil, but this was "outside the perfection of Christ" so believers should have nothing to do with "the devilish weapons of force".[1] This pacifism was a deliberate rejection of Thomas Müntzer's apocalyptic warfare and the other peasant violence which had recently swept through southern Germany. These principles became the keynote of many evangelical Anabaptist communities across Europe during the 1530s and 1540s, far beyond the borders of Switzerland and southern Germany.

While the meeting to establish the Schleitheim Confession was taking place, the Catholic government in Rottenburg uncovered the local Anabaptist network. As soon as Sattler returned home he was arrested and a copy of the Confession was found in his possession with other incriminating documents. Knowing that execution was inevitable, he wrote a valedictory letter to his congregation from his prison cell at Binsdorf, bidding them farewell and urging them to stand firm. He pleaded: "let no man remove you from the foundation which is laid through the letter of the Holy Scriptures, and is sealed with the blood of Christ and of many witnesses of Jesus".[2]

The Habsburg authorities, who had jurisdiction in Rottenburg, were determined to exterminate the Anabaptists. Archduke Ferdinand of Austria, younger brother of Emperor Charles V, proclaimed that the best way to deal with them was by "the third baptism" (drowning).[3] Therefore in May 1527, fourteen defendants were put on trial accused of seven crimes – sedition against the Holy Roman Empire; their rejection of transubstantiation, of infant baptism and of extreme unction; novel practices at the Lord's Supper; despising the Virgin Mary and the saints; and refusal to swear oaths to the government. Sattler also faced two additional charges – that he had abandoned his monastery and married a wife; and that he taught it was wrong to resist the Islamic armies from the Ottoman empire who were pressing forward into eastern Europe.

At first Sattler insisted that this secular court was not competent to judge religious questions. Nevertheless he argued that the Edict of Worms had condemned Lutheranism not Anabaptism, so technically they had not broken the laws of the empire. On the most serious charge, he admitted to preaching against armed resistance to invasion, because the Bible commands "Do not kill". Christians should pray for their enemies, not use violence against them. He even confessed to being more willing to fight against Christian persecutors like the Habsburg authorities than Turkish soldiers, because at least Muslims had the excuse of not knowing the Bible. This was nothing less than treason. Yet the Anabaptist leader proclaimed to the court: "we are ready to suffer and to await what God is planning to do with us. We will continue in our faith in Christ as long as we have breath until we are shown from the Scripture to be wrong... I appeal to the Scriptures".[4]

As anticipated, the sentence on the prisoners was death. Sattler was the first to suffer and his treatment was especially cruel. First he was taken to the Rottenburg market place where part of his tongue was cut out (though he could still speak) and two pieces of his flesh were torn out with red-hot tongs. Then he was dragged to the place of execution on a wagon, and five times the procession stopped along the route so that more parts of his body could be ripped out. He was tied with ropes to a ladder which was pushed into the fire, but continued to call upon the crowd to repent and turn to God. In anguish, he exclaimed: "Almighty, eternal God, you are the way and the truth; because I have not been shown to be in error, I will with your help today testify to the truth and seal it with my blood."[5] When the flames burned through the rope on his hands, he raised his two forefingers to heaven, as a secret sign to his Anabaptist friends of victory and endurance. Perhaps because they witnessed Sattler's torture, some of the Swiss Brethren publicly recanted their views. They were released and expelled from the Habsburg territories in ignominy. Sattler's wife refused to return to Catholicism so was drowned in the Neckar River a week after her husband's death.

Sattler's martyrdom had a considerable impact upon the evangelical Anabaptist movement and won them widespread sympathy throughout Switzerland and Germany, even among those who opposed their theological principles. The magisterial reformers in Strassburg were particularly distressed. Martin Bucer mourned Sattler as "a dear friend of God". Wolfgang Capito wrote immediately to the city council at Horb, protesting that he was a godly man who had shown "great zeal for the honour of God and the Church of Christ".[6] Reublin wrote an influential account of Sattler's execution (including stories of miracles said to have taken place in Rottenburg) which circulated among the Swiss Brethren in Zollikon, Grüningen, Basel, and Appenzell. It inspired many other Anabaptists to lay down their lives in the way he had done.

TRUTH IS IMMORTAL

The leading theologian within the earliest Anabaptist networks was Balthasar Hübmaier, who began his career as a popular Catholic teacher in southern Germany. A protégé of Johann Eck at the universities of Freiburg and Ingolstadt, he quickly rose to prominence as a scholar and preacher, attracting large crowds by his eloquent oratory. He ministered at Regensburg Cathedral in Bavaria and was then appointed as parish priest in the town of Waldshut, on the Swiss border. During 1522, when Hübmaier was in his early forties, his opinions changed dramatically. Already well schooled in patristic and scholastic theology, he began a fresh study of the Bible, especially St Paul's letters in the New Testament. He also toured through Switzerland, examining the style of Reformation in different cities, and met Erasmus at Basel. This experience persuaded him to return to Waldshut determined to reform the town after the model of Zürich. Hübmaier soon came to view his previous ministry in a very negative light. He mourned that for decades he had been "blinded by the doctrine of men" and had "not known the way to eternal life" because he had neglected "the pure word of God". He now realized that Christ had commanded, "Search the Scriptures", not, "Follow the old customs."[7] Hübmaier also complained that instead of godly pastors, the church hierarchy was guilty of promoting "courtesans, fools, whores, adulterers, procurers, gamblers, drunkards and buffoons, whom we would not entrust with our pigs or geese, let alone accept as the shepherds of our souls".[8]

In his desire to imitate Zwingli, Hübmaier issued Eighteen Theses in 1524 and invited all the neighbouring clergy to dispute them at Waldshut. He began to remove images from local churches and proved his rejection of clerical celibacy by marrying Elizabeth Hügline. Some months later he challenged his former mentor, Dr Eck, to a disputation, mocking the Catholic controversialist as "the elephant of Ingolstadt".[9] These activities brought Hübmaier to the attention of the imperial authorities, who put pressure on the Waldshut city council to dismiss him. He was also summoned to stand trial before the Bishop of Konstanz, but refused. Under attack from those who wished him silenced, he was forced to flee for temporary refuge to the Swiss canton of Schaffhausen in September 1524, from where he wrote an influential treatise, *On Heretics and Those Who Burn Them*. Hübmaier argued that unbelievers were to be won for the Christian gospel by gentle biblical teaching, not by coercion. Although he thought it permissible to burn erroneous and irreverent books, the burning of heretics was "an invention of the devil". The treatise ended with his personal motto, printed in almost all his works – *Die warheit ist untödlich* – "Truth is Unkillable" or "Truth is Immortal".[10]

Through his study of the New Testament, Hübmaier gradually became convinced that infant baptism was invalid, which brought him into open conflict with Zwingli, his former mentor and ally. He published *An Open Appeal to All Christian Believers* challenging anyone to defend the traditional rite on the basis of Scripture. Two months later, during the Easter of 1525, he was baptized at Waldshut with sixty others by Wilhelm Reublin, who had been expelled from Zürich. Over the next few days, Hübmaier himself baptized hundreds of other Anabaptist converts from his local parish and the surrounding region. From either side of the Swiss border, Zwingli and

Hübmaier fired treatises at each other. First came Zwingli's *Baptism, Rebaptism and Infant Baptism*, to which Hübmaier responded with *On the Christian Baptism of Believers*, a detailed study of New Testament texts, which received an acerbic reply. Prevented from attending the Zürich disputation on baptism in November 1525 because of the Klettgau peasant uprising, Hübmaier instead published *A Dialogue with Zwingli's Baptism Book*, in the form of a debate between the two men. His years of university training were reaping dividends. For the first time, the Anabaptists could claim an articulate theologian on their own side, who could match the depth of scholarship, biblical knowledge, and oratorical skill of the best magisterial reformers.

Hübmaier's success was short-lived. In December 1525 the Habsburg government in Austria launched a military assault upon Waldshut, in an attempt to capture its radical preacher and quash its reformation. A year earlier the town might have expected protection from its Swiss neighbours, but because of its allegiance to Anabaptism it was now left isolated. It was easily overpowered by Archduke Ferdinand's troops and Hübmaier escaped just in time. He ran across the border to Switzerland and made the mistake of hiding with friends at Zürich, where Anabaptism was a crime. When his hideout was discovered he was taken into custody and interrogated by Zwingli, before making the surprise announcement that he was ready to recant. A delighted city council sent him to the *Fraumünster* to read a statement denouncing Anabaptism, after which he would be set free. Yet as he stood in the pulpit, Hübmaier wavered again. He told the congregation: "Oh what anguish and travail I have suffered this night over the statements which I myself have made. So I say here and now, I can and I will not recant."[11] He then began an impromptu defence of believers' baptism, before Zwingli silenced him and accused him of being possessed by the devil.

Hübmaier was sent to the Wellenberg prison, a tower on an island in the middle of the Limmat River. There he wrote an exposition of his evangelical faith, *Twelve Articles of Christian Belief*, modelled on the Apostles' Creed. He knew that he might be tempted to abandon these views "through human fear and weakness, through tyranny, torture, sword, fire or water", but prayed: "let me not depart in death without this faith... let me not be ashamed in eternity".[12] Before long, Hübmaier did face the terror of torture and buckled under the strain. In April 1526 he was stretched on the rack by the Zürich authorities until he agreed to sign a public recantation of his Anabaptism, and then was dismissed from the city in shame, a broken man.

AN IMMOVABLE ROCK

Attacked by Catholics in Germany and evangelicals in Switzerland, Hübmaier migrated to Moravia, a safe haven for religious radicals of all descriptions. It was viewed by beleaguered Anabaptists across Europe as the "Promised Land", offering safety from persecution and freedom of worship. Many thousands made the difficult journey. Moravia was part of the kingdom of Bohemia, but vast regions were owned by the Lichtenstein family, who welcomed the Reformation. Baron Leonhard von Lichtenstein granted Hübmaier protection and was even baptized by him. The reformer settled at Nikolsburg (Mikulov), from where he engaged in a busy ministry of writing and preaching, free at last from persecution. At least 6,000 converts were baptized in one year and he published seventeen tracts on themes ranging from the freedom of the will to church discipline ("the ban") and the sacraments.

The Austrian authorities had been hunting Hübmaier since 1525, when he slipped through their grasp at Waldshut. Now they were given a second opportunity, when Moravia was acquired by the Habsburg dynasty. King Louis II of Hungary and Bohemia was killed at the hands of the Ottoman forces of Sultan Suleiman the Magnificent while fleeing the Battle of Mohács in August 1526. The king had no children, so many of his lands and titles were absorbed by his brother-in-law, Archduke Ferdinand. As a result, the persecution of evangelicals became more intense in Bohemia and Moravia. The Lichtenstein barons were no longer able to resist the imperial decrees and unwillingly handed over Hübmaier to the authorities in the summer of 1527. After a preliminary hearing in Vienna, the preacher and his wife were sent to Kreuzenstein Castle, a ruined fortress used as a gaol.

When imprisoned before, by Zwingli in Zürich, Hübmaier had collapsed under torture and recanted his Anabaptist views. Now he was tempted to do the same. He requested an opportunity to talk with his former friend, the Catholic theologian, Johannes Fabri (the archduke's chaplain and confessor, and Bishop of Vienna from 1530). After their conversations over several days at Kreuzenstein Castle, Hübmaier issued a formal statement on 3 January 1528 appealing for mercy from Ferdinand. He outlined his theological views, making numerous concessions to Catholic tradition and deliberately distancing himself from other reformers. His apologia began, somewhat ambiguously, "Mere faith alone is not sufficient for salvation", and he went on to welcome fasting, clerical celibacy, holy days, and the intercession of the saints, and to acknowledge the perpetual virginity of Mary.[13] He accepted the doctrine of free will (unlike Zwingli and Luther) and the authority of Christian magistrates to use the sword (unlike the Swiss Brethren).

Although he stood by his teaching on believers' baptism and the Lord's Supper, and wanted everything proved from Scripture, he was willing to submit himself to the authority of an ecumenical council. Hübmaier offered these compromises in the hope that his life would be spared, but it was not a sufficient recantation so Archduke Ferdinand rejected his appeal and the preacher was condemned to death.

In the spring Hübmaier was carried back to Vienna and tortured on the rack, but still would not recant. His execution on 10 March 1528 was witnessed by Stephan Sprügel, Dean of the philosophy faculty at

Vienna University, who reported that the prisoner remained to the end "fixed like an immovable rock in his heresy". Although Sprügel was not a sympathetic observer, he recalled that Hübmaier seemed to experience more joy than pain in his death. Exhorted to courage by his wife, the condemned man recited verses from Scripture as he was led through the city streets to the place of execution. When they arrived at the stake, he cried out: "O gracious God, forgive my sins in my great torment. O Father, I give you thanks that you will today take me out of this vale of tears." As the soldiers rubbed sulphur and gunpowder into Hübmaier's long beard, he joked: "Oh salt me well, salt me well." Then he called out to the crowd, as the flames were kindled, "O dear brothers, pray that God will forgive me my guilt in this my death. I will die in the Christian faith."[14] Three days later, Hübmaier's wife was drowned in the River Danube with a great stone tied around her neck.

TROUBLES IN UTOPIA

Deprived of Hübmaier's influential leadership, the Anabaptist communities in Moravia disintegrated into competing sects. There were frequent arguments, aggressive rivalries, and struggles for power. One controversial theological question which split the radicals was the appropriate Christian attitude to self-defence. The *Stäbler* ("people of the staff") were pacifists and fell out with the *Schwertler* ("people of the sword"), who believed that violence was legitimate in some situations. Their polarized congregations were unable to live at peace together. Frustrated by their persistent bickering, Baron Leonhard von Lichtenstein expelled the *Stäbler* from his Nikolsburg territories in 1529. Yet out of that moment of crisis sprang one of the most innovative Anabaptist experiments: the "community of goods".

The Nikolsburg exiles, led by Jakob Wiedemann, were homeless and destitute. They were fast running out of food and had many

Anabaptist widows and orphans in their midst, so had no option but to pool their resources. This had New Testament precedent, since the early Christians in the book of Acts sold their possessions and "held everything in common" (Acts 2:44; 4:32). Yet the growth of this doctrine among the *Stäbler* was driven as much by economic necessity as by theological principle. They would have died of starvation otherwise. When they found refuge at Austerlitz, in another part of Moravia, they established communal settlements known as *Brüderhofe* ("place of brothers"), where they lived and worked together. Within these communes the Anabaptists took corporate responsibility for agriculture, manufacture, education, and other activities, so that none was in need.

Although the *Brüderhofe* were viewed as a form of Christian utopia, the dissension and schisms continued. Wilhelm Reublin arrived in Moravia with his wife and children in 1530, fleeing persecution by evangelicals in Strassburg, and immediately tried to wrest control from Wiedemann. After an acrimonious dispute between the rival factions, Reublin split from the Austerlitz community, taking about 300 followers to nearby Auspitz. There he set up a new *Brüderhofe*, with himself as the chief minister. Yet Reublin's brief leadership of the commune ended in scandal when money was found hidden under his mattress. He was likened to Ananias in the book of Acts, who lied to the Holy Spirit by pretending to hand over all his possessions while holding some back for himself (Acts 5). The community at Auspitz was reorganized and reformed from 1533 by Jakob Hutter, who assumed control after fleeing the Habsburg authorities in the Austrian Tyrol. Again, his leadership of the community was short. During a preaching tour in Austria he was captured and tortured. His body was lacerated, then brandy was poured into his wounds and set on fire. Eventually he was burned alive at Innsbruck in February 1536. His bereaved followers took the name "Hutterites" in honour of their martyred hero, and became one of the best-known Anabaptist communities in Europe.

An army of martyrs

Lutherans, Zwinglians, and Roman Catholics were deeply divided on many issues, but on one key question all were agreed – that Anabaptism in its multifarious guises must be suppressed. Zürich had led the way with the expulsion and execution of the Swiss Brethren and the drowning of Felix Mantz. Soon the reformed cantons of Switzerland were discussing "how we might curb and eradicate this evil, un-Christian, annoying and seditious weed".[15]

Watching from Germany, Luther was initially distressed by this development. He argued that peaceful Anabaptists should be won back to the truth by patient biblical teaching, not by violent persecution. In his treatise *On Anabaptism* (1528) he proclaimed:

> *It is not just, and I am pained because these miserable people are so wretchedly killed, burned, and horribly slaughtered. One ought to let everyone believe what he will… With the Scripture and God's word shall one defend against and stand up to such people. With fire one accomplishes little.*[16]

However, within a few years Luther was arguing that Anabaptists were guilty of sedition and blasphemy, so should be punished with the sword for undermining gospel ministry and the political order. Likewise Philipp Melanchthon encouraged the death penalty because "they repudiate the public ministry of the word and teach that one can be saved without preaching or worship".[17] Of all Protestant states, the persecution of religious radicals was fiercest in Electoral Saxony. One local Anabaptist leader, Melchior Rinck, accused the Lutherans of departing from the gospel by their "shameful deeds, persecutions, tyrannies, betrayals and the shedding of so much innocent blood".[18]

More than 80 per cent of Anabaptist martyrdoms took place within Catholic territories. The movement was especially vibrant in Austria and therefore caused particular alarm to the Habsburg authorities. From 1527 Archduke Ferdinand issued a series of edicts against this "new, terrible, unheard of teaching".[19] The death penalty for rebaptism was extended to the entire Holy Roman Empire by imperial mandate at the Diet of Speyer in April 1529. This was the same Diet at which "Protestantism" was born, when the Lutheran princes and cities "protested" against the Edict of Worms, but they showed no concern to protect the religious freedom of Anabaptists. As a result there were waves of martyrdoms. Unlike the charge of "heresy", the crime of "rebaptism" was relatively easy to prove and did not require complex theological debate. Therefore dozens of Anabaptists could be swiftly despatched by the hangman. In some regions the intense persecution succeeded in stamping out the movement, but elsewhere it seemed to stimulate growth. At Alzey in the German Palatinate 350 Anabaptists were rushed to their deaths in 1529 in fulfilment of the imperial mandate, and others were deliberately maimed, but the local official complained, "What shall I do? The more I cause to be executed, the more they increase."[20]

Martyrdom and suffering became significant themes in Anabaptist identity. These afflictions were welcomed as the fruit of faithfulness to the gospel and a sign that the return of Christ was imminent. Pacifism in the face of persecution was a dominant motif in Anabaptist hymnody and the precious testimony of the martyrs was carefully preserved in the archives of local congregations. For example, the *Geschichtsbuch* ("Chronicle") of the Hutterite community recorded their witness in dramatic terms:

> *Some of them were racked and stretched so much that the sun could shine right through them, some were torn apart and died under torture, some were burned to ashes and dust as heretics, some were roasted on spits, some were ripped with red-hot pincers, some were imprisoned in houses and then burned together as a group, some were hanged from trees, some were executed by the sword, were strangled or were cut*

to pieces... Like lambs they were often led in groups to the
slaughter and were butchered in devilish ways.[21]

In a later generation the Dutch martyrologist, Thieleman J. van
Braght, compiled many of these stories in his *Martyrs Mirror* (1660).
It became the Anabaptist equivalent of John Foxe's *Book of Martyrs*
in England.

THE CITY OF SAINTS

The first widespread reform movement in the Netherlands was not
Lutheranism or Zwinglianism, but Melchiorism – an apocalyptic
Anabaptist sect following the teachings of Melchior Hoffman, a
German furrier. He began his career as a disciple of Luther, but the
Wittenberg reformer would have nothing to do with his "fanatical
speculations".[22] Hoffman believed that the end of the world was
imminent and that Christ would soon return to inaugurate the reign
of the saints. In these predictions he was strongly influenced by the
prophetic visions of a married couple, Lienhart and Ursula Jost,
whose ecstatic revelations he considered as equivalent to those of
Isaiah or Jeremiah in the Bible. Another prophet declared in 1533
that the second coming would occur after Hoffman was imprisoned
for six months, so he deliberately had himself arrested in Strassburg.
Yet it was a miscalculation. He was never released and died in his
cell a decade later. In Hoffman's enforced absence, leadership of the
Melchiorites was usurped by another radical prophet, Jan Matthijs,
a baker from Haarlem.

Melchiorite theology had devastating consequences for the city of
Münster in Westphalia, in northern Germany. Like many other cities
in that region, the people of Münster decided to throw their weight
behind the Lutheran Reformation. After a struggle to break free from
the local prince-bishop, their independence was formally recognized
by the Treaty of Dülmen in February 1533 and the city council looked

to Wittenberg for direction. Yet soon their leading reformer, Bernhard Rothmann, began to preach Anabaptist principles supported by exiles from nearby Wassenberg. When the council tried to expel the radicals, Rothmann's followers gathered at St Lambert's Church in the city centre, armed with weapons and ready to defend themselves. The council backed down, acknowledging that Münster welcomed theological diversity and freedom of worship. Although Rothmann lost his pulpit, he was not banished and continued to gather allies. In early January 1534, he and the Wassenbergers were baptized by two missionaries sent by Jan Matthijs. Meanwhile a growing number of Anabaptists began to flood into the city, which they called the "New Jerusalem", fleeing persecution in the surrounding district.

Relations between Lutherans, Melchiorites, and Catholics disintegrated under mutual suspicions. There were rumours that the Lutheran-majority council planned to invite the Catholic bishop and his cavalry into the city to destroy the Anabaptists. According to another false report, the bishop had already assembled 3,000 soldiers for an attack. The Anabaptists, led by alderman Hermann Redeker, met in front of the city hall, fully armed, and closed the city gates. There were minor skirmishes in which some Melchiorites were taken prisoner, and the Lutherans sent a message to the bishop appealing for help. Catholic troops arrived at midnight, joined the next morning by several thousand peasants ready for battle. Massively outnumbered, the followers of Redeker and Rothmann agreed to lay down their weapons and claimed to eschew violence. Now the Lutherans made a fatal mistake. They also feared the Catholic bishop, so instead of pressing home their advantage, they accepted the pledge of peace. The peasant army was paid off with free beer and dismissed. Yet the prince-bishop was irate and besieged the city.

In the chaos which followed, many Lutherans and the remaining Catholics fled from Münster to avoid the episcopal assault. At the same time, Melchiorites continued to stream into the city, including Jan Matthijs himself. This led to a dramatic shift in the balance of power. In the annual elections to the city council in February, all the appointments were filled by Anabaptists. They won complete control and began to enact their programme of reform. Those who refused to accept adult baptism were driven from the city, forced to leave their belongings behind. Yet it was not the elected council which exercised the real power, but the prophet Matthijs, often without reference to the rule of law. For example, he summarily executed a burgher who dared to suggest he was possessed by the devil, and imprisoned those who protested at this rough justice. Matthijs's rule did not last long. Told in a vision to attack the bishop's army, he charged out of the city, only to be cut to pieces.

Leadership passed to another prophet, Jan van Leiden, a former journeyman tailor and radical Melchiorite, who immediately abolished the city council and replaced them with twelve elders. Then in September 1534, guided by a prophecy, he proclaimed himself king, claiming to rule "over emperors, kings, princes and all the powers of the earth".[23] Münster was now to be a theocratic monarchy, modelled on the reigns of King David and King Solomon in the Old Testament, but established by the power of the sword. The Melchiorites saw themselves as engaged in an apocalyptic crusade, preparing for the return of Jesus Christ by exterminating the godless. One Münster prophet claimed that King Jan would reign over the whole world and slay all other rulers. In another piece of propaganda, Rothmann, the king's spokesman, proclaimed:

Now, dear brothers, the time of vengeance is here. God has raised the promised David and armed him for vengeance and punishment over Babylon and its people. Therefore, dear brothers, arm for battle, not only with the apostles' humble weapon of suffering, but also with vengeance, the magnificent armour of David, to stamp out the entire Babylonian power and the entire godless establishment with the power and help of God.[24]

When polygamy was introduced into Münster, on the basis of select passages from the Old Testament, it provoked a revolt. Ex-alderman Mollenhecke and about 200 followers launched a surprise attack and managed to capture the key Melchiorite leaders. Yet when the rebels threatened to surrender the city to the bishop, they were overthrown. Forty-seven conspirators were executed by firing squad and buried in two mass graves. From that point on, no one dared speak out. Wives who objected to polygamy suffered imprisonment or worse. When one woman refused to sleep with her husband and prayed, "Heavenly Father, if you are almighty, see to it that I never more in my life have to climb into this marriage bed," she was executed.[25] King Jan himself beheaded one of his own wives for disobedience. He also performed another six or seven decapitations, as a demonstration of kingship. Among the many crimes now punishable by death were blasphemy, sexual immorality, theft, lying, gossiping, and disrespect of parents. The citizens of Münster lived in abject fear under this Melchiorite reign of terror.

STARVED INTO SUBMISSION

Determined to regain control, the prince-bishop of Münster assembled an army of 8,000 men for an assault upon the city. He lacked the finance to afford a long and costly siege, so hoped for a speedy victory. However, his first attack in May 1534 was a disaster, partly because some of the troops were drunk, leaving 200 dead or wounded. The second attempt in August was even less successful and easily repulsed. Münster was well defended with ample fortifications and artillery, surrounded by a moat. In case of surprise, 500 Anabaptists stood constantly on guard on the walls, ready to sound the alarm. They also made frequent sorties against the besiegers. Therefore the bishop changed his strategy. He reduced his army to 3,000 mercenaries and 300 cavalry, and began a blockade.

The kingdom of Münster would now be starved into submission, however long it took.

Despite their defences, the Melchiorites could not survive without reinforcements. Therefore they sent urgent appeals through all the cities of Westphalia, commanding God's people to hasten to their aid. One prophet, Jakob of Osnabrück, predicted that the whole world would soon be destroyed and that only Münster would be preserved in peace and safety. Likewise a letter circulated to the Dutch Melchiorites warned them to come to Münster to escape the Last Judgment:

> *Dear friends, you should know that God has revealed to us that each one of you should set out to journey to the New Jerusalem, a city of the saints. For God wills to punish the world... whoever has a knife or a spear or a gun, take it with him, and whoever does not, buy one, for the Lord will deliver us through his powerful hand, through his servants Moses and Aaron.*[26]

Many Anabaptists responded. The authorities at Kampen in the Netherlands arrested twenty-seven ships carrying 3,000 people including women and children, and loaded with weapons, on their way to rendezvous with the Münsterites. Although the leaders were interrogated and executed, most of the people were pardoned and sent home after the government concluded they were not seditious but simply naïve.

Meanwhile the Münster prophets attempted to stimulate Melchiorite uprisings elsewhere in Westphalia and the Netherlands, to distract attention away from their city. All the spiritual leaders (except King Jan and Rothmann) scattered through the district to drum up support, preaching judgment openly in the streets, but most were quickly arrested and executed. In January 1535 Anabaptist plots were foiled in Wesel, Maastricht, Utrecht, and

Leiden. In March about 300 men fought a pitched battle at the *Oldeklooster* (Old Cloister), a monastery near Bolsward in Friesland, until overpowered by the local militia. Another seventy Anabaptists took to arms in Groningen but were soon dispersed. There were even hopes that Amsterdam might rise up on behalf of Münster. In May, sixty rebels captured the town hall, shouting: "Slay! Slay the godless! Rally round, everyone who loves the Word of God!"[27] Yet the evangelicals of Amsterdam refused to respond and the conspirators were easily killed or captured.

In Münster the situation was desperate. Nothing but a miracle would save them from being starved to death or mown down by the bishop's army. Yet King Jan recalled that in the Old Testament God had once rescued King Hezekiah and the besieged city of Jerusalem by sending an angel with a mighty sword to destroy their enemies. Münster should pray for a similar deliverance. The king prophesied that God would come to their aid before Easter 1535, but he later chastised his starving people: "Do you want to set a deadline for God? No, God will tolerate no deadlines. You must be free from sin, from all sins, then God will rescue us."[28] With Münster on the point of collapse, the bishop finally made his move. Disillusioned Anabaptist deserters had betrayed the weak point in the city's defences, and on 25 June 400 troops broke in and opened the gates for the rest of the army. The city was sacked and looted by the bishop's soldiers. Melchiorites were dragged from their homes and summarily executed. Many fled or tried to hide, but few men escaped with their lives. Those who stood to fight were slaughtered, including Rothmann, who preferred death in battle to the horrors which would await him if captured. The streets were strewn with corpses and awash with blood. The bodies were dumped in mass graves, dug by local peasants.

Special punishment was reserved for King Jan and two of his collaborators, Bernhard Knipperdolling (a former tailor and ecstatic prophet, who rose to become the king's deputy) and Bernhard

Krechting (a former parish priest). In January 1536 they were publicly tortured at length in the Münster market place, where their bodies were ripped apart with red-hot iron tongs. After enduring excruciating pain, they were finally put out of their misery by having their throats torn open and a dagger thrust deep into their hearts. The implements of torture were hung up on the city hall as a deterrent to the local populace. The corpses of the three men were suspended in iron cages on the tower of St Lambert's Church, where they were left to rot and as food for the birds. When the bodies were gone, still the cages remained in perpetuity as a gruesome reminder to succeeding generations of Münster's disastrous experiment in establishing a Melchiorite kingdom.

NO MORE SOFT PILLOWS

After the Münster catastrophe, the Melchiorite movement in Westphalia and the Netherlands took a new turn. Some continued to advocate militancy, notably Jan van Batenburg, who took over the mantle of Jan van Leiden and led marauding gangs through the countryside. Yet these apocalyptic and riotous splinter groups were eventually expunged. Other communities of Melchiorites reacted against their violent Münster heritage by turning to pacifism, notably the Mennonites, who grew to become one of the most influential Anabaptist networks.

Menno Simons was a young Catholic priest in the Dutch villages of Pingjum and Witmarsum in Friesland where he gained a reputation as an "evangelical preacher".[29] In his early ministry his friends joked at the paucity of his Bible knowledge, yet he began to study the New Testament and to question traditional Catholic dogmas such as transubstantiation. He built up a large congregation but came to believe that his preaching was motivated by a desire for prestige: "Although I had now acquired considerable knowledge of the Scriptures, yet I wasted that knowledge through the lusts of my youth in an impure, sensual, unprofitable life, and sought nothing but gain, ease, favour of men, splendour, name and fame."[30]

Menno's comfortable outlook was shaken in 1531 by the beheading of Sicke Snijder, an Anabaptist, in the city of Leeuwarden, the capital of Friesland. He started to doubt the validity of infant baptism, despite scrutinizing the arguments of reformers like Martin Luther, Martin Bucer, and Heinrich Bullinger. The tragic slaughter of Münsterite fanatics in March 1535 at the *Oldeklooster*, not far from his parish, gave him further cause for reflection. Menno denounced their theological mistakes, but was impressed by their wholehearted conviction:

> the blood of these people, although misled, fell so hot on my heart that I could not stand it, nor find rest in my soul. I reflected upon my unclean, carnal life, also the hypocritical doctrine and idolatry which I still practised daily in appearance of godliness, but without relish. I saw that these zealous children, although in error, willingly gave their lives and their estates for their doctrine and faith.[31]

He felt that, unlike the Anabaptist martyrs, he was trying to "escape the cross of Christ" and his conscience was tormented by the question, "if I should gain the whole world and live a thousand years, and at last have to endure the wrath of God, what would I have gained?"[32] In January 1536 Menno finally renounced his career as a Catholic priest and joined the Melchiorites. He interpreted this stark change of allegiance as nothing less than a conversion experience, vividly described in an influential autobiographical sketch twenty years later.

Menno's ability was quickly recognized and by 1540 he had assumed control of the Melchiorite movement. He supplanted rival leaders such as David Joris, and the brothers Obbe and Dirk Philips, and his followers soon became known as "Mennonites". Menno spent the rest of his life as an itinerant preacher and pastor travelling through the Netherlands and northern Germany, often hunted by the imperial authorities but eluding capture. His theological writings such as *Christian Baptism* (1539), *Foundation of Christian Doctrine* (1540), and *True Christian Faith* (1541) helped to re-establish the movement on evangelical foundations. Menno deliberately sought to erase the Anabaptist reputation for heterodoxy and anarchy which had been forged on the blood-stained streets of Münster. Like the Swiss Brethren, he also emphasized the biblical principle of pacifism: "We leave iron, metal, pikes and swords to those who unfortunately consider human blood to be worth no more than the blood of pigs."[33] Despite this policy of non-violence, Mennonite congregations often bore the brunt of persecution wherever they gathered. Emperor Charles V published an edict against them and offered a reward for Menno's capture. After almost two decades on the run, he prosaically observed:

> *when the clergy repose on easy beds and soft pillows, we*
> *generally have to hide ourselves in out-of-the-way corners.*
> *When they at weddings and baptismal banquets revel with*
> *pipe, trumpet, and lute, we have to be on our guard when a*
> *dog barks for fear the arresting officer has arrived.*

Nevertheless, Menno Simons professed himself glad to have abandoned the privileged life of a priest for the dangerous ministry of an outlawed evangelist, seeking "not wealth, nor possessions, nor luxury, nor ease, but only the praise of the Lord, my salvation, and the salvation of many souls."[34]

6

Defender of the Faith

Since the mid-fifteenth century the kings of France had laid exclusive claim to the title *Rex Christianissimus* ("Most Christian King") and the young Renaissance monarch of England, Henry VIII, was eager to win an equivalent plaudit. Watching the spread of Lutheranism on the continent, he saw his opportunity to come forward as a public champion of Catholicism on the international stage and to demonstrate his theological prowess. With a little help from his advisers, the king crafted a doctrinal treatise against Martin Luther, published in the summer of 1521 just a few months after the Diet of Worms.

Luther had argued in *The Babylonian Captivity of the Church* that according to the Bible there were only two sacraments (baptism and the Lord's Supper), but Henry insisted upon the traditional calculation of seven sacraments. His book, *Assertio Septem Sacramentorum*, jeered the Wittenberg reformer as "a knavish little friar". Nor was the king above coarse language. He warned that Luther "spews out viper's venom" and "belches out of the filthy mouth of the hellish wolf those frightful barks which the ears of the whole flock detest, disdain and abhor".[1] Pope Leo X approved. When he was formally presented with a copy of the book at the Vatican in October 1521 he rewarded the king with his coveted title, *Fidei Defensor* ("Defender of the Faith").

Despite Henry VIII's obvious abhorrence of Lutheran literature, it was soon being smuggled into England along with other evangelical books from the continent. There was a particularly warm reception among a small group of scholars in Cambridge associated with Thomas Bilney (fellow of Trinity Hall). He had been converted through reading Erasmus's *Novum Testamentum* where he stumbled across a sentence from the apostle Paul, "This is a true saying, and worthy of all men to be embraced, that Christ Jesus came into the world to save sinners, of whom I am the worst" (1 Timothy 1:15). Bilney recalled:

> *This one sentence, through God's instruction and inward working, which I did not then perceive, did so exhilarate my heart, being before wounded with the guilt of my sins, and being almost in despair, that even immediately I seemed unto myself inwardly to feel a marvellous comfort and quietness.*[2]

He began to testify to his faith in Cambridge, which led to the conversion of other scholars including Thomas Arthur, Robert Barnes, John Lambert, and Hugh Latimer. Latimer acknowledged that he had been "as obstinate a papist as any was in England" before Bilney spoke with him. Latimer's oration for his Bachelor of Divinity degree in 1524 had denounced the teaching of Philipp Melanchthon, but soon he "began to smell the word of God, and forsake the school-doctors, and such fooleries".[3]

BIBLE SMUGGLING

One of those who helped to supply evangelical literature for the English market was William Tyndale. As a tutor in Gloucestershire, Tyndale met a fellow scholar who argued that it would be better to be without God's law than the pope's law. Yet Tyndale replied in words which echoed the famous *Paraclesis* of Erasmus: "I defy the pope and all his laws... if God spare my life ere many years, I will cause a boy that driveth the plough, shall know more of the

Scripture than thou dost."[4] With that aim in mind, he set himself the target of translating the Bible into English, not from the Latin Vulgate but from the original Hebrew and Greek texts. It was a ground-breaking but dangerous initiative, an act of heresy according to the 1407 "Constitutions of Oxford" which had been composed to combat Lollardy and were still in force. Unable to find a patron and protector in England, Tyndale sought a safe haven on the continent.

In 1524 he began work on the New Testament at Cologne in Germany, assisted by a former friar, William Roye. However, before even the Gospel of Matthew was finished, their project was discovered by one of Luther's opponents, Johann Cochlaeus, who informed the authorities. Tyndale and Roye fled down the River Rhine to Worms, where they succeeded in printing a complete New Testament by early 1526, in a slim volume, which was easy to smuggle. It also began to appear in pirated editions from an Antwerp printer, and before long several thousand New Testaments had been shipped secretly into England.

The authorities, led by Cardinal Thomas Wolsey (the Lord Chancellor), tried to stem the flood by hunting down and burning the contraband, warning booksellers, threatening readers, and imprisoning the smugglers. In October 1526 Bishop Tunstal of London preached against Tyndale, claiming to have found 2,000 errors in his translation, before ceremonially burning a pile of New Testaments. He urged the secular authorities in the capital to be diligent in tracking down copies of this dangerous book which was "seducing the common people" with its "wicked and perverse interpretations".[5] Tunstal was correct in discerning that Tyndale's New Testament was a threat to the *status quo* by its translation of key theological terms. For example, Tyndale rendered *presbuteros* as "elder" instead of "priest"; *ekklesia* as "congregation" instead of "church"; *agape* as "love" instead of "charity"; and *metanoeo* as "repent" instead of "do penance". This shift of emphasis had major implications.

Among those caught in the act of smuggling New Testaments was Robert Barnes, under house arrest in Northampton, who concocted an elaborate plan to escape Wolsey's clutches – he wrote a suicide note, left his clothes by the river, and fled. While the authorities searched for his body, Barnes made his way in disguise across to Antwerp, from where he settled in Wittenberg and became a friend of Luther.

Another book-smuggling enterprise was uncovered in February 1528 at Oxford, organized by Thomas Garrard (curate of All Hallows, Honey Lane, in London). He set up a secret network for distributing copies of Tyndale's New Testament, together with books by Luther, Melanchthon, Bucer, Zwingli, Hus, Wycliffe, and others. Garrard was arrested by the university proctors, but managed to flee in disguise toward Wales, hoping to sail for Germany. The ports were watched and he was recaptured at Bedminster near Bristol, before being sent for trial in London.

Others in Oxford were soon caught up in the affair when an unfaithful friend betrayed the names of twenty-two of Garrard's associates. Rooms were searched and floorboards broken in the hunt for heretical books. Among those arrested were several canons from Cardinal College, recently founded by Wolsey himself upon the site of St Frideswide's priory. They were imprisoned for six months in an underground salt-fish cellar, where they became ill and three died. The young scholars were forced to recant and as a humiliating act of penance they marched in procession past a giant bonfire in the centre of Oxford and threw in the forbidden books found in their possession.

One of those arrested was John Frith (recruited, ironically, from Cambridge by Wolsey himself), who was released on condition he remained within ten miles of Oxford, but he also fled to the continent and joined Tyndale in exile at Antwerp. There he began to write evangelical works for English readers, including treatises like *Disputation of Purgatory*, which demolished the doctrine of purgatory as unbiblical, and *Antithesis*, which contrasted the teaching of Christ and the pope.

BLIND GUIDES AND RAVENOUS WOLVES

Alongside his Bible translations, Tyndale published a number of significant theological works from his base in Antwerp. *The Parable of the Wicked Mammon* (1528) was an exposition of the doctrine of justification by faith alone, building on Luther's teaching. For example, Tyndale emphasized that "faith bringeth pardon and forgiveness freely purchased by Christ's blood". Therefore good works were of no benefit at the hour of death, "though thou hast a thousand holy candles about thee, a hundred ton of holy water, a ship-full of pardons, a cloth-sack full of friars' coats, and all the ceremonies in the world".[6] He also asserted that popes, cardinals, and bishops were like the scribes, Pharisees and "Antichrists" of the New Testament who killed Christ. He had expected them to burn his translation of the New Testament, and prophesied: "if they burn me also, if it be God's will it shall so be".[7] Tyndale's book soon began to circulate in England, where it was denounced by Thomas More (a leading humanist scholar and royal councillor) as "a very treasury and well-spring of wickedness".[8]

A few months later Tyndale published his most influential treatise, *The Obedience of a Christian Man*. The reformers had been accused of instigating rebellion, but he denied this charge, arguing instead that the Bible taught submission to kings and governors. Furthermore, he continued to attack the corruption, hypocrisy, and greed of the Church. Tyndale chastised the clergy as "blind guides" who trembled in fear if they made the smallest mistake in their complex religious ceremonies (like pouring too much wine into the chalice, or reciting the wrong words), and yet who considered it "but a trifle" to sleep with prostitutes or send men to their deaths in battle.[9] He mocked their reverence for "holy water, holy fire, holy bread, holy salt, hallowed bells, holy wax, holy boughs, holy candles and holy ashes", and yet lamented their disregard for the Bible.[10] He warned that the church had replaced the promises of God with "open lies", and that "to keep us from knowledge of the truth, they do all things in Latin. They pray in Latin, they christen in Latin, they bless in Latin, they give absolution in Latin: only curse they in the English tongue."[11] Significantly, Tyndale appealed for the king to rid his realm of this ecclesiastical oppression, and argued that anyone who resisted royal decrees resisted God and would be damned, "yea though he be pope, bishop, monk or friar".[12] Thomas More again led the response to Tyndale, mocking the idea that people could understand the Scriptures without the aid of the church. He asserted that evangelical Bible expositors should have "an hot iron thrust through their blasphemous tongues". He abused Tyndale as "a hell-hound in the kennel of the devil" and "an idolater and devil worshipper", who was "discharging a filthy foam of blasphemies out of his brutish beastly mouth".[13]

A similar note was struck in *A Supplication for the Beggars*, an anticlerical satire published by Simon Fish, another English exile in Antwerp. The tract pretended to be an appeal to the king from genuine beggars (like the blind, the sick, and the lame) against the invasion of England by "counterfeit, holy and idle beggars" (bishops, abbots, archdeacons, priests, monks, canons, and friars). It asserted that this multitude of ecclesiastics were not godly shepherds but "ravenous wolves" devouring the flock. They were "holy thieves", squeezing money from the people by their tithes and taxes until they had come to own more than a third of the kingdom. Fish looked to King Henry to deliver England from these "cruel, unclean, unmerciful" hypocrites by confiscating their property and putting them to work. The clergy, he concluded, deserved to be "whipped naked" through every market town.[14]

Burned alive

The appointment of Thomas More as Lord Chancellor in October 1529, and John Stokesley as the new Bishop of London in March 1530, signalled a dramatic shift in the campaign against evangelicalism. Both were energetic heresy-hunters. Instead of burning books, the authorities now began to burn people. The first to suffer was Thomas Hitton – often considered the first martyr of the English Reformation. He was captured in Kent after helping to smuggle copies of Tyndale's New Testament from Antwerp, and was burned at the stake at Maidstone in February 1530. More called him "the devil's stinking martyr", whose soul had been sent straight from the fire of execution "to the fire everlasting".[15]

Hitton's death was a sign of things to come. Soon the prisons began to fill up with evangelicals, the most prominent of whom was Thomas Bilney. Under pressure from Wolsey he had recanted in 1527 but returned to Cambridge in shame and despair, filled with remorse for denying his evangelical principles. Friends were unable to console him and when Bilney read the promises of Scripture he felt as though someone had "run him through the heart with a sword".[16] In a state of spiritual anguish, he travelled through Norfolk in the spring of 1531, preaching in private homes and openly in the fields. At Norwich he spoke with a nun who had been converted through his ministry, giving her a copy of Tyndale's New Testament and *The Obedience of a Christian Man*. Arrest and condemnation were inevitable. Bilney was burned in the Lollard's Pit at Norwich, crying out "Jesus!" and "*Credo!* " ("I believe!").[17]

Further executions followed from the winter of 1531 to the spring of 1532. Richard Bayfield had been a Benedictine monk in the abbey at Bury St Edmunds, but was converted through the ministry of Robert Barnes. He initially recanted after being imprisoned, but then fled to the continent and became one of the leading smugglers of evangelical literature into England. He brought in at least three major consignments of illegal books, via Norfolk,

London, and Colchester, but this operation was uncovered by More. The Lord Chancellor proclaimed that Bayfield had returned to his evangelicalism "like a dog returning to his vomit", and ensured that he was burned at Smithfield, in central London.[18] He was followed a few weeks later by John Tewkesbury, a London leather merchant who had been converted through reading Tyndale's New Testament and *The Wicked Mammon*. Meanwhile, at Devizes in Wiltshire, John Bent was burned for denying transubstantiation. In Essex, three men were hanged after they broke into Dovercourt Church one night, pulled down the rood (the large crucifix above the rood-screen dividing the nave from the chancel), and set it alight. At Chesham in Buckinghamshire, Thomas Harding was spotted secretly reading a book of English prayers in a local wood and when an angry crowd ransacked his house, they found portions of the Bible in English hidden under the floorboards. After trial by Bishop Longland of Lincoln, he was burned at the stake, though someone threw a block of wood at his head and smashed his skull before the fire did its work. At Exeter in Devon, Thomas Benet was burned after fixing anonymous posters to the doors of local churches, including the cathedral, denouncing the pope as "Antichrist", "Thief", "Mercenary", and "Murderer of Christ's Flock".[19]

Thomas More celebrated the deaths of these various heretics, proclaiming: "after the fire of Smithfield, hell doth receive them where the wretches burn forever".[20] He was actively involved in several prosecutions, including that of James Bainham, a London lawyer who had recently married the widow of Simon Fish. After being tortured on the rack in the Tower of London, Bainham recanted his evangelical views but his conscience was troubled. Only a few weeks after his release from prison, he stood up in church one Sunday morning, with tears rolling down his cheeks, and confessed that he had denied God. Holding a copy of Tyndale's New Testament in his hand, he proclaimed: "if I should not return again unto the truth, this word of God would damn me both body and soul at the day of judgment". He was soon executed, praying as the flames took hold, "The Lord forgive Sir Thomas More!"[21]

This spate of burnings included not just the living, but the dead. Bainham's uncle, William Tracy, a prominent member of the Gloucestershire gentry, had made a provocative final will and testament as he lay on his death-bed in October 1530. In a departure from the medieval norm, he refused to ask help from the Virgin Mary and the saints, and instead asserted: "I accept none in heaven or in earth to be mediator between me and God, but only Jesus Christ." Therefore Tracy refused to leave any money to pay for priests to say masses for his soul, insisting, "I trust only to the promises of Christ."[22] This will soon became a *cause célèbre*. It circulated among evangelicals throughout England as a model for others to follow, and was later published in Antwerp with commentaries by Tyndale and Frith. Yet Tracy was pronounced a heretic by the clergy in convocation. His corpse was exhumed from its grave and burned.

Chancellor More also managed to capture John Frith, Tyndale's associate, when he visited England from exile in Antwerp in 1531, another high-profile arrest. He was seized at Milton Shore in Essex as he was about to sail back to Flanders, and sent to the Tower. When he heard the news, Tyndale wrote to encourage him in his prison cell: "Your cause is Christ's gospel, a light that must be fed with the blood of faith... Rejoice and be glad, for great is your reward in heaven." Tyndale urged his friend not to listen to the "sweet words" of hypocrites who would advise him to recant, but instead to pray that God would "ease your pain, or shorten it".[23] Frith was put on trial at St Paul's Cathedral, where Bishop Stokesley condemned him as "the child of wickedness and darkness... guilty of most detestable heresies... an obstinate unpenitent sinner". The bishop feared that Frith would "infect the Lord's flock with thy heresy", and so sentenced him to death.[24] He was burned at Smithfield in July 1533, chained back-to-back with a tailor from Kent.

THE KING'S "GREAT MATTER"

Since the late 1520s a constitutional crisis had been brewing. King Henry was determined to ensure the dynastic survival of the Tudors by providing a male heir to the throne. His marriage to the Spanish princess, Katherine of Aragon, had resulted in several pregnancies but only one surviving child, Princess Mary (born in 1516). Katherine was the widow of the king's brother, Prince Arthur (who had died in 1502, aged fifteen), and Henry began to worry that his lack of children was a sign of divine judgment. The book of Leviticus forbade a man to marry his brother's wife and explicitly warned that they would be childless (Leviticus 20:21). Therefore the king instructed his advisers to find a way for his marriage to be annulled.

From 1527 English diplomats, canon lawyers, and theologians were absorbed by the question. The government's first strategy was to put pressure on Pope Clement VII to grant an annulment, but Rome had recently been sacked by the troops of Emperor Charles V, who was Queen Katherine's nephew. The pope had no desire to alienate either the king or the emperor, so he refused to make a decision. The legal proceedings moved to London, presided over at Blackfriars by Cardinal Wolsey and Cardinal Campeggio (the pope's legate). Campeggio recommended that Katherine become a nun, which would leave Henry free to marry again, but she refused to go quietly and appealed formally to Rome. This lack of progress angered the king and hastened Wolsey's downfall in 1529. The cardinal was a ruined man and was forced to forfeit all his property to his royal master, including his palace at Hampton Court, but died the following year, thus cheating the executioner.

A new group of advisers, led by Wolsey's former secretary, Thomas Cromwell, suggested that Henry take matters into his own hands. Their policy was based upon two ground-breaking new principles. First, they argued that the pope had no authority to overrule the teaching of the Bible, and therefore the king's marriage was invalid. Second, they insisted that the pope had no authority in

England and could not command the king. As a result, Henry began to exercise greater control over the church. He rediscovered the medieval law of "praemunire", which forbade the pope's interference in the appointment of clergy to benefices, and extracted a massive fine from convocation for their guilt. This was followed in March 1532 by the *Supplication Against the Ordinaries* (probably drafted by Cromwell), an appeal from the House of Commons to the king in which they laid down numerous grievances against the church. Yet the clergy refused to submit themselves to lay interference and their resistance seemed to the king like treason. He ominously proclaimed in May:

> *we thought that the clergy of our realm had been our subjects*
> *wholly, but now we have well perceived that they be but half*
> *our subjects, yea, and scarce our subjects: for all the prelates*
> *at their consecration make an oath to the pope, clear contrary*
> *to the oath that they make us, so they seem to be his subjects,*
> *and not ours.*[25]

A few days later, faced by these thinly veiled threats, the bishops and clergy of convocation made their formal "Submission" to the king, surrendering the church to royal authority. Thomas More promptly resigned his post as Lord Chancellor in protest. Meanwhile the death in August of Archbishop Warham of Canterbury, in his early eighties, opened up another significant position for reform. The surprise candidate as his successor was Thomas Cranmer, an obscure evangelical theologian from Cambridge who had argued cogently in favour of the king's divorce. Cromwell and Cranmer, as the key leaders in state and church affairs, now combined their energies to push the Reformation forward.

Over the next two years a raft of new legislation gave the force of law to this shift in spiritual authority from pope to king. Parliament put an end to the financial payment of "annates" or "first-fruits" from

English bishops to the pope, forbade appeals to the ecclesiastical courts in Rome, and gave the crown the right to appoint bishops. It stopped the ancient papal taxation of England, known as "Peter's Pence", and refused to acknowledge papal dispensations from canon law. The pinnacle of this legislation was the Act of Supremacy, passed in November 1534, which declared the king to be "the only Supreme Head in earth of the Church of England". This gave him the right to reform the doctrine and ceremonies of the church, in order to expunge "all errors, heresies, and other enormities and abuses" and to promote "virtue in Christ's religion".[26] The Act of Supremacy made the break with Rome complete. Soon the word *papa* ("pope") was obliterated from English service books. The government no longer called him the "pope", but merely the "Bishop of Rome". Meanwhile the Act of Succession forced the population to acknowledge the king's new wife, Anne Boleyn, as queen and her children as the rightful heirs to the throne. Anne and Henry were secretly married in January 1533 and their daughter, Princess Elizabeth, was born eight months later. Yet Catholic opponents spoke against Boleyn as a "harlot" and a "goggle-eyed whore".[27]

OBEY YE YOUR KING!

The king's policy was to eliminate his opponents and he punished severely all those who rejected the royal supremacy or the new line of succession to the throne. His trusted adviser, Thomas Cromwell, arranged a series of high-profile treason trials which ended in judicial murder. As one of Cromwell's propagandists put it, the most important commandment was "Obey ye your king".[28]

Elizabeth Barton, a young nun from Canterbury, nicknamed "the Holy Maid of Kent", was seen as a particularly dangerous threat. She won fame throughout England for her ecstatic visions and prophecies, and pilgrims sought her out for spiritual advice and intercession. At first her prophecies concerned traditional Catholic devotion and a denunciation of evangelical "heresy", but from 1530 she made the mistake of speaking against Henry's religious policies. Barton announced that if he went through with his divorce of Katherine and married another wife he would cease to be king within a month. When Henry visited Canterbury she declared that he was "so abominable in the sight of God that he was not worthy to tread on hallowed ground".[29] She also warned of divine retribution against England in the form of wars and plagues. This was seditious talk. The example of Jeanne d'Arc in fifteenth-century France showed that a female visionary with a popular following could be a dangerous political threat.

Cromwell took action, and in the autumn of 1533 Barton and her disciples were rounded up. Under interrogation she admitted that her prophecies were forged, and was forced to do public penance at St Paul's Cross in London and again at Canterbury. In April 1534 the Holy Maid and five of her closest associates were executed at Tyburn for high treason. She was hanged and then beheaded. Her male followers suffered the worse fate of being hanged, drawn, and quartered. Barton's head was stuck on a pike on London Bridge, while the other heads were displayed on the gates of the city, as a warning to others.

The following year Cromwell smashed any remaining signs of resistance to the royal supremacy. Those who refused to abandon their allegiance to the pope were hurried to execution. In May 1535 three Carthusian priors were hanged, drawn, and quartered at Tyburn, alongside a Bridgettine monk from Syon Abbey and a parish priest. Others were sent to the gallows in the following months, or were left to starve to death in prison. Two executions in particular sent shock waves around Europe: those of Cardinal John Fisher (Bishop of Rochester) and Sir Thomas More, who both refused to swear the oaths required by the Act of Succession and the Act of Supremacy. More was the only layman in the country to do so, for fear of condemning "my soul to perpetual damnation".[30]

121

At his trial he rejected the royal supremacy as "directly repugnant to the laws of God and his holy church", and warned that England was flying in the face of Catholic Christendom: "I have, for every bishop of yours, above one hundred; and for one council or parliament of yours… I have all the councils made these thousand years. And for this one kingdom, I have all other Christian realms."[31] Fisher and More were beheaded within a fortnight of each other at the Tower of London, granted a swift death by axe rather than the tortures which awaited other traitors at Tyburn.

Henry VIII appointed Cromwell as "vicegerent in spirituals", which gave him sweeping powers to control the reform of the church as the king's deputy. On the king's authority, he issued two sets of significant royal injunctions in 1536 and 1538 which aimed to ensure that all religious dissent was "repressed and utterly extinguished".[32] Yet they included important concessions to the reformist agenda. Parents and teachers were commanded to instruct their children and servants in the Lord's Prayer, the Apostles' Creed, and the Ten Commandments in English. The injunctions also denounced "superstitious" practices "devised by men's fantasies", such as pilgrimages to local shrines, the offering of money or votive candles before religious relics, the kissing or licking of images, and the use of rosary beads.[33]

On the strength of Cromwell's injunctions, a wave of government-sponsored iconoclasm swept through the country. Numerous shrines were stripped and relics destroyed, including those of England's premier saint, Thomas Becket, at Canterbury. The former archbishop had been murdered in his own cathedral in 1170 for defying King Henry II, but now he was declared a traitor against the crown and his bones were burned. Other relics were exposed as fakes, such as the "holy blood" at Hailes Abbey in Gloucester, said to be a phial of Christ's blood; and the "ear of Malchus" at Bangor in Wales, said to have been cut off by the apostle Peter in the Garden of Gethsemane (see John 18:10).

Another popular venue for medieval pilgrims was Boxley Abbey in Kent, which owned the so-called "rood of grace", an ingenious wooden crucifix on which the body of Christ could move and gesture, controlled by the monks with wires and levers. Cromwell's commissioners derided it as a deliberate fraud and smashed it to pieces at St Paul's Cross while Bishop Hilsey of Rochester preached against idolatry. These attacks upon images, shrines, and pilgrimages went hand in hand with the destruction of England's monasteries. About 750 religious houses were suppressed between 1536 and 1540, their wealth confiscated and most of their buildings razed to the ground. Thousands of monks and nuns were evicted from their homes and livelihoods. Those who defied the royal commissioners, like the abbots of Colchester, Glastonbury, and Reading, were executed. Some of the confiscated revenue was redirected toward educational or charitable foundations, but most found its way into the coffers of the king and his friends. This wholesale destruction of England's traditional religious landscape led to uprising across the north of the country from Lincolnshire to Yorkshire in October 1536, the so-called "Pilgrimage of Grace", but the rebels were exterminated in vicious reprisals.

The royal injunctions of 1538 also ordered that a copy of the English Bible be made freely available in every parish church in the country, because it was "the very lively Word of God, that every Christian man is bound to embrace, believe and follow if he look to be saved".[34] Miles Coverdale was entrusted with the work and his "Great Bible" was finally published in April 1539, issued with the king's authority. It was much in demand and went through seven editions in two and a half years. Cranmer wrote an influential preface, urging the populace to immerse themselves in the Scriptures. He called the Bible "a better jewel in our house than either gold or silver" and insisted that all the people of England should read this precious book.[35]

DOWNFALL AND DEFEAT

The English reform movement had begun to lurch forward with faltering steps, but it suffered a series of significant setbacks during the late 1530s and early 1540s. King Henry's personal sympathy for evangelicalism was at best ambiguous, and in many respects he remained wedded to traditional piety, only without the pope. The evangelical reformers in the royal court were weakened by internal divisions and outmanoeuvred by their opponents. As a result the future direction of the English church was left hanging in the balance.

Queen Anne openly identified herself with the evangelical cause and helped to promote several reformers to positions of influence, such as Archbishop Cranmer himself. However, in 1536 there was a fatal rupture between Anne and Cromwell. Both vied for the ear of the king, but they fell out over the best use of the financial assets stripped from the monasteries, which the queen wanted given to charity. One of her chaplains pointedly compared the vicegerent to Haman, the Old Testament royal adviser known for his greed and corruption. Anne's sway over Henry was also hindering Cromwell's foreign policy, so he set out to destroy her. He fabricated charges of adultery, playing upon the king's natural suspicions, and Anne was beheaded at the Tower of London in May 1536 by a French swordsman specially imported from Calais. The king's new wife, Jane Seymour, delivered him a long-awaited male heir, Prince Edward, but she died from septicaemia two weeks after giving birth.

A few months after Queen Anne's downfall, the figurehead of the evangelical movement in exile, William Tyndale, also met his death. He had been living in the "English House" at Antwerp surrounded by English merchants, but their circle was infiltrated by Henry Phillips, a young Oxford graduate and thief. Phillips struck up an association with the Bible translator, pretending friendship, and then betrayed him to the Habsburg authorities for financial reward. He arranged for Tyndale's arrest one evening in the narrow streets of the city, by officers from the imperial court at Brussels.

From London, Cromwell made weak diplomatic efforts to rescue Tyndale and have him deported to England, but to no avail. He was imprisoned at Vilvorde Castle, between Brussels and Leuven, where he was condemned as a heretic after lengthy legal proceedings and executed in October 1536. At the stake he was first strangled by the hangman, probably with rope twisted around his neck, and then his body was burned. With his countrymen still on his heart, the martyr prayed as he died, "Lord! Open the king of England's eyes."[36]

The violent deaths of Anne and Tyndale were major blows for the English reform movement. Meanwhile, an anti-evangelical reaction set in at court and the conservative faction began to regain ground. The reformers were slipping from power, and divisions between them were increasingly apparent. For example, John Lambert (one of the early evangelical circle at Cambridge) was imprisoned by Archbishop Cranmer for his Zwinglian views of the Lord's Supper and put on trial before the king himself in November 1538. Cromwell pronounced the sentence of death on the king's orders and Lambert was burned at Smithfield six days later, crying, "None but Christ, none but Christ."[37]

There was further victory for the conservatives in June 1539 with the passing of the Act of Six Articles, a sign of things to come. It enforced the doctrine of transubstantiation (under pain of death by burning) and upheld communion "in one kind" (bread only), clerical celibacy, private masses, and auricular confession. The reformers nicknamed the act "the whip with six strings", and although Cranmer agreed to submit, Bishop Latimer of Worcester and Bishop Shaxton of Salisbury resigned their sees in protest.[38]

Cromwell's position was now increasingly precarious. With England threatened by invasion from France and the Holy Roman Empire, he had sought to build an alliance with the Lutheran princes of the Schmalkaldic League in Germany. After numerous diplomatic missions, Cromwell finally negotiated the marriage between Henry and a young German noblewoman, Anne, sister of the Duke of Jülich-Kleve. The king was sent a portrait of his beautiful new fiancée, commissioned from Hans Holbein, but when he met her in person he said he found her physically repulsive. The marriage went ahead as planned in January 1540, but it was never consummated (the king was impotent) and was annulled within six months.

This debacle was the final nail in Cromwell's coffin. Although he was created Earl of Essex in April 1540, he was sent to the block three months later, beheaded for treason on Tower Hill. When Cromwell fell, others were brought down with him. The evangelical preacher Robert Barnes had been employed by the vicegerent to negotiate with the Lutherans in Germany and he met his death two days after his patron. Barnes was burned at the stake at Smithfield alongside fellow preachers William Jerome and Thomas Garrard (the former Bible smuggler). In a macabre demonstration of the king's even-handedness, or his religious indifference, three Catholic priests (Thomas Abel, Richard Featherstone, and Edward Powell) were hanged, drawn, and quartered on the same occasion for denying the royal supremacy. The prisoners had been dragged to Smithfield on three hurdles, an evangelical and a Catholic on each.

TRADITIONALISTS TRIUMPHANT

The traditionalist faction at court was triumphant. On the same day that Cromwell was sent to the block, Henry married again, this time into the conservative Howard family. He took as his fifth wife Katherine Howard, the young niece of the Duke of Norfolk. Although she was soon beheaded for treason when the king learned about her previous sexual liaisons, the conservative grip on power remained invincible. The last actions of Henry's reign were almost all in a conservative direction, as the hard-won gains of the reformers were erased one by one. In 1543 the Act for the Advancement of

True Religion withdrew the right to read the English Bible from the majority of the population. Gentry, clergy, and merchants were still permitted to read the book, but women, servants, and labourers were threatened with prison if caught with a copy. The act also enforced a new theological statement, *A Necessary Doctrine and Erudition for Any Christian Man* (nicknamed "the King's Book"), which emphasized Catholic doctrine and denied justification by faith.

There were minor victories for Cranmer, such as a new authorized Litany in English, but he was constantly on the defensive and under threat from his enemies. In 1543 the archbishop himself was almost toppled in the "Prebendaries' Plot", when leading clergy from his cathedral claimed that he tolerated heresy in the diocese. Observing events from exile in Zürich was John Hooper, a former Cistercian monk who converted to evangelicalism after reading the works of Huldrych Zwingli and Heinrich Bullinger. He was deeply depressed by the state of the English church:

> *As far as true religion is concerned, idolatry is nowhere in greater vigour. Our king has destroyed the pope, but not popery... The impious mass, the most shameful celibacy of the clergy, the invocation of saints, auricular confession, superstitious abstinence from meats, and purgatory, were never before held by the people in greater esteem than at the present moment.*

As he surveyed his homeland, Hooper lamented, "I see nothing but the death of all godliness and religion."[39]

By 1546 it was clear that the king's life was drawing to a close. Therefore, with England's political and religious future uncertain, the conservatives intensified their efforts to smash the evangelical networks. Prominent evangelical preachers Edward Crome and Nicholas Shaxton were arrested for preaching against transubstantiation but both recanted when threatened with burning. Others, however, refused to buckle. Anne Askew, a young woman in her early twenties, daughter of Sir William Askew, was sentenced to death for denying the doctrine of the mass. When Bishop Shaxton visited her prison cell and urged her to follow his example by recanting, she likened him to Judas Iscariot. Due to Askew's close connections with ladies in the royal court, her captors tortured her in the hope that she would divulge the names of fellow evangelicals close to the king. She was stretched on the rack in the Tower of London, remarkable treatment for a woman with noble connections and a scandal when the news broke. The lieutenant of the Tower refused to continue the torture, so Sir Thomas Wriothesley (the Lord Chancellor) and Sir Richard Rich racked her with their own hands until she was almost dead. Askew was sent to Smithfield for burning on 16 July 1546, carried there in a chair because she could no longer walk.

The future of the English Reformation looked bleak, especially if the conservative Howard faction gained control of the regency council when the king died. However, in the final weeks of 1546 there was a sudden swing in political fortunes when they were charged with conspiracy against the crown. The Duke of Norfolk (Thomas Howard) was sent to the Tower and his son, the Earl of Surrey (Henry Howard), was beheaded for treason. The Seymour faction, led by the uncle of young Prince Edward, was left back in the ascendancy, so there were glimmers of hope for evangelical recovery in the next reign. Meanwhile the reformers took encouragement from the death-bed scene which Archbishop Cranmer encountered when he was called to Whitehall Palace in the early hours of 28 January 1547. Cranmer reminded King Henry of the evangelical gospel of forgiveness for repentant sinners and asked if he trusted in Jesus Christ for eternal salvation. The dying monarch was no longer able to speak but squeezed the archbishop's hand as a sign of assent.

7

The Most Perfect School of Christ

Paris in the early sixteenth century was home to one of Europe's greatest universities, rivalled only by Oxford and Bologna, and its theology faculty (the Sorbonne) prided itself on being the guardian of Catholic orthodoxy. It was among the first to denounce the spread of Lutheran heresy and condemned the Wittenberg reformer in the *Determinatio*, published on 15 April 1521 just two days before he faced the imperial Diet at Worms. The Sorbonne rooted out Lutheran literature smuggled into France and campaigned for the execution of heretics, backed by legislation from the Parisian *parlement*. The first French martyr was Jean Vallière, an Augustinian monk, burned alive in Paris in August 1523 for reading Luther's works.

Nevertheless, the Sorbonne's conservative zeal was initially restrained by King François I, who was sympathetic toward Renaissance humanism. This royal benevolence allowed early reformers, the *évangéliques*, to be galvanized into action. One such network was the intellectual circle gathered around Bishop Guillaume Briçonnet at Meaux, east of Paris. Among the recruits he attracted was his vicar-general, Jacques Lefèvre d'Étaples, an elderly humanist scholar whose ground-breaking vernacular translation of the New Testament was published in 1523. The bishop also welcomed reforming preachers like Gérard Roussel, Françoise Vatable, Martial Mazurier, and Guillaume Farel, who were sent out to evangelize the district and to teach the Bible. Nevertheless, when Briçonnet was accused of harbouring Lutheran heresy, he grew timid. He revoked the licences of some of his more radical preachers and instructed the others to affirm their belief in purgatory and the invocation of saints. When the Sorbonne finally broke up the Meaux circle in 1525 the bishop abandoned his Reformation experiment and affirmed his commitment to traditional Catholicism. Other *évangéliques* were offered protection at the court of Nérac by the king's sister, Marguerite de Valois, Duchess of Angoulême and (from 1527) Queen of Navarre. Her writings, like *Mirror of the Sinful Soul* (1531), revealed strong sympathies for the humanist cause.

At first, the French reformers sought to work within the Catholic church. However, despite royal protection, this became increasingly difficult. The *évangéliques* grew in confidence and there were regular outbreaks of anti-Catholic agitation. For example, in June 1528 an unknown iconoclast attacked a stone statue of the Virgin Mary on the wall of a house in the Rue des Rosiers in Paris. The heads of the madonna and child were chopped off with a knife and smashed to pieces. In reparation to God for this insult, a series of solemn processions were organized through Paris, culminating at the Feast of Corpus Christi. The king himself played a leading part and donated a costly new image, covered in silver, to replace the one which had been sensationally assaulted.

The following year, the Sorbonne claimed its first high-profile victim, much against the king's wishes, with the execution of a young aristocratic scholar, Louis de Berquin, noted for his Reformation leanings. Roussel was also put on trial for preaching heresy in the presence of Queen Marguerite, but her brother intervened. In November 1533 a further outcry was provoked by Nicolas Cop, the newly elected rector of the University of Paris and son of the king's physician. He was required to deliver the traditional All Saints' Day sermon in the Church of the Cordeliers (the Franciscan Observants), to mark the beginning of a new academic year, but used the occasion to issue an appeal for reform of the French church. His address was based upon the Beatitudes, from the Sermon on the Mount (Matthew 5), but it caused outrage. Marguerite did her best to protect the new rector from his enemies in the Parisian *parlement*, but he was forced to flee to Basel for safety.

The Affair of the Placards

The decisive turning point in the tense relationship between the *évangéliques* and the Catholic church was "the Affair of the Placards". It was a watershed in the early history of the French Reformation. One Sunday morning, 18 October 1534, Catholics on their way to mass in Paris and other cities in northern France were horrified to discover anonymous and offensive "placards" pasted in conspicuous locations. These posters had been put up secretly overnight by the accomplices of Antoine Marcourt, a French pastor and pamphleteer living in exile at Neuchâtel in Switzerland. They were a vitriolic attack upon the Catholic doctrine of the Eucharist and the bold headline spoke of "the horrible, gross and insufferable abuses of the papal mass, invented directly contrary to the Holy Supper of Jesus Christ". The poster denounced transubstantiation as "the doctrine of devils against all truth and openly contrary to all Scripture", and proclaimed:

> *I invoke heaven and earth as witnesses to the truth against this pompous and arrogant popish mass, by which the whole world (if God does not soon remedy it) will be completely ruined, cast down, lost, and desolated; and because our Lord is so outrageously blasphemed and the people seduced and blinded by it, it can no longer be allowed to endure.*[1]

It mocked the mass service as nothing more than "chimes, howling, singing, ceremonies, lights, incense, disguises, and other sorts of monkey business".[2] The final paragraph was a fierce attack upon the Catholic clergy, denouncing them as "bewitching wolves" who devour the flock:

> *They kill, burn, destroy, and murder as brigands all those who contradict them, for now all they have left is force. Truth is lacking in them, but it menaces them, follows them, and chases them; and in the end truth will find them out. By it they shall be destroyed. Fiat. Fiat. Amen.*[3]

According to one account, a placard was even attached audaciously to the door of the king's bedchamber at his château at Amboise, pinned there while he slept. A backlash was inevitable. This was the opportunity for which the conservatives in the Paris *parlement* and the Sorbonne had been waiting.

A reward of 100 écus was offered for any information on the culprits in the placards plot, and those suspected of evangelical sympathies were quickly arrested. By the end of November, six had been burned at the stake – a shoemaker's son (nicknamed "the paralytic"), a draper, a printer, a weaver, a bookseller, and a stonemason. This time King François did nothing to halt the persecution. Indeed, he said that he was pleased for it to continue "so that the damned and abominable sect may neither set foot nor take root in my kingdom".

On 21 January 1535, he took part in a grand procession through the streets of Paris, from Saint-Germain l'Auxerrois to Notre-Dame, to purify the city from the evangelical outrage. All the leading citizens were out in force – those from the law courts, the university, religious orders, magistrates, and guilds. Among the many precious shrines and relics carried in the procession were the heads of Saint Philip and Saint Louis (the former king of France), a fragment of the cross, and the "crown of thorns" normally displayed in Sainte-Chapelle. The sacrament itself (*Corpus Christi*) was reverently carried by the Bishop of Paris, under a canopy held by the king's three sons and the Duke of Vendôme. The king followed immediately behind, bareheaded and dressed in black. After high mass at the cathedral, François exhorted his subjects to report all heretics to the authorities, even close friends or relatives. The city's act of penance was completed by the burning of six more evangelicals that evening, and over the next four months the executions continued.[4]

Many fled from France during this wave of repression. Among them was a young evangelical scholar called Jean Cauvin, destined to become one of the leading reformers of his generation.

FLIGHT TO GENEVA

Jean Cauvin, better known as John Calvin, was brought up at Noyon in Picardy, in northern France, where his father was secretary of the local cathedral chapter. He was sent to the universities of Paris, Orléans, and Bourges, planning to pursue a career as a priest or lawyer, but was increasingly attracted by the ideals of humanism. Perhaps hoping to become the next Erasmus, Calvin initially tried to make his mark as a scholar of classical antiquity. His first book was a commentary on a Latin philosophical treatise, Seneca's *De Clementia* ("*On Clemency*"), published in April 1532, though it failed to sell and left him financially in debt.

At some point during 1532 or 1533, in his early twenties, Calvin moved decisively from humanism to evangelicalism. His passions shifted from scholarship to reform. In later life he was reticent about this conversion experience, revealing few details. The most explicit reference is in the preface to his *Commentary on the Psalms* (1557), where he recalled that as a young man he had been "firmly addicted to the papal superstitions", unable to free himself from "such a deep mire" until divine intervention brought "sudden conversion". Calvin's priorities were transformed:

I was so inspired by a taste of true religion and I burned with
such a desire to carry my study further, that although I did
not drop other subjects, I had no zeal for them. In less than a
year, all who were looking for a purer doctrine began to come
to learn from me, although I was a novice and a beginner.[5]

As a new convert, Calvin was soon caught up in the Parisian conflict surrounding the *évangéliques*. He may have contributed ideas to Cop's provocative speech on All Saints' Day in 1533 and fled immediately afterwards to Angoulême for refuge with a friend, Canon Louis du Tillet. Calvin left the capital just in time, as the authorities searched his room and confiscated his papers. Next he travelled to Nérac, where he met with Lefèvre d'Étaples and other members of the reform circle benefiting from asylum with Queen Marguerite, but returned to Paris.

When the Affair of the Placards burst upon France, several of Calvin's evangelical friends were rounded up and burned at the stake, such as Etienne de la Forge, martyred in February 1535. Like many others, Calvin ran for his life, this time to the safety of Switzerland. At first he settled in Basel, famous as one of the early centres of humanism and Erasmus's last resting place. There Calvin spent his first months in exile writing an introductory handbook to evangelical theology, *Institutio Christianae Religionis* ("*The Institutes of the Christian Religion*"), which was to become one of the most influential Christian books ever written. It was dedicated to King François I and began with a passionate plea for an end to the persecutions in France. Calvin protested that the *évangéliques* were being falsely slandered and asked the king to make an honest investigation of their teaching rather than listening to "the whisperings of the malevolent".[6] He warned that the cause of Christ in France was "completely torn and trampled in your realm today, lying, as it were, utterly forlorn":

> *For ungodly men have so far prevailed that Christ's truth,*
> *even if it is not driven away scattered and destroyed, still*
> *lies hidden, buried and inglorious. The poor little church has*
> *either been wasted with cruel slaughter or banished into exile,*
> *or so overwhelmed by threats and fears that it dare not even*
> *open its mouth.*[7]

Calvin insisted that evangelicalism was not a new invention but was consistent with apostolic and early church doctrine, unlike the Roman church, which was guilty of "a deadly butchery of souls".[8] Therefore, he proclaimed, evangelicals were willing to suffer because of their hope of eternal life:

> *For the sake of this hope some of us are shackled with irons,*
> *some beaten with rods, some led about as laughingstocks,*
> *some proscribed, some most savagely tortured, some forced*
> *to flee. All of us are oppressed by poverty, cursed with dire*
> *execrations, wounded by slanders, and treated in most*
> *shameful ways.*[9]

He declared that those who opposed the gospel were tools of Satan, but that Jesus Christ would one day return to deliver the afflicted and to punish their oppressors.

There was a temporary lull in the French persecutions after the summer of 1535, when the Edict of Coucy proclaimed an amnesty. Fugitives were invited to return to their homes and would be freely pardoned provided they renounced their heretical views within six months. However, the edict also declared that any who went back to evangelicalism after being pardoned would be executed without appeal. Calvin took advantage of the edict to return from Basel to France to settle some family affairs. Then in July 1536, aged twenty-seven, he left his homeland forever. His original intention was to settle now in Strassburg, just across the Swiss border. Yet the road was blocked by troops engaged in the Valois-Habsburg war between King François I and Emperor Charles V. So Calvin made a long detour to Geneva, planning to rest there for only one night.

AFTER DARKNESS, LIGHT

For many centuries the city of Geneva had been dominated by the neighbouring Duchy of Savoy, which exercised considerable political and religious power in the region. However, since the 1490s a growing number of Genevans had been agitating for independence. They began to look instead toward the Swiss Confederation, especially the city of Berne with whom they forged an alliance in 1526. This political reorientation brought spiritual revolution in its wake. After Berne sided with the Reformation, it started to send preachers to Geneva to propagate evangelical views. Guillaume Farel arrived in 1532, in exile from France, joined two years later by Pierre Viret. Copying the model of other Swiss cities, these men engaged in public disputation against the Catholic party (led by a Dominican scholar, Guy Furbity), but the event degenerated into rioting.

Following outbreaks of iconoclasm, the city council abolished the Catholic mass in 1535 and minted its own coins bearing Geneva's new motto, *Post tenebras lux* ("After darkness, light") and the words *Deus noster pugnat pro nobis* ("Our God fights for us"). The Catholic Bishop of Geneva was overthrown and responded by excommunicating his former flock. Eager to seize back control, the Duchy of Savoy put the city under military siege but was forced to retreat by the armies of Berne. Geneva's freedom from Catholic intervention was now assured and it was able to pursue a rigorous reforming agenda. In May 1536 the citizens voted to "live henceforth according to the law of the gospel and the word of God, and to abolish all papal abuses".[10]

When Farel discovered in July that Calvin was in Geneva on his journey to Strassburg, he begged the young man to stay and join forces in transforming the city along evangelical lines. The Reformation settlement was far from secure and it was still possible that Geneva would descend into chaos. Yet Calvin viewed himself more as a scholar and author than a public reformer or preacher. He was determined to settle in Strassburg where he could continue his studies in peace and privacy. Although impressed by Farel, whom he described as a minister "working with incredible zeal to promote the gospel", he resisted the call. Therefore Farel tried another approach and proclaimed that God would curse Calvin's leisure if he held back from helping the gospel cause at such a time of need. This so shocked Calvin that he relinquished his plans, as he later recalled: "Terrified by his words, and conscious of my own timidity and cowardice, I gave up my journey and attempted to apply whatever gift I had in defence of my faith."[11] His first task was not to pastor a Genevan congregation but simply to deliver public lectures on the Bible and quietly to support Farel and Viret behind the scenes.

Within a few months, Calvin was suddenly thrust into the limelight. Berne had captured extensive territory during its military crusade against the Duchy of Savoy. A Bernese army of 6,000 men, commanded by Hans Franz Nägeli, had entered Lausanne in the spring and begun to convert it to the Reformation. A public disputation to determine the city's religious future was held in the cathedral of Notre Dame in October, but Lausanne was French-speaking and Berne was German-speaking, so Berne invited the ministers of Geneva to present the case for reform. Farel and Viret led the delegation but were eclipsed in the debate by Calvin, who demonstrated his skills as a theologian and orator, and won a reputation as a rising star.

Back in Geneva, the ministers brought forward an elaborate and controversial programme of reform. They persuaded the city council to agree in January 1537 to an evangelical Confession of Faith, which every resident was required to accept or be banished.

They also drafted articles concerning ecclesiastical discipline, covering themes such as excommunication from the Lord's Supper, the singing of psalms, the regulation of marriage, and the teaching of children. These provocative policies divided the city. Genevan citizens were especially insulted that Farel and Calvin, both French émigrés and newcomers, should presume to threaten them with excommunication and impose such tight religious restrictions.

The backlash was fierce. Farel and Calvin's supporters were voted off the council and replaced by men who favoured Berne's more moderate style of reform. The ministers were reminded that they were only entitled to work under the council's authority. They were commanded not to bar anyone from holy communion and to stop meddling in political affairs. One of their colleagues was imprisoned by the council for having dared in a sermon to call Geneva a "kingdom of frogs" and the magistrates "drunkards". When Farel and Calvin ignored instructions to use unleavened bread at the Lord's Supper, they were banned from preaching but refused to comply and Calvin defiantly retorted: "If we served men, we would be badly rewarded. But we serve a great master, who will recompense us."[12] Finally the council lost patience and expelled Farel and Calvin from Geneva at the end of April 1538. In their grand attempt at a thorough reformation of the Swiss city, they had badly miscalculated and over-stretched themselves. Calvin's career as a reformer had ended in abject failure after less than two years.

RETURN FROM EXILE

At first Calvin planned to return to Basel and the quiet life of scholarship, but instead was appointed pastor of the French-speaking congregation in Strassburg. That city's leading reformer, Martin Bucer, persuaded him to stay by warning him of the example of the prophet Jonah, who ran away from the call of God. So Calvin settled and thrived. Bucer became his mentor and father figure, and helped to restore his shattered confidence in his abilities as a pastor.

On Bucer's advice Calvin married a young widow, Idelette de Bure, a former Anabaptist whose first husband had died of the plague. He immersed himself in writing and preaching. Several books flowed from his pen – his influential *Reply to Cardinal Sadoleto* (rejecting the accusation that evangelicals were theological innovators), a commentary on Romans, a treatise on the Lord's Supper, and a new edition of the *Institutes* (soon translated from Latin to French). Calvin also accompanied Bucer to a number of international colloquies between Catholics and Protestants during 1540–41 at Hagenau, Worms, and Regensburg, though he grew alarmed at the spirit of doctrinal compromise apparent at those meetings.

The prospect of returning to Geneva was far from Calvin's mind. His leadership in Strassburg was warmly appreciated, unlike the frosty reception he had experienced in Geneva, and he was allowed to enact reforms which the Genevans resisted. Soon after their dismissal, Calvin and Farel had written to Heinrich Bullinger in distress:

After we had been expelled, the audacity of Satan and his acolytes was seen to increase in Geneva... You cannot figure out with what license and what insolence the impious there plunge themselves into all sorts of vices, with what effrontery they insult the servants of God, with what brutality they laugh at the gospel, with what extravagance they behave on every occasion.[13]

Calvin said he would prefer "a hundred deaths" than return to Geneva.[14] He told du Tillet: "there is nothing I dread more than returning to the charge from which I have been set free".[15] Likewise he protested to Viret that it would be "far preferable to perish once for all than to be tormented again in that place of torture".[16]

However, the political situation in Geneva remained volatile. The faction which had driven Farel and Calvin from the city were known as the "Articulants", led by a local militia commander, Jean Philippe. They favoured friendship with Berne but became politically compromised during treaty negotiations and fell from favour in 1540. Some of the leading Articulants were put on trial for treason, accused of betraying Geneva's best interests, and Philippe himself was tortured and beheaded. This turn of events allowed Farel's supporters (known as the "Guillermins") to regain control of the city and to invite the reformers back. Farel was now ministering at Neuchâtel and refused, while Calvin declared that he "shuddered" at the very idea.[17] Nevertheless, after numerous pleas from the Genevan authorities over many months, he was eventually persuaded to give up his Strassburg idyll and re-entered the city on 13 September 1541.

Calvin's second attempt to reform Geneva could not be less successful than his first, and his return came with strings attached. In his letter of acceptance he insisted:

> *If you desire to have me for your pastor, correct the disorder of your lives. If you have with sincerity recalled me from my exile, banish the crimes and debaucheries which prevail among you... I consider the principal enemies of the gospel to be, not the pontiff of Rome, nor heretics, nor seducers, nor tyrants, but bad Christians... Either command me to abandon a second time your town and let me go and soften the bitterness of my afflictions in a new exile, or let the severity of the laws reign in the church. Re-establish there pure discipline.*[18]

Immediately Calvin set about introducing the reforms which had caused such uproar in 1538. He presented the city council with a set of *Ecclesiastical Ordinances*, adopted in November 1541, governing almost every area of church life. They set out a radical new structure for the Genevan church, which in time was to become a model for congregations across Europe. It was organized around four main offices – pastors, doctors, elders, and deacons. The pastors were responsible for preaching, spiritual counsel, and administration of the sacraments. The doctors were to teach Christian theology and to lecture in the Old and New Testaments. The elders were twelve laymen elected from the city council with oversight of every home in Geneva. The deacons were commissioned to care for the poor and the sick. The *Ecclesiastical Ordinances* also included regulations for baptism, the Lord's Supper, marriage, burial, visitation of the sick and prisoners, and the catechesis of children.

MORAL SUPERVISION

At the heart of Calvin's new ecclesiastical order for Geneva, and the key controversial issue, was the establishment of the "consistory". This weekly meeting of pastors and elders, a combination of clergy and laity, claimed the responsibility for doctrinal and moral discipline in Geneva. Sinners were brought before the consistory for admonishment and those who refused to repent were excommunicated from the Lord's Supper (though in practice this sanction was seldom necessary).

Soon these reforms began to transform the cultural life of Geneva. Many appeared before the consistory over the next two decades, from every section of society and for a multitude of offences – a Franciscan who prayed to the Virgin Mary; parents who married their daughter to a Roman Catholic; a goldsmith who made a chalice; a barber who cut a tonsure on a priest; merchants who made rosaries to sell at a fair; a bookseller who carried corrupting literature.[19] At the instigation of the Genevan pastors, new laws were enacted concerning divorce, dancing, promiscuity, blasphemy, swearing, drunkenness, civic festivals, luxurious clothing, and theatrical performances. The city council even regulated the names given to infants at baptism. The names of patron saints linked to medieval superstition were banned, as were biblical titles like Baptiste, Évangéliste, Emmanuel, and Jésus. No child in Reformation Geneva was to be called "Christian", because that was a name belonging to everyone in the city.[20]

These dramatic religious and cultural changes were not welcomed by all Geneva's citizens. Indeed, for many years Calvin was politically isolated and his position was precarious. As a French émigré he had no voting rights in the city and could be dismissed by the council at a moment's notice if public opinion swung against him. Many challenged his authority. For example, in 1546 Pierre Ameaux, a maker of playing cards and dice, was arrested for speaking against Calvin and the council. He was sentenced to walk around the city in penitence, bare-headed and carrying a candle, and to beg for mercy on his knees. The following year Jacques Gruet fixed an obscene poster to the pulpit in Saint-Pierre church, abusing Calvin and the other Genevan pastors. At his house the authorities discovered further papers mocking Christ and the Bible. Gruet was accused of treason against Geneva so was executed, having first been tortured.

The consistory, which exercised close oversight of Genevan morality, was a particular focus of hostility. Many influential families resisted this intrusion upon their private affairs. The fact that Calvin and a majority of his fellow pastors were French refugees rather than Genevan citizens only increased the feelings of resentment. The most vocal faction arrayed against Calvin were the friends and relatives of a local politician and diplomat, Ami Perrin, who called themselves the "Children of Geneva" but were nicknamed the "Libertins" because they rejected moral supervision. In 1547 Perrin's wife, Françoise, appeared before the consistory accused of dancing and spent several days in prison for her intransigence. Meanwhile her father, François Favre, was prosecuted for suggesting that Calvin was like a Catholic priest at auricular confession who wanted to hear the details of everyone's sins. Favre complained that Geneva had been enslaved by the French pastors. In his treatise *On the Scandals that Today Prevent Many People from Coming to the Pure Doctrine of the Gospel and Ruin Others* (1550), Calvin mourned that he was being so frequently attacked for denying people their freedom to sin. Yet he defiantly described his opponents as "fornicators, debauched and dissolute" and disciples of the pope.[21]

There were also more erudite theological challenges to Calvin's teaching. Jérôme Bolsec, a former Carmelite monk from Paris, arrived in Geneva in 1551 and threw his energy behind the Reformation movement. However, he publicly objected to Calvin's doctrine of predestination, arguing that it made God the author of both good and evil. He protested that Calvin's God was "a tyrant and an idol like the Jupiter created by pagans", responsible for saving and damning human beings at random.[22] Bolsec was imprisoned for blasphemy and heresy, and then banished from the city. Toward the end of his life, he returned to France, reconverted to Catholicism and in 1577 published a vitriolic biography of Calvin, assailing his opponent as "a man among all others who were ever in the world ambitious, presumptuous, arrogant, cruel, malicious, vengeful, and above all ignorant".[23] Bolsec's book was filled with malicious lies – for example, that Calvin was caught in the act of sodomy and branded with a hot iron as punishment – but it provided a rich source of material for later critics of the reformer.

The Servetus affair

Calvin's numerous troubles were eclipsed by the controversy which engulfed his dealings with Miguel Servetus, a Spaniard from the Basque country and a radical thinker who enjoyed challenging traditional orthodoxies. Servetus lived at Vienne, in the French province of Dauphin, where he worked as a medical doctor under the pseudonym Michel de Villeneuve – a name chosen from his home town of Villanueva. He put his theological speculations down on paper in a manuscript entitled *Christianismi Restitutio* (*"The Restoration of Christianity"*), which proposed that the church needed to return to its original purity unencumbered by the accretions of the last fifteen centuries. In particular, he argued that the doctrine of the Trinity could not be found in the Bible and mocked the concept as the Christian equivalent of Cerberus, the three-headed dog of Greco-Roman mythology who guarded the gates of hell. From Vienne, Servetus began a lengthy correspondence with Calvin and sent him a copy of his manuscript, but the reformer rejected these ideas as "wild imaginings". When the Spaniard proposed a visit to Geneva in 1547, Calvin told Farel: "I am unwilling to guarantee his safety, for if he does come and my authority counts for anything, I will never let him get away alive."[24]

Throwing caution to the wind, Servetus published his *Restitutio* at Lyons in January 1553, which led the reformers to remark on the inconsistency of the Catholic censors. Five evangelical students from Berne had been arrested while travelling through Lyons the previous summer and were martyred at the stake in February despite vocal protests from Switzerland. Yet Servetus was apparently allowed to publish heresy and remain free. One of Calvin's friends in Geneva, Guillaume Trie, saw this as further evidence of Catholic corruption. He wrote to his Catholic cousin in Lyons, protesting that the French authorities burned evangelicals for no other crimes than believing the Bible and following Jesus Christ, yet they tolerated heretics: "You say that books which keep solely to the pure simplicity of Scripture poison the world, and if they get out, you cannot suffer them. Yet you hatch poisons that would destroy Scripture and even all that you hold of Christianity."[25]

The French inquisitor general began an investigation, and "Michel de Villeneuve" was arrested at Vienne and put on trial. Despite the evidence against him, he brazenly denied that he was the same man as Servetus. "Villeneuve" asserted that he was a medical doctor rather than a theologian, and that he would happily submit himself to the teaching of the Catholic church. Nevertheless only two days into the trial he fled, escaping from prison by jumping over a wall. *In absentia*, Servetus was found guilty of heresy and sedition, and sentenced to death. Since he was on the run, his effigy was executed instead – it was hanged and then burned at the stake, along with five bales of blank paper representing his books.

Servetus planned to seek refuge at Naples in Italy and continue his medical practice, but on his way through Switzerland he foolishly chose to stop at Geneva. There he was recognized and arrested on Sunday, 13 August 1553. Having escaped the clutches of his Catholic enemies, he had now run straight into the hands of his evangelical ones. The inquisition in Vienne promised that the fugitive would be punished if returned to their custody. Yet he pleaded to be judged in Geneva, not France. The case was prosecuted by the city council, not by the consistory (the normal means of ecclesiastical discipline), although Calvin was involved as a witness and their theological clashes in court were often heated. Meanwhile Calvin wrote to the pastors at Frankfurt, where the *Restitutio* was likely to be sold at the local book fair, that it contained "nothing but a farrago of errors... a compendium of the impious ravings of all ages. There is no sort of impiety which this monster has not raked up, as if from the infernal regions." He exhorted the pastors that it was their duty to destroy every copy.[26]

Heretic or martyr?

The trial of Servetus was significant not just for Geneva, but for the whole of Switzerland. There was a wide chorus of agreement from the other reformed cantons that the prisoner should be punished with severity, though there were individual exceptions. For example, an Italian refugee called Vergerio, who gave up his career as a papal nuncio to become an evangelical pastor in the Swiss canton of Graubünden, argued that heretics should be constrained but not killed. He explained: "I hate such disturbers more than a dog and a snake, but I should have preferred that they be incarcerated in the foulest dungeon rather than that they be destroyed by fire and sword." Likewise the former Anabaptist leader David Joris, now living in Basel under an assumed name, urged them not to listen to "the bloodthirsty counsel of the learned".[27]

Having won support from their Swiss allies, the Genevan authorities condemned Servetus on 27 October 1553, not for sedition or immorality but for theological error, and announced that he would be burned "to ashes". When he heard the verdict he broke down in tears, crying out in Spanish, "*Misericordia! Misericordia!*" ("Mercy! Mercy!")[28] To avoid the horrors of the stake he asked to be beheaded rather than burned, and Calvin tried to persuade the council to adopt this more compassionate method of execution, but they refused. So Servetus was taken to the plain of Champel, outside the city gates, and condemned to the flames. His last recorded words were a heartfelt prayer: "Jesus, son of God eternal, have mercy on me!"[29] This final cry was perfectly consistent with Servetus's anti-Trinitarian views. As Farel observed, even in his dying moments the heretic had obstinately refused to acknowledge Jesus as "*eternal* son of God".

The brutal execution of Servetus resulted in a backlash against Calvin. Although it was the city council which had prosecuted the case, Geneva's chief pastor bore the brunt of the scandal. He was accused of cruelty and vindictiveness, while some began to call Servetus a "martyr of Jesus".[30] The most articulate and vociferous attack upon Calvin was a treatise published in Basel by his former ally, Sebastian Castellio, a French humanist scholar. Castellio had been a teacher in Geneva, but was barred from becoming a pastor in 1543 because of his suspect doctrinal views. In particular he had declared that the Song of Songs should be cut out of the Bible because it was "simply a lascivious or obscene song describing Solomon's objectionable love affairs".[31]

The Genevan pastors would not countenance this disrespect for Scripture and Castellio was forced out of the city. In 1553 he became professor of Greek at the University of Basel, from where he launched a tirade against Calvin for his handling of the Servetus affair. In his treatise, *On Heretics*, Castellio argued that Christians spent far too much time arguing about unprofitable doctrines like the Trinity, the work of Christ, predestination, free will, angels, and the immortality of the soul. He maintained that such debates were irrelevant since salvation was achieved not by doctrinal precision but through faith in Christ, as tax-collectors and prostitutes realized in New Testament times. Castellio went further and asserted that it was futile to punish "heresy", because Christians could not agree among themselves which views were heretical. Surveying the bewildering multitude of Christian opinions in evidence across sixteenth-century Europe, he wrote:

There is hardly one of all the sects, which today are without number, which does not hold the others to be heretics. So that if in one city or region you are esteemed a true believer, in the next you will be esteemed a heretic. So that if anyone today wants to live he must have as many faiths and religions as there are cities or sects, just as a man who travels through the lands has to change his money from day to day...[32]

Castellio looked for an emphasis upon Christian morality rather than doctrinal correctness, and maintained: "It would be better to let a hundred, even a thousand heretics live than to put a decent man to death under pretence of heresy."[33]

This apparent lack of concern for biblical truth provoked a stern response from the Swiss reformers. Théodore de Bèze replied from Lausanne with an influential treatise *On the Authority of Magistrates in the Punishment of Heretics*, justifying the actions of the Genevan city council. He later warned that Castellio "advises everyone to believe whatever he wants, opening the door by this means to all heresies and false doctrines".[34] Calvin described Castellio's teaching as "malignant, unmanageable and pernicious".[35] He defended the burning of Servetus as perfectly lawful in his 1554 treatise on the doctrine of the Trinity, and in his final edition of the *Institutes* continued to assail this executed heretic as a "foul dog".[36]

Triumph at last

Calvin's position in Geneva remained vulnerable for many years, and he was nearly forced out by the Perrin faction, who gained political control of the city during the early 1550s. The last major challenge to his leadership took place in the midst of the Servetus affair and again the focal point was the authority of the pastors over ecclesiastical discipline. One of Perrin's relatives, Philibert Berthelier, had been excommunicated by the consistory, but he appealed to the city council, which overturned the ruling. This was direct political interference in the spiritual oversight of Geneva, which Calvin believed was the sole responsibility of the pastors. He refused to back down and threatened to resign. There was a stand-off between the two sides and as Communion Sunday approached in September 1553, it was unclear whether the Calvinists or the Perrinists would emerge triumphant. If Berthelier was allowed to receive communion, then Calvin's authority would be publicly undermined and he would be forced to leave the city. From the pulpit, the reformer defiantly proclaimed: "Since we should now receive the holy communion of our Lord Jesus Christ, if anyone wants to intrude at this holy table to whom it has been forbidden by the consistory, it is certain that I will show myself, at the risk of my life, what I should be." He later added: "As for me… I would rather have been killed than have offered the holy things of God with this hand to those declared guilty as scorners."[37] In the event, Berthelier did not attend the communion service and Calvin's authority in Geneva remained intact. The city council still claimed the right to have the final verdict in all matters of church discipline, and to veto the consistory if necessary, but they did not force the issue.

Two years later there was a dramatic and decisive shift in the balance of power in Genevan politics. During the 1550s thousands of evangelicals fled to the city for refuge, especially to escape the persecutions in France, as well as groups from England and Italy. The population rose from about 13,000 at the start of the decade to a peak of 21,400 ten years later. Most of these émigrés were firm defenders of Calvin, attracted to the city partly because of his reputation. One exile, John Knox from Scotland, wrote home in ecstasy: "this place… is the most perfect school of Christ that ever was in the earth since the days of the apostles. In other places, I confess Christ to be truly preached; but manners and religion so sincerely reformed, I have not yet seen in any other place."[38]

Wealthy incomers were granted the status of *bourgeois*, for a fee, and thus entitled to vote. Therefore in the elections of February 1555 Calvin's supporters wrested control of the city council back from the "Children of Geneva". In the turmoil which followed, there was rioting in May 1555 and it was claimed that Perrin himself was trying to lead a *coup d'état*. The new council responded with repressive measures. Perrin fled the city, but was condemned to death *in absentia*, along with his accomplices. Other members of his faction were beheaded, including Berthelier's brother. In the elections of 1556 the last vestiges of opposition to Calvin were purged from the council.

Calvin had been ministering in Geneva for two decades, often under severe strain. Now at last his position was secure. For the remaining few years of his life he was able to work unhindered, with the full backing of his political masters. Though suffering from increasing physical ailments, such as migraines, bowel problems, gout, and gallstones, he continued to write and to preach. His Bible teaching drew large crowds every week and he also set about revising his *Institutes* for the final time.

As the pinnacle of his success, Calvin launched the Geneva Academy in June 1559, which he had been planning for twenty years. It was a Bible college for evangelical pastors, headed by Théodore de Bèze who migrated from Lausanne, which enabled Calvin to train young preachers and deploy them as missionaries across Europe. This was the final phase of his great reform programme. After years of uncertainty, the Reformation in Geneva was secure. Now its distinctive brand of Christianity – "Calvinism" – was set to become an international phenomenon.

8

Cleansing the Augean Stables

Evangelicals did not have a monopoly on "reform". Long before Luther or Calvin rose to prominence, many within the Catholic church had expressed their desire for its renewal and revitalization. This movement for "Catholic Reformation" blossomed during the sixteenth century among those who remained fiercely loyal to the Church of Rome and distanced themselves from schismatic Protestantism. Indeed, a number of reform initiatives were driven by the papacy itself.

When the Dutch theologian Cardinal Adrian Florenszoon from Utrecht was elected as Pope Adrian VI in January 1522, he immediately made known his willingness to reform the church from the top downwards. One Italian bishop advised him, "*Purga Romam, purgatur mundus*" ("Cleanse Rome and the world will be cleansed").[1] He despatched a papal nuncio to the imperial Diet at Nuremberg the following autumn to lay out his views of the church's most pressing needs. Like Leo X before him, the new pope urged the German princes to act swiftly against the Lutheran "pestilence" and to enforce the edict of the Diet at Worms, because he believed that evangelical teaching was endangering people's salvation: "we see countless souls who have been redeemed by the blood of Christ and entrusted to our pastoral care being turned away from the true faith and religion and going to perdition".[2] Nevertheless, in a departure from normal papal policy, Pope Adrian went on to make a public admission of guilt. He believed that the schism which was rending the church in Western Europe was a sign of the judgment of God upon the failings of the Roman hierarchy:

> *we frankly confess that God permits this persecution to afflict his Church because of the sins of men, especially of the priests and prelates of the Church... We know that for many years many abominable things have occurred in this Holy See, abuses in spiritual matters, transgressions of the commandments, and finally in everything a change for the worse. No wonder that the illness has spread from the head to the members, from the Supreme Pontiffs to the prelates below them. All of us (that is, prelates and clergy), each one of us, have strayed from our paths; nor for a long time has anyone done good; no, not even one.*[3]

The pope promised to reform Christ's "deformed bride", the Catholic church, and to "cure the sickness at its source" by beginning with the Roman curia. Nevertheless, he knew that vested interests and ancient traditions were at stake, so was resolved to proceed cautiously:

> *For the sickness is of too long standing, nor is it a single disease, but varied and complex. We must advance gradually to its cure and first attend to the more serious and more dangerous ills, lest in a desire to reform everything at the same time we throw everything into confusion... He who scrubs too much draws blood.*[4]

Despite these resolutions by the new papal regime, the German princes doubted his competence to initiate change. The Nuremberg Diet issued a list of grievances against Rome and demanded "a free Christian Council" in Germany to resolve the crisis.[5]

Pope Adrian hardly had time to begin his cleansing work. By September 1523 he was dead, aged sixty-four, and the papacy was dragged back into the murky realms of Italian power politics – indeed, he was the last non-Italian pope until John Paul II in 1978. The Florentine Medici family once again claimed the see of St Peter with the election of Pope Clement VII (Giulio de Medici), cousin of Pope Leo X (Giovanni de Medici), and reform was low on his agenda. The Vatican became embroiled in the continual warfare sweeping across southern Europe and joined the League of Cognac, an alliance with France, Venice, Milan, and Florence against Spain and the Holy Roman Empire. As a result, the troops of Emperor Charles V laid siege to Rome in 1527 and sacked the city. Unpaid and mutinous, they rampaged through the streets, looting, raping, and murdering. The Swiss Guards were massacred. Shrines and palaces were destroyed and desecrated. The pope escaped with his life, but was forced to take refuge in the Castel Sant'Angelo, where he became a virtual prisoner.

From Germany, Luther watched in amazement as his Catholic enemies destroyed each other: "Rome and the pope have been terribly laid waste. Christ reigns in such a way that the emperor who persecutes Luther for the pope is forced to destroy the pope for Luther. It is evident that all things serve Christ and those who belong to him."[6] Yet some Catholic commentators also interpreted the Sack as a sign of God's wrath upon the sins of the Roman church. For example, Bishop Egidio da Viterbo wrote:

> You must understand just how wicked are these days and how angry is Heaven at the rabble now admitted everywhere to the exalted office of the priesthood (lazy, untrained, disorganized and immoral, mere youths, bankers, merchants and soldiers, not to mention usurers and pimps)... The Emperor's army, tearing to pieces the barbaric filth, have overthrown and burnt everything in this dunghill. They have triumphed over pride, wealth and power. The ungodly say, "If God cares for sacred things, why does he allow this?" I reply that it is because God

cares that he not only allows this thing, but even carries it out himself.[7]

The Sack of Rome seemed to be a dire warning from heaven that if the papacy and priesthood did not embrace reform then they would soon be obliterated.

New beginnings

The drive toward reform within the Catholic church took a leap forward with the election of Cardinal Alessandro Farnese as Pope Paul III in October 1534. In many ways he was a Renaissance pope in the old style, notorious for his decadence and nepotism. He had fathered several illegitimate children, appointed two of his teenage grandsons as cardinals soon after becoming pope, and later acquired the Duchy of Parma for the Farnese family. Like his predecessors, he was a generous patron of artists and architects, such as Titian and Michelangelo. Paul III also threw his energies into renewing the church and one of his first acts was to summon an ecumenical council to tackle the task. Emperor Charles V had been demanding a council since the early 1520s, and even threatened to call one himself if the popes did not take a lead.

Leo X and Clement VII had consistently blocked this move, fearing the return of conciliarism (the fifteenth-century movement which argued that bishops-in-council had greater authority than the pope). Indeed, Cardinal Aleandro advised Pope Clement, "Never offer a Council, never refuse it directly. On the contrary, show yourself willing to comply with the request, but stress the difficulties in the way. Thus you will be able to ward it off."[8] Nevertheless, Pope Paul was serious about reform and called all the bishops of the church to gather at Mantua, in northern Italy, from May 1537.

In preparation for the council, Paul III established a nine-man commission at the Vatican to identify abuses in need of remedy.

It was headed by the leading Catholic reformer, Cardinal Gasparo Contarini (a Venetian diplomat), supported by several other sympathetic cardinals and bishops, such as Gian Pietro Carafa, Jacopo Sadoleto and Reginald Pole (a young English aristocrat). Together they produced a secret report, *Consilium de Emendanda Ecclesia* ("*Advice concerning Church Reform*"), presented to the pope in March 1537.

It was a devastating critique of the church's moral turpitude, exposing the avarice and corruption which lay at the heart of the Roman curia. It lambasted the indiscriminate ordination of immoral clergy, the sale of benefices, the greed of power-hungry cardinals, the laxity of monasticism, and the ineffectiveness of episcopal discipline: "This scandal, most blessed Father, so greatly disturbs the Christian people that words cannot express it. Let these abuses be abolished, we implore your Holiness by the Blood of Christ... Let these stains be removed." The commissioners assailed the tendency for bishops and priests to live far from their dioceses and parishes, perhaps hundreds of miles away in another country, while raking off the income:

For, by the Eternal God, what sight can be more lamentable for the Christian man travelling through the Christian world than this desertion of the churches? Nearly all the shepherds have departed from their flocks, nearly all have been entrusted to hirelings.

The *Consilium* especially focused the spotlight upon Rome, which was meant to be a model for the rest of Christendom, and yet "in this city harlots walk about like matrons or ride on mules, attended in broad daylight by noble members of the cardinals' households and by clerics".[9] Nevertheless, the commissioners looked to the leadership of Pope Paul III to cleanse the church and make it:

*beautiful as a dove, at peace with herself, agreeing in one
body... to restore in our hearts and in our works the name of
Christ now forgotten by the nations and by us clerics, to heal
the ills, to lead back the sheep of Christ into one fold, to turn
away from us the wrath of God and that vengeance which we
deserve, already prepared and looming over our heads.*[10]

It was a remarkable report and strictly confidential. Yet someone
leaked it and soon it found its way into the hands of the Protestants.
Latin editions were published in Rome, Cologne, and Strassburg
in 1538, and Luther gleefully issued a German translation with
a commentary. He ridiculed the idea that the papacy was serious
about reform and accused Paul III of "hypocritical flattery".[11] The
front cover of his booklet showed a woodcut of three cardinals
trying to sweep clean the Augean Stables with foxtails. Having only
strengthened Protestant propaganda, the *Consilium* was quietly
buried by an embarrassed papacy. It led to little decisive action. In a
further setback for the Catholic reformers, the ecumenical council
at Mantua failed to get off the ground, primarily because of political
wrangling between France and the Holy Roman Empire, and Pope
Paul was forced to postpone it indefinitely.

There were, however, other signs of renewal within the
Catholic church such as the vibrant growth of new religious orders.
Dedicated communities of monks and nuns were established
across southern Europe from the 1520s, often with episcopal or
papal encouragement. They ministered in the midst of the massive
social misery, especially poverty and plague, which followed in
the wake of the Italian Wars. Unlike some of the older orders,
these new groups won a reputation for austerity, self-sacrifice,
and zealous evangelism. A young Franciscan, Matteo da Bascio,
won papal approval for his community of hermits in 1528 and
deployed them throughout Italy's poorest rural districts. They
were nicknamed *scapuccini* or "hooded men", and so became

known as the Capuchins, one of the largest and most influential new orders.

At the same period the elitist Theatines were formed in the Italian diocese of Chieti (*Theate* in Latin), attracting young noblemen to their ranks by their strong commitment to social welfare. The Somaschi – formally known as the "Society of Servants of the Poor" – were founded in 1531 in the village of Somasca near Milan and worked alongside the newly launched Barnabites, who had a particular focus on education. There were also new female communities, such as the Ursulines, named after the legendary early Christian martyr, St Ursula. They were led by Angela Merici from Brescia and worked especially in hospitals, orphanages, and schools, a model for other Catholics to follow.

THE CHIVALROUS KNIGHT

The most significant of the new religious orders were the Jesuits, dominant in Italy but with their roots in Spain. They were founded by a Basque nobleman, Don Íñigo López Recalde de Oñaz y de Loyola (better known as Ignatius of Loyola), and became powerful champions of Catholic reform.

Ignatius was brought up in the province of Guipúzcoa in northern Spain and launched upon a military career. In May 1521, in his late twenties, he found himself caught up in the ongoing conflict between the Valois and Habsburg dynasties. Spanish troops loyal to Emperor Charles V sought to defend the fortress of Pamplona from French assault, but were overrun. In the early skirmishes of the battle, Ignatius was seriously wounded, perhaps by a cannonball. One of his legs was shattered and the other also badly damaged, so he could neither fight nor escape. Nevertheless his captors showed mercy and allowed him medical treatment. After a fortnight recuperating in Pamplona, Ignatius was carried back home to Loyola, where the doctors had to break his leg again to set it properly. His wounds would not heal and seemed fatal. Approaching death, he was advised to make his final confession and receive the last rites, yet on the feast of St Peter and St Paul (29 June) he took a turn for the better and within a few days was out of danger. It was a miraculous recovery which the young soldier attributed to his prayers to St Peter.

Still Ignatius could not walk and required weeks in bed convalescing. To reduce the hours of boredom he hoped to read romantic tales of chivalry, but none could be found in the house. So he was supplied instead with two religious books, both classics of medieval Catholic piety – *Vita Christi*, a life of Christ by Ludolf of Saxony (died 1377) and *Flos Sanctorum*, known as the *Golden Legend*, a collection of lives of the saints compiled by Jacopo da Varagine, Archbishop of Genoa (died 1298). Ignatius was gripped by these stories, reading them over and over again. They provoked a new desire and a change of focus for his future life – no longer to emulate the courageous acts of a champion knight, but to imitate the bold deeds of the great Christian saints such as St Francis and St Dominic. It was a spiritual reorientation which Ignatius later looked back upon as his conversion experience. He resolved that when he recovered from his wounds he would not rejoin the army but make a pilgrimage barefoot to Jerusalem, where he would live out his days in acts of penance and self-denial for the sins of his youth. This desire was confirmed, he recalled, by a vision of the Virgin Mary with the Christ child which gave him "very extraordinary consolation" but also left him sickened at his former way of life.[12] Now he spent his days in prayer and in making notes on the lives of the saints, transcribing the words of Jesus in red and the words of Mary in blue.

In the spring of 1522, when Ignatius was well enough to travel, he set out for Jerusalem, heading first for Barcelona. En route, his new found religious zeal and his dedication to the Virgin Mary were obvious. His first stop was at Oñate, where he kept a night vigil at the shrine of Our Lady of Aránzazu (Our Lady among the Thorns), on a site where a young Basque shepherd boy claimed to have seen a vision of the Virgin Mary in a thornbush in the 1460s. Next he met with his former employer, the Duke of Nájera, at Navarrete, accepting money from the duke to pay off his debts and to repair a damaged image of Mary. While riding on his mule, Ignatius struck up conversation with a Muslim, who questioned how Mary could have given birth if she was a virgin. This left the Christian burning with such anger that he even considered hunting down and murdering the Muslim to vindicate the Virgin's honour.

When he reached Montserrat he kept another vigil in the abbey church of the great Benedictine monastery, where there was a famous "black madonna" (a statue of the Virgin Mary with a black face). It was the Feast of the Annunciation (25 March), the day commemorating the angel Gabriel's appearance to Mary, and Ignatius spent all night kneeling or standing before Mary's altar. Here was the final renunciation of his former ambitions, though he still perhaps viewed himself as a chivalrous Christian knight serving "Our Lady". Instead of his sword and dagger, which were left hanging above Mary's altar, he carried a pilgrim's staff. Instead of his fine clothing he wore a garment made from sackcloth – though the pauper in Montserrat to whom he donated his rich attire was arrested on suspicion of theft!

All was now ready for Ignatius' departure for the Holy Land, but instead he made a detour to the small town of Manresa – perhaps because there was an outbreak of plague at Barcelona, from where he was due to set sail. He remained there for almost a year, going through intense spiritual struggles. To demonstrate his rejection of worldly values and vanities, he refused to cut his hair or his nails and relied on begging for food and alms. He spent many hours in prayer, fasting, and acts of penance, imitating the austerity of the Desert Fathers of the early church.

Ignatius also experienced strange and disturbing visions, and was beset by temptations and depression. Like Martin Luther before his conversion experience, he was troubled by the burden of his sins, fearing that he could not be completely forgiven. He could not remove the stain of his wrongdoing from his mind. Each time Ignatius confessed his sins to a priest, he would remember others he had not confessed. No matter how lengthy his prayers (he was often on his knees for seven hours a day) or how detailed his confession, he found no peace. For months he felt spiritually tormented. Ignatius decided to starve himself to the verge of death, in search of liberation, but his confessor commanded him to break the fast after only a week. In desperation he even considered suicide, but knew it would be a sin to kill himself, so he shouted out many times, "Lord, I won't do anything that would offend you". In his distress he cried, "Help me, Lord: I can find no cure from human beings nor in any creature. If I thought I could find it, no struggle would be hard for me. You, Lord, show me where I am to find it. Even if I have to follow a little dog so that it can give me the cure, I'll do it."[13]

Eventually Ignatius concluded that these burdens were an attack from the devil, so he decided not to confess sins from the past any more, but to trust that God would mercifully liberate him. Nevertheless his sense of unrighteousness remained with him. After recovering from a dangerous fever, he urged his friends that the next time he was near death they must shout at him at the top of their voices, "Sinner!" and remind him of his many offences against God. This spiritual wrestling in Manresa formed the seed which later came to flower in *The Spiritual Exercises*, Ignatius' influential guidelines for prayer and contemplation.

FOOT SOLDIERS OF THE POPE

In the spring of 1523, Ignatius set out again for the Holy Land, at last hoping to fulfil his ambition to lead a life of penance in Jerusalem.

His journey took him from Barcelona via Rome to Venice, begging food and sleeping rough along the way. Several times his life was in danger – from illness, from the weather, and when he intervened to protect a woman and her daughter from being gang-raped by a group of soldiers. In Rome, the pope gave blessing to his pilgrimage. In Venice, the doge ordered him to be given free passage to Cyprus.

There were fewer pilgrims to Jerusalem that year than usual, because of the precarious security situation across the Mediterranean region. Rhodes Island had been captured in December 1522 by the massive Turkish armies of Suleiman the Magnificent, who expelled the remaining Christian knights. There were only about twenty pilgrims in Ignatius' party. The Venetian doctors warned that if he journeyed to the Holy Land he would die there, but he ignored their advice. On the boat he still refused to restrain his outspoken nature and chastised the sailors so severely for their obscene behaviour that they considered marooning him on a Greek island.

Eventually Ignatius arrived in Jerusalem, in September 1523, eager to begin his life's work. Yet his ardent hopes were quickly dashed by the Franciscan friars in charge of the Christian shrines in the Holy Land, who refused him permission to remain. They feared that he would either be killed or be taken prisoner by the Turks and need to be ransomed. Although he managed to pray in some of the "holy places" (like the Mount of Olives, where he searched for the stone on which it was said Jesus left his footprints before ascending to heaven), he was soon compelled to start on the long journey back to Italy. All his religious ambitions now lay in tatters and Ignatius was forced to rethink his priorities. He decided to train for the priesthood, so studied theology back in his native Spain at Barcelona, Alcalá, and Salamanca. Soon he began to attract a following, but also came under suspicion from the Spanish Inquisition, who sent him to prison for heterodoxy. So Ignatius migrated to the Sorbonne in Paris from 1528, continuing his habit of begging for money to pay for his food and his fees.

161

In the French capital, a group of fellow students began to gather around Ignatius, mostly young men training for the priesthood attracted by his *Spiritual Exercises*. The early recruits included Francisco Xavier, Diego Laínez, Alfonso Salmerón, and Nicolás Bobadilla (all from Spain), Pierre Favre (from Savoy in France), and Simão Rodrigues (from Portugal). On 15 August 1534 – just two months before the Parisian *évangéliques* provoked outrage in "the Affair of the Placards" – these seven friends made a vow in the Chapel of St Denis in Montmartre to lead lives of poverty, chastity, and "the service of souls".[14] It was not intended as a religious order and the men were soon dispersed around Europe, but they had a mutual commitment to performing the *Spiritual Exercises* and in October 1537 took the name *Compañía de Jesús* (the Company of Jesus). At first they hoped to minister in the Holy Land, but war between Venice and the Turks made the journey to Jerusalem impossible, so they offered themselves instead to Pope Paul III, in total obedience, to be deployed wherever he thought fit.

Pope Paul welcomed the opportunity to command the energies of these young "reformed priests" and in September 1540 he published a bull, *Regimini Militantis Ecclesiae*, establishing the Society of Jesus (or "Jesuits") as a new religious order. In militaristic language, he urged them "to bear the arms of God under the banner of the Cross, and to serve the one God and the Roman Pontiff, his Vicar upon earth".[15] Their focus was to be public preaching, works of charity, and the catechetical instruction of children. Ignatius, now almost fifty years old, was elected their first "superior general" and lived out his days at the Jesuit headquarters in Rome revising their *Constitutions* and directing their activities. In a radical departure from the traditional pattern of a religious order, they abandoned set times of corporate prayer, to give greater flexibility and focus to their evangelistic and educational endeavours.

Missions were established throughout Europe, Asia, and the "New World". Francisco Xavier was sent to Goa in India in

1541, travelling from Lisbon via Mozambique under Portuguese protection. He evangelized as far as the Maluku Islands in Indonesia and Satsuma in Japan, before dying of fever off the coast of China in December 1552. Jesuits were also the first missionaries to arrive in Brazil with the Portuguese colonists in 1549, and helped to found cities like Salvador ("Saviour") and São Paulo ("Saint Paul"), from where their work spread throughout the rest of Latin America. The dynamism and dedication of the Society of Jesus won them a reputation as "foot soldiers of the pope", the vanguard of the Catholic Reformation. Their loyalty to the papacy was absolute, believing the pontiff to speak with the voice of the Holy Spirit, and among Ignatius' rules for his followers was the bold instruction, "we must always maintain that the white I see, I shall believe to be black, if the hierarchical Church so stipulates".[16] By the time of his death in 1556 there were a thousand Jesuits worldwide, with thirty-three educational institutions, and the movement continued to grow at a phenomenal rate.

CALLING A COUNCIL

Frustrated by Pope Paul III's reluctance to call an ecumenical council, Emperor Charles V took matters into his own hands. He summoned an imperial Diet to the German city of Speyer in February 1544 in an attempt to settle the religious conflict within his empire. At war with France in the west and with the Turks in the east, Charles was willing to make concessions to the Lutheran princes of the Schmalkaldic League in exchange for their military support. He suspended lawsuits against Protestants in Germany, granted them ecclesiastical revenues and also promised to convene a national council to discuss further reformation. Watching from the sidelines at Geneva, John Calvin sent the emperor an urgent appeal, entitled *The Necessity of Reforming the Church*, an apologia for the evangelical movement. He catalogued the many doctrinal abuses still in need of correction and looked to the Diet to come to the rescue of the church in its "grievous distress".[17]

The pope's reaction was to insist that only he had the right to call a Christian council. He denounced the emperor's concessions to Protestantism and rejected the authority of the imperial Diet to decide religious questions. Instead, he summoned his own council of bishops to meet at Trento (known in English as "Trent" and in Latin as *Tridentum* because it was surrounded by three mountains). The location was a compromise solution in the tug-of-war between emperor and pope, since it lay within the boundaries of the Holy Roman Empire but was an Italian-speaking city on the Roman side of the Alps.

Evangelicals responded to the news that Pope Paul had called an ecumenical council by deriding his authority and mocking the idea that Rome was able to reform itself. Calvin likened it to a thief arranging a tribunal at which the criminal was to act as both judge and jury in his own case. He denounced Rome as "a sink of wickedness scarcely better than hell itself" and the pope as "a high priest of all impiety, a standard-bearer of Satan, a fierce tyrant, a cruel murderer of souls".[18] From Wittenberg, Luther entered the fray with *Against the Roman Papacy, an Institution of the Devil* (1545), filled with bitter invective. He believed the Council of Trent would be "nothing but a farce, a carnival act put on to amuse the pope... The very devil himself would thank him for such a council."[19] From Luther's pen poured a ceaseless tirade of abuse against Paul III. Rather than the Most Holy Father, he called him the "Most Hellish Father", "a forger of Scripture, a liar, a blasphemer, a desecrater of all the apostles and the whole of Christendom, a lying villain, a tyrant over emperor, kings, and the whole world, and a thief, knave, and robber of both the goods of the church and the goods of the world".[20] Luther derided the idea that the pope was the head of the Christian church or the vicar of Christ:

> *Instead, he is the head of the accursed church of all the worst*
> *scoundrels on earth, a vicar of the devil, an enemy of God, an*
> *adversary of Christ, a destroyer of Christ's churches; a teacher*
> *of lies, blasphemies, and idolatries… an Antichrist, a man of*
> *sin and child of perdition; a true werewolf.*[21]

Against the Roman Papacy was one of the most violent of all Luther's polemical writings, the final tirade of the elderly reformer in his Herculean contest against the Church of Rome. Yet his ire fell on deaf ears, and within a few months he was dead, aged sixty-two, probably of heart failure. His followers were soon split into rival camps, squabbling over his theological inheritance. The Philippists (named after Melanchthon) and the Gnesio (or "Genuine") Lutherans both claimed to be the authentic representatives of his legacy, and their arguments rumbled on for decades, threatening to derail the Lutheran movement.

OPENING PANDORA'S BOX

After years of delays and false starts, the pope's ecumenical council was at last convened in Trent on Sunday, 13 December 1545. Then they promptly adjourned for Christmas! At the opening session there were just four archbishops, twenty-two bishops, five generals of religious orders, and three papal legates. They were supported by a team of theological consultants and canon lawyers, who were allowed to advise the council and its committees but not to vote on the resolutions. The bishops promised, in their *Decree Concerning the Manner of Living During the Council*, to model prayerful and godly behaviour while at Trent. They would observe "sobriety and moderation at table", with Bible reading during meals instead of "idle conversations", and fasts every Friday. There was to be no "chattering or gossiping" during church services. All their theological debates would be temperate, and there was a ban on "uncontrolled shouting" and stamping of feet.[22] Yet these promises proved difficult to keep during heated debates between opposing theological schools, where tempers often flared.

Although the council was not merely a tool of the pope, it was led by his three legates, cardinals Giovanni del Monte, Marcello Cervini, and Reginald Pole, with del Monte as president. The first question to be settled was the agenda. Which should take priority – the reform of ecclesiastical corruption or the definition of Catholic doctrine? Pope Paul wanted a focus on doctrine, to clarify Catholic teaching in response to Protestantism and the challenges of Luther. Charles V knew that restating traditional doctrinal positions would only alienate Protestants in his empire even further, whereas reform of moral abuses would help to conciliate them. Yet the pope feared this might lead to theological compromise. Therefore at the suggestion of Bishop Tommaso Campeggio the council agreed to discuss questions of doctrine and reform alternately.

The council showed no patience for evangelical theology. Indeed it drove a deep and permanent wedge between Catholicism and Protestantism. Its very first doctrinal resolution, the *Decree Concerning the Canonical Scriptures* (April 1546), dismissed the central evangelical principle of *sola scriptura*. The council insisted that church traditions should be ranked alongside the Bible as a source of divine revelation, since those traditions were "dictated by the Holy Spirit" and had been preserved in the Catholic church "in unbroken sequence" since the time of the apostles.[23] They did not explain which traditions were Spirit-inspired, but a Catholic theologian had recently compiled a list including the Apostles' Creed, the sign of the cross, infant baptism, and confession to a priest. This decree attacked the very foundation stone of the Protestant Reformation and was bound to provoke an outcry. One Lutheran commentator, Martin Chemnitz, warned in his massive *Analysis of the Council of Trent* (1565–73) that this Roman doctrine of tradition

*is very far-reaching, embracing in its bosom whatever the
papalist church transmits and preserves of things which
cannot be taught and proved with testimonies of Scripture.
It is truly a Pandora's box, under whose cover every kind of
corruption, abuse and superstition has been brought into the
church.*[24]

The council also affirmed that Jerome's old Latin Bible translation
(the Vulgate) was to be used for all theological discussions, and that
its "true meaning and interpretation" could only be judged by the
church, not by private individuals. Books and commentaries which
erred from authorized teaching were banned, and their authors
were to be punished by the bishops as "violators and profaners of
the word of God".[25]

In its early months the council also tackled another major theme
which lay at the heart of the Protestant Reformation: the doctrine
of justification, and related topics such as original sin, free will, and
predestination. There was protracted debate among the bishops at
Trent on these key and controversial questions, but they eventually
reached unanimous agreement. The apostle Paul had declared in
the New Testament that men and women are "justified by faith" not
by observing the Old Testament law (Romans 3:28), and the council
agreed: "If anyone says that a person can be justified before God
by his own works, done either by the resources of human nature
or by the teaching of the law, apart from divine grace through
Jesus Christ: let him be anathema." Nevertheless, they drew back
from Luther's bold declaration that justification is "by faith *alone*"
(*sola fide*). Good works still contributed something to salvation,
according to Catholic dogma: "If anyone says that the sinner is
justified by faith alone... let him be anathema."[26] Trent's decrees
on the seven sacraments followed on naturally, another point of
dispute with Luther and his allies.

HIATUS

In the spring of 1547, just as the council was beginning to debate the thorny subject of the Eucharist, Trent was beset by the plague (probably a fatal strain of influenza). Therefore the bishops hurriedly transferred their proceedings to Bologna, in the papal states, for the rest of the year. This left Charles V irate that the council was now beyond the boundaries of his Holy Roman Empire. His power struggle with Pope Paul III reached a new low, exacerbated when imperial troops supported the assassination of the pope's illegitimate son, Pier Luigi Farnese, by the aristocracy of Piacenza in September 1547. Charles even threatened to command the bishops from his empire to continue meeting at Trent, which opened the prospect of two rival Catholic councils running in parallel. This would only lead to schism and further confusion, so the pope suspended the council in February 1548. Nothing more could be done until Paul's death the following year, aged eighty-one.

The new pope was Giovanni del Monte, former president of the council, who took the name Julius III. At the emperor's urging he soon summoned the bishops back to Trent, from May 1551, to continue their deliberations. They picked up where they had left off with discussion of the sacraments, issuing resolutions on transubstantiation, penance, and extreme unction. Yet within a few months, by the spring of 1552, the security situation in Trent had become too volatile. War erupted again between the emperor and King Henri II of France, who had forged a new alliance with the Protestants in Germany and the Farnese family in Italy. Trent was in danger of being overrun by Lutheran soldiers, so the pope again suspended the council, lamenting that "everything, and Germany in particular, was aflame with arms and disputes".[27] The adjournment was meant to be for two years – in the event it lasted a decade.

Pope Julius hoped to continue reforming the church without the help of the council, but died in March 1555 before he could promulgate his reform bull, *Varietas Temporum*. His successor, Cardinal Marcello Cervini (another of the original presidents of the council), was also known as a Catholic reformer, but died from exhaustion only twenty days after his election, aged fifty-four – one of the shortest-reigning popes in history. This left the way open for the appointment of the ancient Cardinal Carafa as Pope Paul IV, a reactionary and autocratic traditionalist. As a younger man Carafa had helped to compose the *Consilium de Emendanda Ecclesia*, but the prosecution of heterodoxy had become his overarching concern as the first head of the Roman Inquisition from 1542. He promised: "Even if my own father were a heretic, I would gather the wood to burn him."[28] Some described his pontificate as the "regime of terror".[29] Catholic reformers faced heresy trials and many authors found themselves on the first papal Index of Forbidden Books (which included the entire works of Erasmus). The pope was highly suspicious of the conciliar movement, believing it to be a hotbed of reforming zeal and a threat to his powers.

ANATHEMAS AND TEARS OF JOY

Only after Pope Paul IV's death was the Council of Trent allowed to finish its work. It was reconvened by Pope Pius IV from January 1562 and quickly issued doctrinal decrees on the mass, ordination, marriage, purgatory, the veneration of saints and relics, and indulgences. Once again the council firmly condemned Protestant critiques of contemporary Catholicism and pronounced "anathema" upon them. In other significant reforms, bishops were commanded to reside in their dioceses and to establish seminaries to train a new generation of Catholic priests.

When the council finally drew to a close in December 1563 there was a chorus of celebration at Trent's achievements and it was reported that even "the most grave prelates wept for joy".[30] Having been stretched out over almost two decades, it was the longest council in the history of the church. The consultation had involved 270 bishops (almost 190 of them from Italy) during the reign of five popes, and was a major milestone in the internal reform of Catholicism. It eliminated many blatant moral and financial abuses, proclaimed a more rigorous pastoral ideal for its clergy, and helped to clarify Catholic teaching on the serious doctrinal issues in dispute with the Protestant reformers. Pope Pius IV formally approved the council's decrees in his bull *Benedictus Deus* (1564), while at the same time insisting that only he had the power to interpret what they meant. He also issued the *Tridentine Profession of Faith*, a summary of the council's doctrine, which all Catholic clergy, teachers, and students were required to subscribe – a deliberate counterpoint to the many reformed confessions in circulation across Europe. These theological distinctives were elaborated in the *Roman Catechism* (1566) and the *Roman Missal* (1570), which further emphasized Catholic uniformity, Roman centralism, and submission to papal authority.

After the Council of Trent the battle lines between Protestantism and Catholicism were much more rigidly drawn than they had been in Luther's day. There was no longer any doubt about where the Church of Rome stood. Although its moral purity and pastoral zeal were markedly improved, Protestants continued to believe that the Augean Stables had been cleansed only superficially. They argued that true Catholic Reformation would mean a return to evangelical doctrine. Moral corruption within the church, such as clerical ignorance and indolence, was not the key issue at stake. As Luther had admitted many years before, "there are just as many bad Christians among us as under the pope".[31] He wrote elsewhere, "Even had Rome observed her religion with the zeal of the hermits, her false doctrine must still have been overthrown."[32] The primary concern of the evangelical reformers was not to improve Christian ethics but to return to the New Testament understanding of salvation. The doctrinal clarity of the Council of Trent revealed that on this central issue the chasm between the two sides was just as wide as ever.

9

King Josiah and Queen Jezebel

In the late 1540s, the evangelical movement in continental Europe was in disarray. Luther was dead, the Schmalkaldic League had been smashed in battle by Emperor Charles V, and the Council of Trent was in full swing. Therefore all eyes turned to England as a beacon of hope for the reformers.

NEW BEGINNINGS

The death in January 1547 of King Henry VIII left the political and religious future of England in a precarious position. The crown passed to his son, Edward VI, who was just nine years old, and the precedent was not encouraging. England's previous boy-king, Edward V, had reigned for less than two months in 1483 before being deposed by his uncle and murdered in the Tower of London. This time power was also seized by the young monarch's uncle, Edward Seymour, Earl of Hertford, soon created Duke of Somerset. He was made "Lord Protector" and granted near-sovereign powers during the king's minority. Nevertheless, Somerset and the regency council made it clear that their allegiance lay with evangelicalism. At Edward's coronation at Westminster Abbey, Archbishop Thomas Cranmer called him "a second Josiah", likened to the Old Testament boy-king who cleansed the Temple, rediscovered the Scriptures, and destroyed idolatry (2 Kings 22–23).[1] Here was a potent signal to the watching world that England's new monarch would encourage reform. From Geneva, John Calvin urged Somerset forward with the encouragement: "This is the age of salvation when God's word has been revealed."[2]

The new government quickly set about replacing much of the Henrician religious legislation. They issued royal injunctions in July 1547 which ushered in a fresh wave of reforming activity in churches and chapels across the country. Although the population were warned not to take the law into their own hands, the clergy were commanded to become iconoclasts and to "utterly extinct and destroy all shrines, coverings of shrines, all tables and candlesticks… pictures, paintings and all other monuments of feigned miracles, pilgrimages, idolatry and superstition".[3] Other traditional objects connected with Catholic piety, such as holy water and palm crosses, were also banned. There was widespread destruction, encouraged by evangelical preachers. Images were burned and wall-paintings whitewashed. At St Paul's Cathedral in London the great rood was pulled down, though when some of the iconoclasts were injured in the task, Catholics interpreted this as the judgment of God upon their irreverent vandalism.

Instead of idolatrous images, the royal injunctions ordered every parish church to invest in a pulpit "for the preaching of God's Word".[4] Clergy were also now required to read a government-endorsed "Homily" every Sunday. The *Book of Homilies* was a collection of a dozen "model sermons", several of them written by Cranmer himself, expounding Reformation theology. For example, in the opening homily, "A Fruitful Exhortation to the Reading and Knowledge of Holy Scripture", the archbishop described the Bible as the "fountain and well of truth" and "food of the soul". He urged his hearers to "diligently search for the well of life in the books of the New and Old Testament, and not run to the stinking puddles of men's traditions, devised by man's imagination, for our justification and salvation". Cranmer called the people of England to feast upon the Bible, which "ought to be much in our hands, in our eyes, in our ears, in our mouths, but most of all in our hearts".[5] This *Book of Homilies* was intended to drill evangelical theology into local congregations. Next on the agenda was the abolition of chantries – religious foundations where priests were employed to sing, or "chant", masses for souls in purgatory. They were denounced for obscuring the true message of "perfect salvation through the death of Jesus Christ" and dissolved by parliament.[6] The confiscated endowments were meant to be redirected to education or the poor, but most were spent on Somerset's war against Scotland and France.

Meanwhile the personnel of the Church of England began to change. In the early years of Edward's reign a number of conservative bishops were imprisoned and deprived of their sees for resisting the government's Reformation policy. Stephen Gardiner (Bishop of Winchester) and Cuthbert Tunstal (Bishop of Durham) were sent to the Tower of London, while Edmund Bonner (Bishop of London) was incarcerated in the Marshalsea. They were replaced by a new crop of evangelical bishops, such as Nicholas Ridley, John Ponet, and Robert Ferrar. The aged Hugh Latimer, already in his sixties, turned down the opportunity to return to the episcopal bench but became one of Cranmer's key advisors. In the London diocese Bishop Ridley gathered together an influential team of preachers, appointed to significant pulpits, including John Bradford, John Rogers, and Lawrence Saunders. Evangelical exiles who had fled the repressive regime of Henry VIII also began to return home in droves. Miles Coverdale, the Bible translator, came back from Germany and was appointed Bishop of Exeter. John Hooper left his Zürich refuge and was appointed Bishop of Gloucester, set to become, according to one prediction, "the future Zwingli of England".[7] There was no love lost between the rival Henrician and Edwardian regimes. Hooper, for example, celebrated Bonner's imprisonment and denounced him as "the most bitter enemy of the gospel".[8]

The tables were turned and England now offered shelter to evangelical refugees from the continent, several of whom were leading reformers in their own right. Martin Bucer, Paul Fagius, and Pietro Martire Vermigli were expelled from Strassburg in 1549 when the city was forced by Charles V to submit to the "Augsburg Interim" (which restored Roman practices). They all accepted Cranmer's invitation to settle in England, where Vermigli and Bucer were appointed regius professors of divinity at Oxford and Cambridge respectively. Fagius became regius professor of Hebrew at Cambridge, though he died of the plague after a few months. Vermigli's compatriot, the Italian reformer Bernardino Ochino, was also welcomed by Cranmer after escaping the clutches of the imperial army at Augsburg. Ochino had once been head of the Capuchin order in Italy but dramatically defected to evangelicalism in 1542 and fled across the Alps for refuge in Calvin's Geneva before taking up a preaching position in Germany.

The defeat of the Schmalkaldic League also pushed out Jan Łaski, a former Catholic priest whose uncle had been Archbishop of Gniezno and primate of the Catholic church in Poland. Łaski was one of a number of Polish clergy converted to evangelicalism in the early 1540s and became pastor of the reformed church in Emden, in East Frisia, but was expelled when the Augsburg Interim came into force. He settled in England and became superintendent of the "Strangers' Church" in London, a community of refugees with Dutch, French, and Italian congregations. Archbishop Cranmer was able to harness the experience and advice of these distinguished continental colleagues as he drove forward the reform agenda in England. Bucer, Vermigli, and Łaski pushed him toward a clear Calvinist approach in doctrine and discipline.

PRAYERS FOR THE PEOPLE

One of the Archbishop of Canterbury's grandest projects was a wholesale revision of the medieval liturgies, to enable English Christians to pray evangelically in their own language. An Act of

Uniformity swept away the Latin mass and enforced the use of Cranmer's *Book of Common Prayer* in every parish across the country from Pentecost Sunday, 9 June 1549. The only exception allowed was in the universities of Oxford and Cambridge, where England's intellectual elite were still allowed to pray in Latin. The emphasis of the new liturgy was upon simplicity, intelligibility, edification, and biblical truth. Nothing was to be read in church except "the very pure word of God, the holy Scriptures, or that which is evidently grounded upon the same". Cranmer hoped that by daily meditation upon the English Bible the clergy would be "stirred up to godliness" and the congregation would "continually profit more and more in the knowledge of God, and be the more inflamed with the love of his true religion".[9]

At the back of the prayer book the archbishop inserted an influential essay, entitled "Of Ceremonies: Why Some Be Abolished and Some Retained". Again he warned that many English church traditions had "blinded the people, and obscured the glory of God" and therefore deserved to be "cut away, and clean rejected". He accused his opponents of being "addicted to their old customs" and complained that in times past "our excessive multitude of ceremonies was so great, and many of them so dark, that they did more to confound and darken, than declare and set forth Christ's benefits unto us". Nonetheless, he insisted that the prayer book was not "newfangled" since it maintained much that was ancient for the sake of "unity and concord".[10]

Some rejoiced in the *Book of Common Prayer*; others were outraged. It provoked insurrection in Devon and Cornwall (the so-called "Western Rebellion"), where traditionalists burned the book and took to arms. Angry villagers hurried together from various locations and marched upon Exeter, carrying the banner of the Five Wounds of Christ, incense, and a pyx (ornate box) for the consecrated Eucharistic bread. They issued a series of demands including the reintroduction of Henry VIII's Act of Six Articles, the banning of the Bible in English and the restoration of abbey and chantry lands. They appealed for the return of images and the right to pray for souls in purgatory "as our forefathers did". They asserted that those who refused to venerate the sacrament should "die like heretics against the holy Catholic faith", and rejected the new English service as no better than "a Christmas game".[11] Archbishop Cranmer replied that to recite Latin without understanding was no better than being a parrot, whereas "true Christian men… pray unto God in heart and faith". Meanwhile an evangelical activist in Devon proclaimed that the rebels had been led astray by Catholic priests to "embrace superstition and idolatry for true worship of God, the puddles and suds of men's traditions for the pure and clear fountain of the apostles' ordinances".[12]

The uprising was crushed by a royal army sent from London, after bloody skirmishes in which thousands were killed. The ringleaders were executed, including a priest near Exeter who was hanged on gallows erected on his own church tower, wearing his Eucharistic vestments. There were numerous other outbreaks of violence across the country, from Hampshire to Yorkshire, harnessed by religious and economic malcontent. The most serious was in Norfolk, where Robert Kett led a rebel army against Norwich. Their demands fell on deaf ears and they were slaughtered by the troops of John Dudley, the Earl of Warwick.

After the uprisings, Somerset was toppled. He had driven the country to the brink of bankruptcy with his war against Scotland and France, and had lost all political credibility through misjudged actions like the execution of his own brother, Thomas Seymour. In the ensuing power struggle it seemed that the Reformation might be stopped in its tracks, and there was danger of a coup led by the earls of Southampton and Arundel. After months of uncertainty the Earl of Warwick seized control. He was made "Lord President" of the regency council in February 1550, though not "Lord Protector" of the realm, and became Duke of Northumberland. Although he lacked Somerset's religious convictions, he remained willing to protect the work of the reformers.

"FOR THE MORE PERFECTION"

Archbishop Cranmer and his allies would not be satisfied until their reformation of the English church was as thorough and complete as possible. More work was necessary and they pushed forward into fresh territory with determination and speed. In 1550 Cranmer issued a new ordinal (a liturgy for the ordination of clergy) which presented a model of ministry radically different from that of the Catholic priesthood. Although the word "priest" was retained (an abbreviation of the old English word "presbyter") their function was now pastoral not sacerdotal. To emphasize the priority of gospel preaching, clergy were now presented at ordination with a copy of the Bible rather than a chalice and paten. A few months later, the authorities ordered that all stone altars be destroyed and replaced by wooden tables.

The time was ripe for revision of Cranmer's 1549 *Book of Common Prayer*, which had provoked heated argument among the theologians. The ambiguous nature of some of the liturgy and its concessions to traditionalists meant that conflicting interpretations were inevitable. Some conservatives were still using the communion service in a way not dissimilar to the Latin mass. Indeed, from his prison cell in the Tower of London, Bishop Gardiner praised the book for teaching transubstantiation, which was not Cranmer's intention at all. Meanwhile evangelicals attacked the book for its lack of Reformation clarity. Bishop Hooper called it "very defective" and even, in places, "manifestly impious".[13] Bucer and Vermigli also offered detailed criticisms. Spurred on by these objections, Cranmer produced a radical revision, far more unambiguously evangelical in its emphases. The new *Book of Common Prayer* was introduced across the country on All Saints' Day 1552. It was enforced by another Act of Uniformity, which acknowledged that the 1549 book had been "a very godly order… agreeable to the Word of God and the primitive Church", but that a new book was needed "for the more plain and manifest explanation" and "for the more perfection".[14]

The revisions were numerous and significant. The word "mass" was dropped completely, in favour of "Lord's Supper" or "holy communion". The "altar" became the "Lord's Table". Catholic vestments, such as albs and copes, were abolished. Prayers for the dead ceased. Traditional circular wafers were replaced by normal wheat bread, and ministers were instructed to place the sacrament directly into the hands of the communicants. The entire structure of the communion service was revised to lay particular emphasis upon justification by faith, and to remove any idea of sacramental consecration or Christ's real presence. The words "consecrate", "bless", and "sanctify" were deleted, and the clergyman was no longer allowed to make the sign of the cross over the bread and wine. The prayers which were retained from 1549 laid particular stress upon the grace of God and the atoning death of Christ:

> *We do not presume to come to this thy table (O merciful Lord) trusting in our own righteousness, but in thy manifold and great mercies. We be not worthy, so much as to gather up the crumbs under thy table. But thou art the same Lord, whose property is always to have mercy…*

> *Almighty God, our heavenly Father, which of thy tender mercy didst give thine only son Jesus Christ, to suffer death upon the cross for our redemption, who made there (by his one oblation of himself once offered) a full, perfect and sufficient sacrifice, oblation and satisfaction for the sins of the whole world…*[15]

In 1549 the sacrament was administered with the ambiguous words: "The body of our Lord Jesus Christ which was given for thee, preserve thy body and soul unto everlasting life." This was changed in 1552 to a more evangelical instruction: "Take and eat this, in remembrance that Christ died for thee, and feed on him in thy heart by faith, with thanksgiving."[16] The repeated emphasis was upon the benefits of Christ's passion on Calvary, appropriated by the faith of the believer, without any hint of offering to God.

This new prayer book was Cranmer's most radical move yet. Nevertheless some evangelicals still remained dissatisfied. John Knox, a Scottish exile in London and royal chaplain, protested against kneeling at the Lord's Supper as an unbiblical tradition. Cranmer dismissed Knox and his allies as "unquiet spirits", though Northumberland considered appointing the Scot as Bishop of Rochester "to be a whetstone to sharpen the archbishop of Canterbury".[17]

The final plank in Cranmer's reform programme was to establish a new confession of faith for the Church of England, to which all clergy would be required to subscribe. Evangelical doctrine could be deduced from his revised *Book of Common Prayer*, but it was now carefully defined in the Forty-Two Articles, which betrayed significant influence from continental Protestantism. The Articles covered key Christian doctrines, from the Trinity to the resurrection of the dead, while the errors of Catholicism and Anabaptism received particular censure. On the central issue of justification Cranmer was crystal clear: "Justification by only faith in Jesus Christ... is a most certain and wholesome doctrine for Christian men" (Article 11).[18] He repeatedly condemned Catholic teaching as without biblical basis, and Article 5 set the tone for what was to follow:

Holy Scripture containeth all things necessary to salvation: so that whatsoever is neither read therein, nor may be proved thereby... no man ought to be constrained to believe it as an article of the faith, or repute it requisite to the necessity of salvation.[19]

The Roman doctrines of purgatory, indulgences, the veneration of images and relics, and the invocation of saints were denounced as "a fond thing vainly invented, and grounded upon no warrant of Scripture, but rather repugnant to the Word of God" (Article 23).[20] Transubstantiation was rejected because it "cannot be proved by Holy Writ, but is repugnant to the plain words of Scripture, and hath given occasion to many superstitions" (Article 29) and sacrifices of the mass were decried as "forged fables and dangerous deceits" (Article 30).[21]

REFORMATION UNDONE

The Forty-Two Articles were promulgated on 19 June 1553, and still on Cranmer's agenda was a wholesale revision of canon law, already in draft form as the *Reformatio Legum Ecclesiasticarum*. England seemed on the verge of becoming Europe's reformed kingdom *par excellence*. Yet the king's premature death on 6 July, probably from tuberculosis, dashed evangelical hopes for a secure future.

According to the will of Henry VIII, the crown was due to pass to Edward's oldest half-sister, Princess Mary (daughter of Katherine of Aragon). Yet she was a convinced Catholic who, according to the privy council, would bring "the bondage of this realm to the old servitude of the Antichrist of Rome, the subversion of the true preaching of God's word and of the ancient laws, usages, and liberties of this realm".[22] Therefore in Edward's dying days and with persuasion from Northumberland, the councillors agreed to alter the order of succession in a futile attempt to protect the evangelical establishment. Lady Jane Grey, the Protestant daughter of the Duke of Suffolk and a great-niece of Henry VIII, was proclaimed as queen in London on 10 July. She was fifteen years old and had been married two weeks earlier to Northumberland's teenage son, Lord Guildford Dudley. Thus Northumberland had arranged that he would be father-in-law to the new monarch.

However, Mary refused to acknowledge Jane's claim to the throne. She took refuge at Framlingham Castle in Suffolk, where she could withstand a siege if necessary, and declared that she herself was queen. A wave of popular support for Mary swept the country and many Catholic nobles and gentry flocked to her aid. Northumberland marched to East Anglia with an army of mercenaries, but his support melted away and he was forced to retreat to Cambridge. In his absence from the capital, the privy council changed sides and Mary was proclaimed queen on 19 July. Lady Jane's reign was over before it had begun and she was remembered with the pathetic sobriquet "the nine days' queen".

The first indications were that Mary would grant religious liberty. In August 1553 the mayor and aldermen of London were informed that she "meaneth graciously not to compel or constrain other men's consciences".[23] She appealed for religious harmony between her subjects, "leaving those new-found devilish terms of papist or heretic".[24] Yet the queen's tolerance did not last long. Northumberland was beheaded for high treason, despite his appeals for clemency and his return to the Catholic faith. On Mary's orders, evangelical preaching licences were revoked and the leading reformers were rounded up and sent to prison. They changed places with the conservative bishops who had been imprisoned under Edward VI but were now reinstituted to their sees.

In October the Convocation of bishops and clergy affirmed the doctrine of transubstantiation and in December parliament repealed all the Edwardian religious legislation. The *Book of Common Prayer* was banned and the Latin mass restored. Altars were rebuilt, processions revived, images re-hung, and vestments re-embroidered. Within a few short months the face of the English church had reverted to the pre-reform days of Henry VIII, although Mary lost her battle to reclaim the monastic and chantry lands. The reformers were dismayed that despite their years of evangelical preaching the country had followed the queen back to Catholicism with such alacrity. Vermigli told Bullinger that even the most resolute were "now wavering, and even yielding".[25] Bishop Ridley concluded of many clergy and civic leaders that "for the most part... they were never persuaded in their hearts, but from the teeth forward, and for the king's sake, in the truth of God's word".[26]

There was further alarm when the marriage treaty was announced between Queen Mary and Prince Philip of Spain, son of Emperor Charles V. This alliance with the Catholic Habsburg dynasty provoked an outcry among Protestant patriots. In November 1553 a parliamentary delegation beseeched the queen not to wed a foreigner, but was turned away. Two months later Sir Thomas Wyatt attempted a *coup d'état* in reaction against the "Spanish Match", perhaps with the intention of placing Princess Elizabeth on the throne. He raised a rebellion in Kent and marched upon London with a force of 3,000 men, but was outnumbered and beheaded. In the wake of Wyatt's plot, Lady Jane Grey was sent to the block with her husband, on 12 February 1554, soon followed by Jane's father, the Duke of Suffolk. Princess Elizabeth was also committed to the Tower, before being placed under house arrest at Woodstock near Oxford.

Still the Marian regime continued to dismantle the Protestant Reformation. The "Strangers' Church" in London was closed down and foreign evangelicals were expelled from the country. In March 1554 clerical celibacy was restored and all married clergy were deprived of their benefices. The next month the three most prominent reformers, Cranmer, Latimer, and Ridley, were sent from the Tower of London up to Oxford to take part in a theological disputation before the university. It was little more than a show trial intended to discredit their teaching and resulted in the bishops being pronounced heretics and excommunicated. Ridley warned Cranmer that the choice which faced them now was "Turn, or burn".[27]

By the end of the year all was ready for England to be received back into fellowship with the Church of Rome, after twenty years of hostility. Cardinal Reginald Pole returned from his lengthy Italian exile to absolve parliament of "all heresy and schism" on behalf of Pope Julius III. On the last day of November, amidst scenes of great jubilation, he pronounced the realm of England reconciled with "our mother the holy church" and the schism begun by Henry VIII formally at an end.[28] Soon the Catholic Reformation began to blossom under Mary and Pole's leadership, as England led the way in enacting the theological and pastoral ideals laid down by the Council of Trent.

PURGED BY FIRE

In January 1555 the government adopted a new strategy in its efforts to eradicate evangelicalism by reviving the old medieval heresy laws, *De Haeretico Comburendo* ("*On the Burning of Heretics*"). With these new powers of persecution Cardinal Pole and Bishop Gardiner (Mary's new Lord Chancellor) began a purge. They struck quickly and decisively at the evangelical leadership with a series of high-profile heresy trials, hoping either to prove the weakness of the reformers and thus discredit them or else to terrify the rank and file into submission. Hooper wrote to Bullinger: "They are daily threatening us with death, which we are quite indifferent about; in Christ Jesus we boldly despise the sword and the flames. We know in whom we have believed, and we are sure that we shall lay down our lives in a good cause."[29]

The first to be executed, on 4 February 1555, was the London preacher John Rogers, who went to the stake at Smithfield insisting, "That which I have preached I will seal with my blood."[30] Soon John Bradford wrote with the news to Cranmer, Latimer, and Ridley at Oxford: "Our dear brother Rogers hath broken the ice valiantly."[31] Four days later Lawrence Saunders suffered at Coventry where (according to one account) he embraced the stake with the words, "Welcome the cross of Christ! Welcome everlasting life!"[32] The following day Bishop Hooper was burned at Gloucester outside his cathedral and Rowland Taylor at Hadleigh in Suffolk in front of his parishioners.

Over the next four years, more than 280 men and women were executed by the same method – an average of more than six every month, from February 1555 to November 1558. Another thirty died in prison before they could be burned. The martyrs came from every section of society. Although five were eminent bishops and sixteen were clergymen, the vast majority were tradesmen or obscure gentry. Approximately one in five were women, including teenage girls, pregnant mothers, and elderly widows. Even a baby boy on the island of Guernsey, born at the stake to a condemned woman, was consigned to the flames with his mother, grandmother, and aunt – though the sheriff in charge was later convicted of murder.

The persecution was fiercest in the south-east of England, where reformed views had taken deepest root and where the Marian bishops were particularly diligent in their hunt for heresy. Edmund Bonner of London led by example, presiding over numerous heresy trials, and he sent more evangelicals to the stake than any other bishop. The fires of Smithfield claimed forty-three lives, more than any other location in the country. Bonner's diocese also stretched to Essex, where the single largest mass execution of thirteen evangelicals took place at Stratford-le-Bow in June 1556. At Colchester there were twenty-three martyrdoms, including ten within ten hours on one bloody day in August 1557. Others were burned throughout numerous towns and villages in Suffolk, Norfolk, Kent, and Sussex. Canterbury, the ecclesiastical capital of England, witnessed forty-one martyrdoms, almost as many as at Smithfield.

However, outside the south-east the persecution was spasmodic and isolated. Only three were killed in Wales (all of whom were

Englishmen). Robert Ferrar, the deposed Bishop of St Davids, was burned at Carmarthen in his former diocese in March 1555 on the same day that Rawlins White, an elderly and illiterate fisherman, suffered at Cardiff. In the north of England there was only one martyr, George Marsh, a former curate of Lawrence Saunders and an itinerant preacher in Lancashire. He was killed in April 1555 outside Chester, where Bishop George Cotes proclaimed that he was "a heretic, burnt like a heretic, and was a firebrand in hell".[33] In the south-west there was likewise only one martyr, Agnes Prest, burned outside Exeter. She was promised her life would be spared if she recanted and returned home to her Catholic husband, but replied: "Nay, that I will not. God forbid that I should lose the life eternal, for this carnal and short life. I will never turn from my heavenly Husband, to my earthly husband; from the fellowship of angels, to mortal children."[34]

A PROPAGANDA DISASTER

The government's policy of persecution was broadly successful in suppressing heterodoxy, and Cardinal Pole could celebrate that English religion was at last "beginning to recover its pure form".[35] However, the burnings also supplied a continual fund of heroic narratives from which the underground evangelical movement drew inspiration. Some of the executions were propaganda disasters for the Marian regime, most notably at Oxford. Bishops Latimer and Ridley were burned in a ditch just outside the city walls in October 1555, where (according to a later edition of John Foxe's *Book of Martyrs*) Latimer was said to have exhorted his friend: "Be of good comfort, master Ridley, and play the man. We shall this day light such a candle, by God's grace, in England, as I trust shall never be put out."[36]

Archbishop Cranmer was kept in prison, where his Reformation principles began to waver. In the face of death his resistance broke.

Lonely, tired, bewildered, and often in tears, he was worn down psychologically by his captors and signed his first recantation late one night towards the end of January 1556. A few days later he signed a second, submitting himself to the Church of Rome and the authority of the pope. After long conversations with two Spanish Dominican theologians, Pedro de Soto and Juan de Villagarcia (Oxford's new regius professor of divinity), Cranmer's evangelical views completely evaporated. By the middle of March he had signed six separate recantations, repenting of his heresy, anathematizing Luther and Zwingli, acknowledging the pope to be the vicar of Christ, and assenting to the doctrines of purgatory and transubstantiation. He asked for sacramental absolution and heard the Roman mass, celebrated specially for him in prison. The reformed teaching to which Cranmer had dedicated his life was now in tatters.

However, the Marian regime failed to exploit this propaganda coup. The queen was determined that the archbishop should be burned, despite his recantations, which gave him an opportunity to rescue his reputation in the final moments of his life. At Oxford's University Church on 21 March 1556, Cranmer was invited to testify to his Catholic faith. He confessed to the congregation of "the great thing, which so much troubleth my conscience, more than anything that ever I did or said in my whole life". The authorities were following his prepared text and knew what to expect – a denunciation of his own reformed writings, followed by a declaration of his belief in transubstantiation.

Yet suddenly, to their alarm, they realized that Cranmer was departing from his script. The writings which he was renouncing were in fact his various recantations, "contrary to the truth which I thought in my heart, and written for fear of death". As he was pulled from the platform, he continued to shout out, "And as for the pope, I refuse him as Christ's enemy and antichrist with all his false doctrine."[37] As chaos ensued, the archbishop was dragged through the streets to the place where Latimer and Ridley had suffered six months before. He had promised that his right hand would be the first to burn for "writing contrary to my heart", so stretched it out into the flames, crying loudly: "This unworthy right hand... this hand has offended." Although it was a wet morning, the fire burned fiercely and the archbishop died quickly with the words of St Stephen on his lips: "Lord Jesus, receive my spirit... I see the heavens open and Jesus standing at the right hand of God."[38]

The monstrous regiment of women

When the Marian persecution began, some chose deliberately to face it. For example, Bishop Hooper proclaimed: "Once I did flee, and take to my feet; but now, because I am called to this place and vocation, I am thoroughly persuaded to tarry, and to live and die with my sheep."[39] However, many others sought exile. Approximately 1,000 English refugees fled to the continent during Mary's reign and established evangelical communities in cities such as Basel, Emden, Frankfurt, Geneva, Strassburg, and Zürich. From there they launched a propaganda campaign against the Catholic regime in England.

The most notorious resistance tracts were those published in January 1558 by Christopher Goodman and John Knox, pastors of the English exiles in Geneva. Goodman's *How Superior Powers Ought to be Obeyed* and Knox's *First Blast of the Trumpet Against the Monstrous Regiment of Women* both advocated rebellion against ungodly rulers. Knox likened Mary to Jezebel, the idolatrous Old Testament queen who had slain the prophets of the Lord, and called for her to be overthrown. He proclaimed that "the day of vengeance" against her "monstrous cruelty" was near, "And therefore let such as assist her take heed what they do. For assuredly her empire and reign is a wall without foundation."[40] Other pamphleteers began to remark upon portents of divine displeasure with England. For example, in 1557 and 1558 two waves of influenza swept through the country in which tens of thousands perished. Meanwhile in January 1558 England's last continental possession, the city of Calais, was seized by the French during the Habsburg-Valois war. Both these setbacks were interpreted as a sign of God's judgment upon the Marian regime.

Nevertheless, unknown to Knox and the Genevan exiles, there was no need for rebellion. Queen Mary was terminally ill and died of stomach cancer at St James' Palace in Westminster on 17 November 1558, aged only forty-two. That same evening, twelve hours later, Cardinal Pole died at Lambeth Palace of influenza. Just a few days earlier evangelicals had been burned alive at Ipswich and Canterbury, the last of the Marian martyrs. On the queen's death, the persecution promptly ceased. Others had already been condemned for heresy in London and Salisbury and were waiting to be taken to the stake, but were soon released.

Mary's half-sister, Princess Elizabeth, succeeded to the throne aged twenty-five and immediately made clear her intention to restore the Reformation. She did not hide her abhorrence for Mary's policies or her contempt for the conservative bishops who had led the purge. Elizabeth signalled the government's change of direction by appointing distinguished evangelicals to her privy council, most notably William Cecil (the future Lord Burghley) as Secretary of State and Nicholas Bacon as Lord Chancellor.

During 1559 they pushed through parliament a series of religious measures known as the "Elizabethan Settlement", largely restoring the legacy of the Edwardian regime. The Act of Supremacy made the queen "supreme governor" of the Church of England (a more nuanced title than the "supreme head" chosen by her father).[41] The Act of Uniformity abolished the Roman mass and restored Cranmer's 1552 *Book of Common Prayer*, with a few minor modifications – though it barely squeezed through the House of Lords by twenty-one votes to eighteen. These acts were followed by a new set of royal injunctions, modelled on those of 1547, which restored the evangelical face of the church. Only one of Mary's bishops was willing to conform, while the others resigned in protest or were deprived of their sees. This gave Queen Elizabeth the opportunity to appoint an entirely new leadership for the church. Most were drawn from the steady stream of exiles returning from Switzerland and Germany, bishops who were more determined than ever to ensure that the evangelical foundations of the Church of England should never again be in jeopardy.

10

Wars of Religion

From the late 1550s to the end of the century, Europe was convulsed by a series of devastating religious wars. The conflicts spread through Scotland, France, and the Netherlands, also entangling the major superpowers of England and Spain. Countless thousands lost their lives as the geographical boundaries of the Reformation were permanently etched in blood.

FIE, FIE, ALL IS GONE!

When England broke with the Church of Rome in the mid-1530s, King Henry VIII had urged his young nephew, King James V of Scotland, to follow suit. However, James was firmly committed to the old church and sought instead to build Catholic alliances in Europe, especially with France. He was married in Paris on New Year's Day 1537 to Princess Madeleine de Valois, eldest daughter of King François I, though she soon died, so James was granted a replacement bride, Princess Marie de Lorraine (better known as Mary of Guise). The king was eager to prove his loyalty to the papacy and to root out Lutheranism. Fourteen evangelicals were executed during his reign, nine of them in the years 1538 and 1539, under Scotland's new stringent heresy laws. It was even rumoured that the pope might reassign Henry VIII's title, *Fidei Defensor*, to James.

When England declared war on France in 1542, Henry VIII launched a pre-emptive strike against Scotland to protect his northern border. The Scots were routed at the Battle of Solway Moss in November, when hundreds were taken prisoner, including dozens of lords and lairds. Just three weeks later James died suddenly of a mysterious illness at the age of thirty.

He was succeeded as monarch by his new-born daughter, Mary, who was only six days old. James Hamilton (Earl of Arran), head of the influential Hamilton clan, was appointed to rule the country as "Lord Governor" during the queen's minority. As a result there was a dramatic but brief shift in Scotland's religious allegiance. Arran announced that he had become a Protestant and began to woo his English neighbours. He encouraged the circulation of the English Bible and appointed two evangelical chaplains to preach the gospel across the country. He also tried to arrange the marriage of Queen Mary to the future Edward VI, which would strengthen the dynastic ties between the two nations. However, this sham conversion was short-lived. Soon Arran reverted to Catholicism, the marriage pact was broken and the Anglo-Scots war was renewed. France promised military aid to its old ally on condition that Queen Mary was pledged in marriage to the infant dauphin (the future King François II). She was shipped over to the French court in 1548, aged five, and Arran was rewarded with the title of Duc de Châtelherault. However, he was soon replaced as regent of Scotland by the queen mother, Mary of Guise. In effect, Scotland had become merely a northern outpost of Catholic France.

Scotland's topsy-turvy religious policy in the mid-1540s resulted in the high-profile martyrdom of George Wishart, an evangelical preacher and former Catholic priest. He was tempted back to his homeland from exile in Cambridge by the prospect of a Protestant Reformation under the Earl of Arran, and began to preach to large congregations from Dundee and Montrose on the east coast to Ayrshire on the west coast. Yet his hopes of revival were dashed by Arran's inconsistency. His life was constantly under threat and he survived an assassination attempt by a priest with a dagger before being captured and burned to death for heresy in March 1546.

The judge at Wishart's trial was Cardinal David Beaton, the French-educated Archbishop of St Andrews and Chancellor of Scotland. Three months later a group of Protestant lairds from Fife broke into St Andrews Castle early one morning in a reprisal attack, possibly sponsored by Henry VIII. The cardinal was smoked out of his bedchamber as he cried in alarm, "I am a priest! I am a priest! Ye will not slay me!" Two of the assassins struck at their victim with daggers before another pulled them back and announced that it must be a solemn execution because they were carrying out the judgment of God. Pointing his sword at Beaton, he proclaimed:

> *Repent thee of thy former wicked life, but especially of the*
> *shedding of the blood of that notable instrument of God,*
> *Master George Wishart… we from God are sent to revenge*
> *it… thou hast been, and remains an obstinate enemy against*
> *Christ Jesus and his holy Evangel.*

At that, he thrust the sword into the cardinal's body two or three times. As Beaton breathed his last, he was heard to murmur, "I am a priest, I am a priest! Fie, fie, all is gone."[1] The verdict of John Foxe, the English martyrologist, was typically polemical: "like a butcher he lived, and like a butcher he died".[2]

DOWN WITH IDOLATRY!

During the regency of Mary of Guise, evangelicalism continued to spread among the Scottish nobility. Local lairds protected Protestant preachers and helped to arrange secret gatherings where the English Bible was read and explained. From 1557 they grew bolder. In December five nobles came forward publicly for the first time to demand religious reform and to pledge themselves in defence of "the

Evangel of Christ".[3] Their numbers grew and soon they were styling themselves "the Congregation", a reference to the true Christian church. They demanded the introduction of vernacular prayers and the right to reform their local estates along evangelical lines.

Under pressure from France, Mary of Guise and her bishops hit back. On 28 April 1558 – just four days after Mary Queen of Scots and the dauphin were married in Notre-Dame Cathedral – an elderly Protestant was burned alive at St Andrews. Walter Mylne was eighty-two years old and physically frail, but offered a sprightly defence of his views on clerical celibacy, pilgrimage, and the sacraments. Before his execution, he pleaded with the gathered crowd to "be no more seduced with the lies of priests, monks, friars, priors, abbots, bishops, and the rest of the sect of Antichrist; but depend only upon Jesus Christ and his mercy, that ye may be delivered from condemnation."[4]

Mylne was the last evangelical to be executed for heresy in Scotland. The movement quickly gathered momentum and in the autumn there were iconoclastic riots in Edinburgh. The famous statue of St Giles from the city's principal church was stolen and ceremonially "drowned" in Nor' Loch before being burned. Its replacement was carried through the streets in the annual St Giles' Day procession (1 September), but a group of evangelicals rushed forward and smashed it to the ground, breaking off its head and hands, with cries of "Down with the idol! Down with it!"[5] Then in January 1559 an anonymous "Beggars' Summons" was nailed to the door of friaries throughout Scotland. It accused the friars of stealing from the poorest members of society and commanded them to hand back their wealth or be forcibly ejected.

Meanwhile from his Genevan exile, John Knox issued a series of revolutionary tracts addressing the religious crisis in Scotland. He published an open letter to the Queen Regent accusing her and her family of "the maintenance and defence of most horrible idolatry with the shedding of the blood of the saints". He exhorted her to discipline the Scottish bishops whose "blasphemy is vomited forth against the eternal truth of Christ's Evangel" and warned that she would "drink the cup of God's vengeance" if she refused to grant freedom of worship.[6] Knox also urged the Scottish nobility to take responsibility for reforming the church, and not to leave it to the bishops, who were nothing better than "deceivable thieves and ravening wolves" who allowed "souls to starve and perish for lack of the true food which is Christ's Evangel sincerely preached".[7] Nevertheless, Mary of Guise remained resilient, threatening to banish all evangelical ministers from Scotland even if they preached "as truly as ever did Saint Paul".[8]

In this volatile atmosphere, Knox was summoned home from Geneva by the lords of the Congregation. He arrived in May 1559 and headed immediately for Perth, where his preaching sparked another iconoclastic riot. According to one report, he urged his hearers: "Pull down the nests, that the crows might not build again!"[9] The statues in St John's parish church were smashed and the Grey and Black friaries ransacked by an angry crowd. The Queen Regent saw this as a defiant act of rebellion and marched upon Perth at the head of a detachment of French soldiers, but was met by a large Protestant force. Although a truce was negotiated, the battle lines were now clearly drawn. Scotland's religious turmoil had escalated into civil war. The following month the army of the Congregation occupied Edinburgh. Mass books were burned, images erased, and religious ornaments confiscated from the city's many churches and friaries. The coining irons from the mint at Holyrood House were also seized. From London, Bishop John Jewel wrote a celebratory report for Pietro Martire Vermigli in Zürich:

Everything is in a ferment in Scotland. Knox, surrounded by a thousand followers, is holding assemblies throughout the whole kingdom… The nobility with united hearts and hands are restoring religion throughout the country, in spite of all

*opposition. All the monasteries are everywhere levelled with
the ground: the theatrical dresses, the sacrilegious chalices, the
idols, the altars, are consigned to the flames; not a vestige of
the ancient superstition and idolatry is left.*[10]

Another truce was signed and the Queen Regent returned to the
capital, but the peace did not hold. In October 1559 the Congregation
decided to depose her as regent and rule the country by means of
a "Great Council" of thirty Protestant leaders. The Earl of Arran
had switched to the rebel side and became the council president.
However, faced by internal dissensions and lack of finance, the
Protestant cause was near collapse. Mary of Guise was determined to
fight on and military assistance from France was expected to arrive
at any moment.

Help from England tipped the balance in favour of the
Congregation. For several months they had been pleading for aid
from London, emphasizing their common desire "to advance the
glory of Christ Jesus, the true preaching of his gospel".[11] Queen
Elizabeth was cautious about encouraging rebellion north of the
English border, but in early 1560 she sent a small flotilla of ships and
an army of 9,000 men to fight alongside the Scottish Protestants. In
February a treaty was signed at Berwick by which Elizabeth agreed
to take Scotland under her protection and to preserve "their old
freedoms and liberties" from French interference.[12] Mary of Guise
took refuge in Edinburgh Castle but she was terminally ill and died
there in June from dropsy, aged forty-four.

France eventually agreed to negotiate and the Treaty of
Edinburgh was signed on 6 July 1560. All French soldiers were
to be sent home, and King François and Queen Mary were to
renounce their claim to the English throne. Reparation was to be
made for any ecclesiastical property damaged during the fighting,
but religious toleration in Scotland was now assured. In celebration
of the treaty, a grand service of thanksgiving was held at St Giles'

Church in Edinburgh where Knox was now installed as minister. He prayed fervently for God to continue the work of reform, which was rapidly gathering pace:

> *We beseech thee, O Father of mercies, that as of thy*
> *undeserved grace thou has partly removed our darkness,*
> *suppressed idolatry, and taken from above our heads the*
> *devouring sword of merciless strangers, that so it would please*
> *thee to proceed with us in this thy grace begun.*[13]

THE TRUE KIRK OF GOD

The Scottish parliament immediately began to draft legislation which would establish Protestantism as the law of the land. First, in August 1560, they agreed upon a Scots Confession of Faith, a doctrinal basis which laid out reformed Calvinistic theology in twenty-five articles. Next they abolished papal authority and forbade the mass, with the threat of imprisonment, banishment, and death for those who defied the law. In January 1561 parliament approved the Book of Discipline, laying down the structure of the new reformed church in Scotland. The country would be divided into ten dioceses, each administered by an elected superintendent. There would be Bibles in every church, schools in every parish, and prayers in every household. Godliness would be encouraged by weekly "kirk sessions" in each parish, through which ministers and lay elders had responsibility to uphold moral discipline in the local community. The syllabus at the three universities at Aberdeen, Glasgow, and St Andrews would be revised and scholastic theology abandoned. Monasteries were to be suppressed and holy days abolished. The influence of Calvin's Geneva upon the Book of Discipline was obvious, though this Reformation blueprint was easier to devise than to implement or regulate. It was followed by the introduction of the Book of Common Order, the reformed liturgy in use among the English and Scottish exiles in Geneva in the 1550s.

When news of parliament's exploits reached France, King François II was furious. He refused to ratify the reform legislation and there were rumours that he was planning to send a French army to Scotland in defiance of the Treaty of Edinburgh. However, in December 1560 the young king died from an ear infection, caught in a cold wind while out hunting, which led to an abscess on the brain. He was just fifteen years old. The union between France and Scotland was therefore dissolved, much to the rejoicing of evangelicals in Edinburgh. Yet they still owed loyalty to their queen, now one of the most eligible young widows in Europe. Lord James Stewart (an illegitimate son of James V, and Mary's half-brother) travelled to France to invite her to return to the land of her birth, where she was welcomed in August 1561 amid jubilant celebrations.

Mary Queen of Scots was in a peculiar predicament. She was an eighteen-year-old Catholic queen raised in the French court, now ruling over a Protestant nation. A compromise was agreed with parliament, by which Mary would recognize the reformed church on condition she still be allowed to hear mass in her private chapel. This provoked a split in the evangelical community. As some were quick to point out, parliament had already outlawed the mass, on pain of death to persistent offenders. The Earl of Arran went as far as to proclaim that any of the queen's servants or French courtiers who attended the private mass should be executed.

On Mary's first Sunday in Edinburgh, Lord James Stewart himself stood guard outside the door of her chapel royal at Holyrood House to prevent furious Protestants bursting in upon the service. Knox denounced the compromise from the pulpit at St Giles in front of a large congregation, arguing that the queen's one mass was more dangerous than the invasion of Scotland by an army of 10,000 men. He reasoned that God would protect the nation from its enemies, "but when we join hands with idolatry, it is no doubt but that both God's amicable presence and comfortable defence leaveth us, and what shall then become of us? Alas, I fear that experience shall teach us, to the grief of many."[14]

Queen Mary summoned the preacher to Holyrood House to explain himself, an interview later recorded in detail in Knox's *History of the Reformation in Scotland*. She told him directly, "ye are not the Kirk that I will nourish. I will defend the Kirk of Rome, for I think it is the true Kirk of God." Yet Knox continued to speak brazenly of "the vanity of the papistical religion, and the deceit, pride and tyranny of that Roman Antichrist... I call Rome a harlot, for that Church is altogether polluted with all kind of spiritual fornication, as well in doctrine as in manners." He did not believe that Catholic scholars could win a theological argument "except fire and sword and their own laws be judges". The queen, however, remained unconvinced: "Ye interpret the Scriptures in one manner, and they interpret in another. Whom shall I believe?"

It was the first of several angry altercations between Knox and his sovereign. After he left the palace, he told his Protestant friends: "If there be not in her a proud mind, a crafty wit and an indurate heart against God and his truth, my judgment faileth me."[15] Over the next few years Knox preached persistently against the queen, as her most relentless critic. He was fond of praying:

O Lord, if thy pleasure be, purge the heart of the Queen's Majesty from the venom of idolatry, and deliver her from the bondage and thraldom of Satan, in the which she has been brought up, and yet remains, for the lack of true doctrine; and let her see, by the illumination of thy Holy Spirit, that there is no means to please thee but by Jesus Christ thy only Son, and that Jesus Christ cannot be found but in thy holy word...[16]

The preacher also continued vociferously to chastise the Protestant nobles whom he believed had betrayed the Christian gospel by their friendship toward the queen.

ASSASSINATION AND ABDICATION

Mary's downfall was her ill-advised marriages. In July 1565 she wed her cousin, Henry Stewart (Lord Darnley), an arrogant and vain nineteen-year-old whom the Cardinal of Lorraine dismissed as "a girlish nincompoop".[17] Their son, Prince James, was born a year later and baptized at Stirling Castle with full Catholic rites. Yet Darnley was implicated in the murder of the queen's Catholic secretary, David Riccio, and then was murdered himself in February 1567 at Kirk o'Field in Edinburgh, probably strangled or asphyxiated. Mary was delighted at her husband's death, glad to be rid of him, though the crime has never been solved. She ensured that the prime suspect, James Hepburn (Earl of Bothwell), was acquitted of the murder before promptly marrying him.

This behaviour horrified the Protestant nobility, who mobilized an army to depose the queen in June 1567. Bothwell fled to Scandinavia and Mary was forced to abdicate in favour of her infant son. After escaping from her captors at Lochleven Castle, she was defeated at the Battle of Langside near Glasgow in May 1568, and then ran south across the border into England. It was a desperate error of judgment because she was promptly imprisoned by Queen Elizabeth and never again returned to her native land.

Mary's abdication triggered six years of civil war in Scotland, from 1567 to 1573. On one side were the Queen's Men, who hoped to restore her to the throne. On the other were the King's Men, fighting in favour of her son, James VI. Although the King's Men had the firm backing of John Knox and other reformers, there were Protestants in both camps. They were years of turbulence and chaos. The first regent during the king's minority was Lord James Stewart, who was shot and killed by an assassin at Linlithgow in January 1570. The second regent was the Earl of Lennox (the king's grandfather) but he was fatally wounded in a skirmish with the Queen's Men at Stirling in September 1571. Only when England finally intervened did the civil war and the ceaseless blood-letting come to an end, and a truce was signed. Queen Elizabeth had initially advocated compromise, but eventually she gave her full backing to the King's Men. With this strategy she was able to secure Scotland's Protestant legacy.

The nation's greatest reformer, John Knox, died at his home in Edinburgh in November 1572, during the final months of the civil war. It was the Scottish nobility who were responsible for forcing through the dramatic religious changes of the previous fifteen years, but it was Knox who gave the Scottish Reformation its distinctive Calvinistic flavour. His reforms were consolidated in the next generation by Andrew Melville, who returned from Geneva in 1574 having worked alongside Théodore de Bèze. Melville was influential in the drafting of the second Book of Discipline (1578), which introduced a more rigorous Presbyterian polity as laid down by Calvin's *Institutes*.

THE BLOOD OF THE MARTYRS

In France the early Calvinists were known as "Huguenots", though they preferred the name *Réformés* ("the Reformed"). Secret congregations were established in several towns and cities across the kingdom, and they looked to Geneva for theological inspiration and pastoral support. Literature and personnel flowed across the border from Switzerland, but these activities were fiercely repressed by the French authorities. One of the first actions of King Henri II on his accession in 1547 was to establish a special criminal court at the Paris *parlement* to deal with heresy. It became known as *la chambre ardente* ("the burning chamber") and within its first three years had consigned thirty-nine evangelicals to death by fire or hanging. Next the Edict of Châteaubriant in June 1551 gave lower courts the authority to condemn heretics to death without reference to *parlement*, which left Calvin appalled that evangelical Christians had fewer legal rights than sorcerers, forgers, and thieves. He proclaimed to Bullinger in Zürich: "The flames are already kindled everywhere, and all highways are guarded lest any should seek an asylum here… The sword is whetted for our throats."[18]

Martyrs were multiplied and their testimonies diligently recorded in Jean Crespin's *Livre des Martyrs*, first published in Geneva in 1554, the French equivalent of John Foxe's *Book of Martyrs*. Usually they were burned at the stake, often with their tongues first cut out to prevent them making a final confession of evangelical faith. Calvin wrote frequently to encourage his persecuted brethren. For example, in September 1557 he exhorted the evangelicals in Paris: "God desires to try our faith, like gold in the furnace… let us never abandon the conviction that the hairs of our head are numbered, and that if he sometimes permits the blood of his people to be shed, yet he fails not to treasure up their precious tears."[19] Two years later he urged the reformed church in France: "the more the wicked strive to exterminate the memory of Christ's name from the earth, the more efficacy will he bestow on our blood to cause that memory to flourish more and more."[20] And again, "As for you, my brethren, hold in reverence the blood of the martyrs which is shed for a testimony to the truth, as being dedicated and consecrated to the glory of God; then apply it for your edification, stirring yourselves up to follow their example."[21]

Despite the persecution, conversions continued and congregations spread. They organized themselves into a national network and in May 1559 representatives of thirty congregations met for a secret synod in Paris where they agreed a Gallican confession of faith which had been drafted by Calvin. To help these new underground churches, Geneva began to send missionary pastors to France from 1555, many of them trained at the Geneva

Academy. Calvin observed that the beleaguered Huguenots hungered for reformed ministry "with a desire as great as the sacraments are coveted among papists", and he was determined to meet the demand.[22]

By the time of his death in May 1564, approximately 100 pastors had been deployed from Geneva, at the risk of their lives. One encouraging sign was the steady trickle of conversions among the French aristocracy. The king's cousin, Jeanne d'Albret (Queen of Navarre), transferred her allegiance from Catholicism to evangelicalism in the late 1550s, as did her brother-in-law, Louis de Bourbon (Prince of Condé). Her husband, Antoine de Bourbon (King of Navarre), was also sympathetic to the evangelical cause and Calvin urged him to declare his colours more boldly:

> *If men of low condition can sacrifice themselves so that God may be purely worshipped, the great should do all the more. God, who has pulled you from the shadows of superstition... and illumined your understanding of the gospel, which is not given to all, does not want this light hidden, but rather wishes you to be a burning lamp to lighten the way of great and small.*[23]

There were prominent conversions too in the Châtillon family, among the nephews of Anne de Montmorency, the Constable of France and a loyal deputy of Henri II. The Venetian ambassador in Paris wrote in distress, "This plague has spread into every layer of society... even the clergy are tainted."[24]

A KINGDOM DIVIDED

The political landscape changed suddenly in June 1559 when Henri II was mortally wounded in a freak accident during a jousting competition while celebrating the Cateau-Cambrésis peace treaty with the Holy Roman Empire. A sharp splinter from his opponent's lance passed through the tiny gap in his visor, pierced his eye-ball and lodged in his brain, and he died ten days later. However, there was no immediate lull in the persecution because the new king, François II (the teenage husband of Mary Queen of Scots), was dominated by his wife's uncles, the Duke of Guise and the Cardinal of Lorraine, both arch-conservatives. Calvin lamented to Vermigli that "all things are tending toward a horrible butchery".[25] In March 1560 some members of the Huguenot nobility hatched a plot to kidnap the young king from the royal château at Amboise, in a desperate attempt to free him from Guise control, but their conspiracy was discovered and they were summarily executed as traitors. Condé was also implicated and sentenced to death. Several Genevan pastors were involved, though Calvin warned the plotters: "if a single drop of blood were spilled, floods of it would deluge Europe... it were better we should perish a hundred times, than expose Christianity and the gospel to such opprobrium."[26]

The sudden demise of François II after his fatal ear infection in December 1560 was welcomed by the reformed churches as a sign of divine judgment upon the opponents of the gospel. His younger brother became King Charles IX but was only ten years old, so their mother, Catherine de Medici (niece of a former pope), immediately declared herself Queen Regent. In order to wrest control from the Guise faction and to establish her own power base, she sought to conciliate the Huguenots. Condé was released from prison and the King of Navarre was appointed lieutenant-general of France.

Catherine also tried to engineer theological reconciliation between Catholics and evangelicals by inviting representatives to a colloquy at Poissy in September 1561 – the last conference in the sixteenth century which aimed to bring the two sides together. Théodore de Bèze travelled from Geneva to lead the Calvinist delegation, supported by Vermigli from Zürich, but they made no headway with the French cardinals and bishops. Nevertheless the

Edict of St-Germain-en-Laye in January 1562 granted freedom of worship to the Huguenots for the first time, provided they met outside towns, unarmed, by day and under supervision. The Parisian *parlement* remonstrated with the Queen Regent, urging her to withdraw the edict and quoting the words of Jesus Christ, "Every kingdom divided against itself goes to ruin" (Matthew 12:25).[27] Yet evangelicals celebrated this limited toleration as a sign that a more widespread reformation was imminent. There were already at least 1,250 reformed congregations in France, remarkably rapid growth, encompassing perhaps 10 per cent of the population. Jean Morély, sire de Villiers, proclaimed: "We have, thanks to God, churches in nearly all the cities of the realm, and soon there will be scarcely a place where one has not been established."[28]

The toleration of Huguenots lasted little more than a month. On 1 March 1562 the Duke of Guise and his troops encountered a large evangelical congregation gathered in a barn at Vassy and attacked the unarmed worshippers, killing seventy and wounding many more. This unprovoked massacre sparked a cycle of violence and bloodshed which tore the kingdom apart over the next thirty years. The reformed churches asked the Prince of Condé to protect them from further assault, so he issued a call to arms and a formal declaration of war at Orléans in April. His *Protestation* stressed the loyalty of evangelicals to the crown but also the necessity to fight for the "matter of religion".[29]

Condé led the Huguenot military campaign alongside Gaspard de Châtillon, Admiral de Coligny, but the early battles went against them. Their troops were defeated at Rouen, Dreux, and Orléans and they were soon forced to sue for peace in March 1563. Condé's elder brother, the King of Navarre, had switched sides and marched into battle arm in arm with Catherine de Medici, but he was mortally wounded at the siege of Rouen. Having switched backwards and forwards between Catholicism and evangelicalism, he was attended on his death bed by both a Dominican friar and a Calvinist preacher, and was derided by the Huguenots as *l'Échangeur* ("the Changeling").

The civil war continued in bursts for the next generation, punctuated by pitched battles and temporary truces. The violence was fiercest in the south-west of France, but sporadic elsewhere, while assassinations and massacres were endemic. One pamphlet in 1568 called upon Catholics "to spill your blood for God, even to the last drop".[30] Condé was killed in the Battle of Jarnac in March 1569, so the mantle of leadership passed to Coligny, who appeared to win favour with King Charles IX and was welcomed to the royal court. The treaty of St-Germain in August 1570 promised lasting peace and there were hopeful signs of rapprochement with the marriage between the king's sister (Marguerite de Valois) and Condé's nephew (Henri de Bourbon, the new King of Navarre). However, the wedding celebrations in Paris in August 1572 became the pretext for the most notorious bloodshed of the religious wars, the St Bartholomew's Day massacre.

Many prominent Huguenot nobles were in the capital for the festivities when the royal command was given for all heretics to be killed. Coligny was assassinated in his home by a servant of the Duke of Guise and his body thrown out of a window onto the street and mutilated. This was the signal for systematic slaughter to begin, lasting several days. The frenzy spread to a dozen provincial cities, where there were similar massacres of the evangelical populace. At a conservative estimate, 2,000 Huguenots were murdered in Paris and 3,000 elsewhere in France. Over 1,000 corpses were washed up on the banks of the River Seine downstream from the capital. The Calvinist leadership was decimated and many fled into exile or returned to Catholicism for fear of death. For example, the reformed community at Rouen in Normandy shrank from approximately 16,500 members to fewer than 3,000 in the wake of the massacres. From Geneva, de Bèze wrote in despair: "God have pity upon us. Never has the like of such perfidy and atrocity been seen. How many times have I predicted it! How many times have I averted it! God has let it happen, God who is justly angered; and yet he is our Saviour!"[31] Meanwhile in Rome the pope was celebrating. He commissioned frescoes of the massacre for the Vatican and struck a special commemorative medal showing an angel with drawn sword, lifting high the cross of Christ as evangelicals were slain.

THE DUTCH BEGGARS

After forty years of burdensome political responsibilities, Emperor Charles V took the unusual decision to abdicate. He transferred power over his vast dominions to his Habsburg relatives during 1555–56, a complex procedure. His son, Prince Philip (consort of Queen Mary of England), became king of Spain and the Americas, while Charles' younger brother, Archduke Ferdinand of Austria, became Holy Roman emperor. Philip also inherited the Low Countries (known in Dutch as *Nederlanden*, or "Netherlands"), a loose collection of seventeen provinces in northern Europe, including Holland, Zeeland, Flanders, Luxemburg, Friesland, and Utrecht. The new monarch remained in Brussels from his accession in 1555, but eventually departed for Spain in 1559 and never returned. Instead he appointed his half-sister, Margaret of Parma, to rule over the Netherlands as regent.

During the early 1560s members of the Dutch nobility began to reveal their evangelical sympathies and to protect preachers and congregations on their estates, in parallel to the pattern seen in Scotland and France. King Philip wrote from Spain to insist that heresy be exterminated, but the nobles continued to press for religious freedom. Led by Hendrik van Brederode, they founded the League of Compromise in November 1565 to campaign for a relaxation of the heresy laws. Five months later they presented Margaret of Parma with their Petition of Compromise, hinting at armed rebellion, and forced her to suspend the prosecution of evangelicals. The nobles were derided as *Les Gueux* ("The Beggars"), a title which soon became their badge of honour. The regent's grip on power was rapidly disintegrating and she could do nothing to halt a wave of Calvinistic open-air preaching which swept through the Netherlands. This was followed by iconoclastic violence as churches and cathedrals were stripped bare of their images and ornaments. In Utrecht, Catholic works of art, vestments, and all the books from the library of the Friars Minor were destroyed on the bonfire. In Antwerp all forty-two churches were ransacked as crowds shouted, "*Vivent les Gueux!*"[32] By Christmas, evangelicals had organized congregations in most cities, modelled on the policy laid down in Calvin's *Institutes*, and they even erected their own buildings in Antwerp and Ghent. They described 1566 as the *Wonderjaar* ("Wonderyear").

Margaret of Parma managed to suppress the rebellion, but she was soon replaced by the Duke of Alva, who arrived in Brussels in August 1567 at the head of an army of 10,000 Spanish and Neapolitan troops sent by the king. Alva was a veteran military commander and was ruthless in re-establishing royal authority. Over the next four years his notorious *Conseil des Troubles* ("Council of Troubles"), also known as the "Council of Blood", condemned almost 9,000 people for heresy or treason and executed more than 1,000. Many evangelicals fled into exile, especially to Germany, Switzerland or England, while others reconverted to Catholicism. After Brederode's death, the rebel leadership passed to Prince Willem of Orange, who retreated to his estates at Nassau in Germany. His Dutch property was confiscated by Alva, and his teenage son was kidnapped and taken to Spain to be raised as a Catholic. Orange reluctantly agreed that armed resistance was the only way to save the Netherlands from Alva's "unbearable slavery", though he continued to acknowledge Philip's sovereignty.[33] His stated war aims were the withdrawal of all Spanish and other foreign troops from Dutch territory and the legal toleration of Calvinism and Lutheranism.

A PRICE ON HIS HEAD

Orange's early sorties were no match for Alva's military prowess, but guerrilla warfare turned to full-scale revolt in 1572. In April, a pirate fleet of 600 *Gueux* (known as the Sea-Beggars) captured the port of Brill and raided other towns along the coast. In August, just after the St Bartholomew's Day massacre in Paris, Orange marched into Brabant with an army of 16,000 men, mostly German mercenaries. Rebellion against the Spanish soon spread across the country. Alva responded with brutality, slaughtering the population of towns which stood in his way, like Mechelen, Zutphen, and Naarden. He managed to quell the uprising in the south, but not in the north, where evangelicalism took root. By the end of the decade the Netherlands was deeply and permanently divided along theological lines. The southern provinces signed the Union of Arras in January 1579, affirming their allegiance to Catholicism and welcoming Spanish rule. The northern provinces, where Calvinism was dominant, responded with the Union of Utrecht, a defensive alliance against Spanish intrusion.

Spain renewed its efforts to regain control over the whole of the Netherlands during the early 1580s under its new governor-general, Alessandro Farnese (Duke of Parma). He was a brilliant military strategist and soon reconquered Brussels, Ghent, and Antwerp, leaving the local Calvinist congregations in disarray. Meanwhile Philip II formally outlawed Willem of Orange. He called the prince "the chief disturber of the whole state of Christendom", absolved his subjects of their allegiance and authorized them "to do him injury or take him from this world as a public enemy".[34] The king placed a reward of 25,000 écus on Orange's head and promised that his assassin would be raised to the nobility and pardoned from all his crimes. Several men sought the prize but were foiled in their attempts. Juan de Jáuregui, a merchant's clerk from Spain, came closest in March 1582 when he shot Orange in the neck and face at Antwerp, but the prince survived despite massive blood loss.

Two years later, in July 1584, he was not as fortunate. Balthasar Gérard, a cabinet-maker's apprentice from France, infiltrated Orange's retinue at his headquarters at Delft and shot him at close range. The bullets tore through his lungs and stomach. Falling to the ground, the prince cried out: "*Mon Dieu, ayez pitié de mon âme; mon Dieu, ayez pitié de ce pauvre peuple*" ("My God, have mercy on my soul; my God, have mercy on this poor people"). In the next few chaotic moments the Countess of Schwartzburg took the hand of her dying brother and asked, "Do you die reconciled with your Saviour, Jesus Christ?" He struggled to open his eyes and mouthed "Yes", before passing from consciousness.[35] Gérard was captured as he made his escape and executed with gruesome cruelty, but his parents in France received the reward which King Philip had promised.

With Orange dead and Parma on the march, it seemed as if the evangelical movement in the Netherlands would soon be extinguished. Yet in August 1585 Queen Elizabeth agreed to send an expeditionary force from England to help the rebels, at the risk of provoking the wrath of Philip II. Her intervention restored the uneasy stalemate between north and south, deliberately undermining Spanish dominance in the region, and helped to secure the permanent future of Dutch Calvinism. The northern provinces became the Dutch Republic, though Spain did not officially recognize their independence for another sixty years.

THE PRETENDED QUEEN AND SERVANT OF CRIME

Not everyone in England welcomed the Elizabethan Settlement of 1559, which established Protestantism as the law of the land. All but one of the Catholic bishops resigned, as did a large number of other ecclesiastical dignitaries. Approximately 100 academics at Oxford University were deprived of their posts and went into exile, with Rome and Leuven as popular destinations. The parish clergy mostly conformed, though some hoped for the restoration of Catholicism.

One minister proclaimed that "he had said mass and did trust to live to say mass again". Another told his congregation that "this Church of England is a defiled and spotted church" and that the reformed Lord's Supper was worthless.[36] Although the Act of Uniformity made attendance at evangelical worship obligatory, some refused as a matter of conscience and became known as "recusants" (from the Latin *recusare*, to refuse). To bolster the Protestant establishment, the first English edition of John Foxe's *Book of Martyrs* was published in 1563, with its emotive warnings about the dangers of Catholicism. At the same period Bishop John Jewel wrote his *Apologia Ecclesiae Anglicanae*, an influential defence of the Church of England in the face of Catholic criticism. The evangelical doctrine of the church was also explicitly reaffirmed in the Thirty-Eight Articles (soon expanded to Thirty-Nine Articles), a mild revision of Thomas Cranmer's confession of faith.

Nevertheless, the best efforts of the Elizabethan bishops could not quash the agitation of discontented recusants. The situation was exacerbated by the arrival of Mary Queen of Scots in England in 1568 after her defeat by the Lords of the Congregation, and she became the focus of several pro-Catholic conspiracies aimed at toppling the Protestant regime. The most serious was the so-called Northern Rebellion of 1569, led by the earls of Northumberland and Westmoreland. They issued a summons across the north-east of England urging all men between the ages of sixteen and sixty to defend the ancient traditions of the church against the innovative "heresy" which had infiltrated the country. They appealed for support "as your duty toward God doth bind you, for the setting forth of his true and Catholic religion".[37]

The rebels marched upon Durham, where they tore up the Protestant prayer books in the cathedral and celebrated the mass. This pattern was repeated in other parish churches throughout Yorkshire and County Durham. At Sedgefield the parishioners threw down the communion table and dragged the stone altar back into the church. Meanwhile in Durham Cathedral, one clergyman took it upon himself to absolve the congregation of their schism with the Church of Rome. A correspondent in York warned Sir William Cecil that even those who had not openly joined the rebels were hostile to the queen:

> *There are not ten gentlemen in all this country that favour*
> *her proceedings in the cause of religion. The common people*
> *are ignorant, superstitious, and altogether blinded with the*
> *old popish doctrine, and therefore so favour the cause which*
> *the rebels make the colour of their rebellion, that, though their*
> *persons be here with us, their hearts are with them.*[38]

He observed: "The ancient faith still lay like lees [sediment] at the bottom of men's hearts and if the vessel was ever so little stirred came to the top."[39]

The rebel army marched south, planning to free Mary Queen of Scots from Tutbury Castle in Staffordshire. Yet when they reached Leeds they lost their nerve and turned back. Queen Mary had been moved to a more secure fortress at Coventry and a massive royal force of 10,000 men was heading north to confront them. The rebels retreated in confusion, unable to recruit sufficient allies. Just before Christmas 1569, Northumberland and Westmoreland slipped over the border into Scotland, hoping to join forces with the Queen's Men in the Scottish civil war.

Their followers in England were left to pay the price for their folly. Queen Elizabeth demanded the severest punishments, so approximately 450 of the rank and file were executed under martial law. Eight rebel leaders were taken to Tyburn in London where they were hanged, drawn, and quartered for treason, though many of the other northern gentry were allowed to live on condition that they surrendered their lands and possessions to the crown. In order to curry favour with the queen, the Scottish government handed back Northumberland, who was beheaded at York in August 1572. Westmoreland managed to escape to the Netherlands, where he lived out his days enjoying a pension from Spain. Their attempt to overthrow English Protestantism had ended in disorganized failure.

In a belated attempt to encourage the Northern Rebellion, Pope Pius V issued a bull from Rome in April 1570 entitled *Regnans in Excelsis* ("*Ruling in the Highest*"). In inflammatory language, it excommunicated Queen Elizabeth as "a heretic and favourer of heretics". The pope denounced her as "the pretended queen of England and the servant of crime", responsible for reducing her kingdom to "a miserable ruin". He proclaimed that she was no longer queen and absolved her subjects from all their oaths of obedience to the English crown. He warned that anyone who dared to obey Elizabeth's laws would also be excommunicated, a punishment with eternal consequences since there was "no salvation" outside the Catholic church.[40] Rome appeared to be explicitly encouraging the overthrow or assassination of the Queen of England.

The government's worst fears were substantiated a few months later when royal spies uncovered a planned coup, coordinated by the Italian banker, Roberto di Ridolfi. A Catholic army would invade from the Spanish Netherlands and install Mary Queen of Scots on the throne after her marriage to the Duke of Norfolk. When the plot was discovered, Norfolk lost his head and parliament pressed the queen to execute Mary too. The bishops warned that God would judge Elizabeth if she showed "unreasonable clemency" to her rival.[41] Meanwhile from Scotland, John Knox urged William Cecil that the destruction of Mary Queen of Scots was the only way to stop these ceaseless Catholic conspiracies: "If you strike not at the root, the branches that appear to be broken will bud again (and that more quickly than men can believe) with greater force than we would wish."[42] For the time being, Elizabeth resisted these calls to exterminate her relative. However, parliament made it "high treason" for any English subject to be reconciled to the Bishop of Rome.[43]

THE PURITANS

Although the Elizabethan Settlement of 1559 was explicitly Protestant, with strong Calvinistic leanings, there were many in England who wanted to push the Reformation further in order to eradicate every last vestige of unbiblical practice. They looked to Geneva for the best model of a purified church and were mocked as "precisians" or "puritans", though they preferred to call themselves "the godly". As early as 1563 they petitioned convocation to abolish a series of minor rituals and traditions which still lingered from the Middle Ages, such as holy days, the sign of the cross at baptism, kneeling at the Lord's Supper, vestments, and pipe organs.

The puritan agenda was laid out most clearly in an anonymous *Admonition to Parliament* (1572), which complained that "we in England are so far off from having a church rightly reformed, according to the prescript of God's word, that as yet we are not come to the outward face of the same". It appealed for the gospel to be preached with "purity", the sacraments administered with "simplicity", and church discipline enforced with "severity". The *Admonition* demanded an end to the Thirty-Nine Articles and the *Book of Homilies*, and derided Cranmer's *Book of Common Prayer* as "an unperfect book, culled and picked out of that popish dunghill, the mass book, full of all abominations".[44] It also looked for the eradication of bishops and the inauguration of a Presbyterian polity. The authors of the *Admonition* were two young puritan ministers in London, John Field and Thomas Wilcox, who were punished with a year in prison. However, there were many others to take their place, like Thomas Cartwright, who was dismissed in 1571 from his post as Lady Margaret professor of divinity at Cambridge because he publicly advocated Presbyterianism.

One of the first major clashes between the puritans and Queen Elizabeth was the so-called "vestiarian controversy", over clerical dress. Although medieval Eucharistic vestments were abolished, the queen insisted that her clergy must wear a surplice when leading public prayer – a rule explicitly laid down in 1565 in Archbishop Parker's *Advertisements*. The puritans believed that the surplice was a sacerdotal garment and preferred to wear academic gowns to emphasize their theological learning, but they lost this battle. Those who refused to conform were dismissed from their posts, beginning with Thomas Sampson (Dean of Christ Church, Oxford), England's first evangelical "nonconformist".

Next the queen complained at the proliferation of puritan meetings known as "prophesyings", named after and modelled upon the *Prophezei* in Zürich. These Bible classes enabled local ministers to study the Scriptures together and trained them in evangelical methods of exegesis. Yet Elizabeth reckoned there were already too many preachers in England and that these unauthorized gatherings would lead to factions and anarchy. She therefore ordered Edmund Grindal (the new Archbishop of Canterbury) to suppress them. He refused and wrote at length to the queen in December 1576 explaining: "Public and continual preaching of God's word is the ordinary mean and instrument of the salvation of mankind." He defiantly told Elizabeth: "I choose rather to offend your earthly majesty, than to offend the heavenly majesty of God."[45] This diplomatic *faux pas* put an end to Grindal's ministry and he was confined to Lambeth Palace in enforced retirement until his death six years later. The next archbishop, John Whitgift, had less sympathy for puritanism and forced the clergy to affirm their belief that every detail of the *Book of Common Prayer* was compatible with biblical teaching. As many as 400 refused to subscribe and were suspended from ministry in the Church of England.

MISSIONARY PRIESTS

The Protestant establishment in England faced a challenge from a different direction with the arrival of missionary priests from the continent in the mid-1570s. William Allen, principal of St Mary's Hall in Oxford, was among the first exiles who fled to Leuven and in 1568 he established a college at Douai to provide a Catholic education for young Englishmen. He hoped his students would become the future leaders of the church when Elizabeth was toppled: "For we thought it would be an excellent thing to have men of learning always ready outside the realm to restore religion when the proper moment should arrive, although it seemed hopeless to attempt anything while the heretics were masters there."[46] The college was such a success that within a few years there were more than 200 on the books – several of whom were disillusioned dons and students from Oxford University. Indeed the Earl of Leicester (chancellor of the university) compared Oxford unfavourably with Cambridge, complaining at the toleration "of secret and lurking papists among you, which seduce your youth and carry them over by flocks to the seminaries beyond the seas".[47]

After their training at Douai, many of these seminary priests were sent back across the English Channel to strengthen the Catholic underground. Their numbers rose year upon year. More than 140 missionaries were dispatched between 1574 and 1581, while Allen coordinated the strategy for smuggling in Roman books, vestments, and personnel from the safety of the continent. Soon there were similar colleges training English priests in Rome and Spain. The Jesuits were particularly enthusiastic in their supply of missionaries. Secret Catholic congregations began to multiply, which caused one evangelical in Lancashire to lament: "We hoped that, these papistical priests dying, all papistry should have died and ended with them, but this brood will never be rooted out."[48]

In a climate of fear and suspicion, the Protestant authorities clamped down upon the recusants with increasing severity. The early toleration of Elizabeth's reign was replaced by draconian measures. In 1581 the anti-Catholic legislation was tightened. Anyone reconciled to Rome faced the death penalty for treason; those who heard or said mass would be punished with a year in prison; and the fine for non-attendance at the parish church was increased 400-fold, from a shilling to twenty pounds. Four years later it was made treason for Catholic priests ordained abroad to even enter the country, and any who provided them with aid or shelter would face the same charge.

EDMUND CAMPION

More than 130 missionary priests were executed during Elizabeth's reign, beginning with Cuthbert Mayne, who was hanged, drawn, and quartered at Launceston in Cornwall in November 1577. At least sixty lay accomplices also met the death penalty. The most notorious case was that of Edmund Campion, who had deserted Oxford for Rome but returned as part of the first Jesuit mission to England. He arrived at Dover in June 1580 pretending to be a travelling salesman, and began to tour through Berkshire, Oxfordshire, and Northamptonshire ministering in secret to Catholic families, saying mass and hearing confessions. It was a risky strategy, which necessitated frequent moves from one safe house to the next, often in disguise and under a false name. Many Catholic homes had built a "priest hole", a secret room in which the missionaries could quickly be hidden if government agents came too close. Yet Campion was not optimistic that he would evade capture, as he reported to his superiors: "I cannot long escape the hands of the heretics, the enemy have so many eyes, so many tongues, so many scouts and crafts."[49]

Shortly after arriving in England, Campion was persuaded to compose an address to the privy council, which was meant to remain secret until his arrest or execution, but copies were soon in circulation. The document was nicknamed *Campion's Brag* and became a manifesto for the Jesuit mission. He proclaimed that they had come to England "for the glory of God and benefit of souls", but he disavowed any political motivation: "My charge is, of free cost to preach the gospel, to minister the sacraments, to instruct the simple, to reform sinners, to confute errors – in brief, to cry alarm spiritual against foul vice and proud ignorance, wherewith many of my dear countrymen are abused."

Campion believed that the claims of the Church of Rome were unanswerable and hoped that the privy councillors would heed the teaching of the missionary priests "who would spend the best blood in their bodies for your salvation". He ended with the provocative announcement that many young English seminarians on the continent were praying daily for the conversion of England, determined "either to win you heaven, or to die upon your pikes". Likewise the Jesuits had made a binding agreement

> *cheerfully to carry the cross you shall lay upon us, and never to despair your recovery, while we have a man left to enjoy your Tyburn, or to be racked with your torments, or consumed with your prisons. The expense is reckoned, the enterprise is begun; it is of God, it cannot be withstood. So the faith was planted; so it must be restored.*[50]

Campion's Brag put the Jesuit at the top of the government's list of "most wanted" criminals. He provoked them further with the publication of *Decem Rationes* ("*Ten Reasons*"), a pamphlet attack upon the Protestant Reformation, copies of which were left on the benches of the University Church in Oxford in June 1581. Campion proclaimed that the same heaven could not hold both Calvin and the heroes of Catholic Christendom. He finished with an appeal to Queen Elizabeth, promising that "the day will surely come, that will show thee clearly which of the two have loved thee, the Society of Jesus or the brood of Luther".[51] A month later he was arrested in

Essex, along with two other priests and seven laymen, when betrayed by a Catholic informer.

Campion was interrogated under torture at the Tower of London. He was stretched on the rack and, according to some reports, had his fingernails pulled out. He was also subjected to four days of disputation against a team of Reformed theologians, answering questions about justification by faith, the church, the Lord's Supper, and the authority of the Bible. When put on trial before a grand jury at Westminster Hall, along with seven other priests, Campion was found guilty of conspiracy to overthrow the queen and the Protestant establishment by fomenting Catholic rebellion and foreign invasion.

He was dragged to Tyburn for execution on 1 December 1581, but protested from the gallows that he was "altogether innocent" of the charge of treason: "I am a Catholic man and a priest; in that faith have I lived and in that faith I intend to die. If you esteem my religion treason, then am I guilty; as for other treason I never committed any, God is my judge." When a reformed minister offered to pray with the condemned man, he replied: "Sir, you and I are not one in religion, wherefore I pray you content yourself. I bar none of prayer; but I only desire them that are of the household of faith to pray with me, and in mine agony to say one creed."[52] Campion was hanged, drawn, and quartered alongside two seminary priests from Douai, Ralph Sherwin and Alexander Briant. In defence of this barbarity the English government insisted that these men were not martyrs, having been killed not for their religion but for political sedition.

THE CATHOLIC UNDERGROUND

Campion's courageous example inspired many within the recusant community. Philip Howard (Earl of Arundel and son of the Duke of Norfolk) testified that he had turned to Catholicism after hearing Campion dispute theology in the Tower of London. He tried to flee from England but was arrested as he sailed to the continent and spent the rest of his life in prison. Henry Walpole attended Campion's execution and stood so close to the gallows that when the martyr's entrails were dragged from his body and his heart held aloft, some of Campion's blood splashed onto Walpole's coat. He was so affected that he decided to become a Jesuit and later paid with his life at York.

Among the other notorious executions was that of Margaret Clitherow, a young mother from York. She converted to Catholicism and was arrested in March 1586 for harbouring priests. She refused to enter a plea at her trial and therefore was crushed to death, though she was probably pregnant at the time. She was tied to the ground, naked, with a sharp stone in the small of her back, then a door was laid on top of her body and seven or eight hundredweight were added (totalling approximately a third of a ton). As her ribs were broken and her torso ruptured, she cried out in agony, "Jesu! Jesu! Jesu! Have mercy on me!"[53] Two years later Margaret Ward was hanged at Tyburn for helping a Catholic priest to escape from prison, though she rejoiced in "delivering that innocent lamb from the hands of those bloody wolves".[54]

Meanwhile at Oxford, where the precious memory of Cranmer, Latimer, and Ridley was celebrated as a focal point for Protestant hagiography, four Catholics were executed too. They were arrested in May 1589 at the Catherine Wheel Inn, part of an elaborate network of safe-houses for priests. Like Campion, they protested from the gallows that they were being ruthlessly persecuted because of theology not politics: "Behold, we are brought here to die for the confession of the Catholic faith, the old religion, in which our forefathers and ancestors all lived and died."[55] Their heads were displayed on the walls of Oxford Castle and two days later were nailed to the city gates.

Despite the Elizabethan regime's determination to destroy the Catholic underground, threats to the queen's life and to English sovereignty continued unabated. In 1586 Anthony Babington, a Catholic gentleman from Derbyshire, organized a plot to kill

Elizabeth and to place Mary Queen of Scots on the English throne. This was to be followed by invasion from Spain and France, and the restoration of Catholicism. Government spies discovered the plans and the conspirators were brutally executed, along with Mary Queen of Scots, who was beheaded in February 1587, aged forty-four, after almost two decades in captivity. The following year the planned Catholic invasion ended in debacle when Philip II's Spanish Armada was routed in the English Channel and then battered by gales. Although they lost only four ships in combat, twenty-eight were sunk by the atrocious weather. English Protestants saw this as a sign of God's good providence and gave him heartfelt thanks for protecting their religious freedoms.

EPILOGUE

Salvation at Stake

Back in 1523, in the early days of the European Reformation, the great Christian humanist, Erasmus of Rotterdam, had triumphantly declared, *Summa nostrae religionis pax est et unanimitas* ("The essence of our religion is peace and unanimity").[1] However, by the end of the century it was apparent that Europe was deeply divided politically, culturally, and theologically. The armed conflict between reformed and Catholic cantons in Switzerland in the 1530s, or between the Lutheran princes of the Schmalkaldic League and the Holy Roman emperor in the 1540s, had been a sign of things to come. Many thousands lost their lives on the battlefield in the religious wars which wreaked havoc in Scotland, France, and the Spanish Netherlands, and which threatened to embroil England too. Hundreds of others were willing to endure the agonies of execution from hostile regimes, whether burned at the stake or hanged, drawn, and quartered.

The Reformation was a clash of ideologies, and the confessional divide became sharply defined as the century progressed. Alongside heated debates on justification and the Eucharist, there was an explosion of fresh thinking and argumentation on themes such as kingship, nationhood, freedom of conscience, and obedience to authority. The disruption was driven partly by a thirst for political power and economic supremacy, as princes, popes, and peasants sought to build their empires and defend their sovereignty. When evangelicals and Catholics went their separate ways they rapidly developed divergent cultures, with their own foundational narratives, community rituals, and contrasting attitudes to music, literature, and artistic expression.

While monasteries, pilgrimages, shrines, altars, and icons continued to dominate the visual landscape of Catholic nations, they were almost entirely erased from Protestant domains. The Reformation even left Europe divided chronologically. In February 1582 Pope Gregory XIII published a bull, *Inter Gravissimas*, which reformed the ancient Julian calendar of the Roman Republic and replaced it with the more accurate Gregorian calendar. The Catholic governments in Spain, Portugal, Italy, and France immediately adopted the new system, beginning the new year on 1 January instead of 25 March, but Protestants were suspicious of this papal interference. Several territories, including England, Scandinavia, and parts of Germany and the Dutch Republic, resisted the change until the eighteenth century.

Underlying all these multifarious conflicts was the question of religious allegiance. European subjects and citizens in the sixteenth century were all agreed that there was more at stake than the material prosperity or happiness of their family, city, or nation. They looked toward an eternal future, which made questions about the Christian gospel of surpassing importance, beyond temporal concerns. The deepest chasm between Catholicism and evangelicalism concerned the questions, "How can I be saved? How can I be in right relationship with Almighty God? How can I be sure of a place in heaven?" The two movements offered conflicting and incompatible answers. Men and women on either side of the confessional divide laid down their lives for these theological convictions, but they could not recognize each other as fellow believers because the chasm was too wide. Robert Southwell, a Jesuit priest who was hanged, drawn, and quartered at Tyburn in 1595, spoke for many when he wrote: "For if all were martyrs, that die for their religion, then many heresies both contrary among themselves, and repugnant to the evident doctrine of Christ, should be truths, which is impossible."[2] The Reformation caused a cataclysmic and permanent rupture throughout Europe, dividing families and communities as never before. Yet they were willing to pay that painful price in their pursuit of eternal salvation.

222

Notes

Prologue

1. Euan Cameron, *The European Reformation* (Oxford, 1991), p. 1.

Chapter 1

1. Diarmaid MacCulloch, *Reformation: Europe's House Divided, 1490–1700* (London, 2003), p. 106.

2. *Collected Works of Erasmus* (86 volumes, Toronto, 1974–2009), vol. 1, p. 203.

3. *Collected Works of Erasmus*, vol. 4, p. 261.

4. John C. Olin (ed.), *Catholic Reform from Cardinal Ximenes to the Council of Trent, 1495–1563* (New York, 1990), pp. 63–64.

5. *Collected Works of Erasmus*, vol. 1, pp. 308–309.

6. *Collected Works of Erasmus*, vol. 2, p. 87.

7. *Collected Works of Erasmus*, vol. 6, p. 108.

8. John C. Olin (ed.), *Desiderius Erasmus: Christian Humanism and the Reformation* (London, 1965), p. 95.

9. Olin, *Erasmus*, pp. 105–106.

10. Olin, *Erasmus*, p. 105.

11. Olin, *Erasmus*, pp. 98–100.

12. Olin, *Erasmus*, p. 96.

13. Olin, *Erasmus*, p. 97.

14. Erika Rummel, *Erasmus* (London, 2004), p. 43.

15. *Collected Works of Erasmus*, vol. 66, pp. 79, 81.

16. *Collected Works of Erasmus*, vol. 66, p. 71.

17. Cameron, *European Reformation*, p. 67.

18. John C. Olin (ed.), *The Catholic Reformation: Savonarola to Ignatius Loyola* (new edition, New York, 1992), p. 76.

19. Olin, *Catholic Reformation*, p. 80.

20. Olin, *Catholic Reformation*, p. 88.

21. MacCulloch, *Reformation*, p. 52.

22. A. G. Dickens and Dorothy Carr (eds.), *The Reformation in England to the Accession of Elizabeth I* (London, 1967), p. 15.

23. Olin, *Catholic Reformation*, p. 31.

24. Olin, *Catholic Reformation*, p. 53.

25. Olin, *Catholic Reformation*, p. 55.

26. Erasmus, *Praise of Folly*, edited by A. H. T. Levi (new edition, London, 1993), p. 66.

27. Erasmus, *Praise of Folly*, p. 74.

28. Erasmus, *Praise of Folly*, p. 88.

29. Erasmus, *Praise of Folly*, p. 107.

30. Erasmus, *Praise of Folly*, p. 109.

31. Erasmus, *Praise of Folly*, p. 110.

32. *Collected Works of Erasmus*, vol. 27, p. 169.

33. *Collected Works of Erasmus*, vol. 27, p. 194.

34. Erasmus, *Praise of Folly*, pp. 147, 154.

CHAPTER 2

1. Gordon Rupp and Benjamin Drewery, *Martin Luther* (London, 1970), p. 2.

2. Heiko A. Oberman, *Luther: Man between God and the Devil* (New Haven, 1989), p. 93.

3. Rupp and Drewery, *Luther*, p. 4.

4. Oberman, *Luther*, p. 137.

5. Oberman, *Luther*, p. 128.

6. Norman P. Tanner (ed.), *Decrees of the Ecumenical Councils* (2 vols, London, 1990), vol. 2, p. 712.

7. Richard Marius, *Martin Luther: The Christian between God and Death* (Cambridge, Mass., 1999), p. 59.

8. Rupp and Drewery, *Luther*, p. 4.

9. *Luther's Works* (56 vols, Philadelphia, 1955–86), vol. 48, p. 65–66.

10. *Luther's Works*, vol. 36, pp. 83, 85.

11. *Luther's Works*, vol. 41, p. 279.

12. Oberman, *Luther*, p. 147.

13. *Luther's Works*, vol. 54, p. 309.

14. Rupp and Drewery, *Luther*, p. 6.

15. Rupp and Drewery, *Luther*, p. 6.

16. Oberman, *Luther*, p. 165.

17. Alister McGrath, *Luther's Theology of the Cross* (Oxford, 1985), pp. 133–34.

18. *Luther: Lectures on Romans*, edited by Wilhelm Pauck (London, 1961), p. 322.

19. Oberman, *Luther*, p. 188.

20. Marius, *Luther,* p. 135.

21. Rupp and Drewery, *Luther*, pp. 17–18.

22. Oberman, *Luther*, p. 195.

23. Roland Bainton, *Here I Stand: A Life of Martin Luther* (New York, 1950), pp. 69–70.

24. Rupp and Drewery, *Luther*, p. 32.

25. Marius, *Luther*, p. 164.

26. Rupp and Drewery, *Luther*, p. 26.

27. *Luther's Works*, vol. 48, p. 107.

28. Marius, *Luther*, p. 178.

29. *Luther's Works*, vol. 48, p. 114.

30. *Luther's Works*, vol. 44, p. 123.

31. *Luther's Works*, vol. 44, pp. 129–30.

32. *Luther's Works*, vol. 44, pp. 143, 197.

33. *Luther's Works*, vol. 44, p. 153.

34. *Luther's Works*, vol. 36, pp. 31, 35.

35. *Luther's Works*, vol. 36, pp. 71–73.

36. *Luther's Works*, vol. 31, pp. 344, 348, 359.

37. *Luther's Works*, vol. 31, p. 343.

38. *Luther's Works*, vol. 31, p. 336.

39. Rupp and Drewery, *Luther*, p. 37.

40. Martin Brecht, *Martin Luther: His Road to Reformation 1483–1521* (Philadelphia, 1985), p. 424.

41. Rupp and Drewery, *Luther*, p. 64.

42. *Luther's Works*, vol. 48, p. 189.

43. *Luther's Works*, vol. 48, pp. 198, 390.

44. *Luther's Works*, vol. 32, p. 107.

45. *Luther's Works*, vol. 32, pp. 109–11.

46. Marius, *Luther*, p. 292.

47. *Luther's Works*, vol. 32, pp. 112–13.

48. Marius, *Luther*, p. 294.

49. Oberman, *Luther*, p. 199.

50. Marius, *Luther*, p. 294.

51. Rupp and Drewery, *Luther*, p. 70.

52. Rupp and Drewery, *Luther*, pp. 61–62.

53. *Collected Works of Erasmus*, vol. 8, p. 72.

54. *Luther's Works*, vol. 48, p. 263.

55. *Luther's Works*, vol. 32, p. 259.

56. Owen Chadwick, *The Early Reformation on the Continent* (Oxford, 2001), p. 234.

57. Marius, *Luther*, p. 319.

58. Oberman, *Luther*, pp. 229–30.

59. *Luther's Works*, vol. 51, p. 76.

60. *Luther's Works*, vol. 51, pp. 77, 81.

61. *Luther's Works*, vol. 51, p. 91.

62. *Luther's Works*, vol. 40, pp. 79, 89.

CHAPTER 3

1. Peter Matheson (ed.), *The Collected Works of Thomas Müntzer* (Edinburgh, 1988), p. 22.

2. Matheson, *Collected Works*, p. 30.

3. Michael G. Baylor (ed.), *The Radical Reformation* (Cambridge, 1991), pp. 2, 6, 8.

4. Baylor, *Radical Reformation*, pp. 3–5.

5. Baylor, *Radical Reformation*, p. 10.

6. Matheson, *Collected Works*, p. 54.

7. Matheson, *Collected Works*, p. 67.

8. Tom Scott, *Thomas Müntzer: Theology and Revolution in the German Reformation* (Basingstoke, 1989), p. 66.

9. Baylor, *Radical Reformation*, pp. 12, 16, 20–23, 25.

10. Baylor, *Radical Reformation*, p. 28.

11. Baylor, *Radical Reformation*, p. 31.

12. Matheson, *Collected Works*, p. 90.

13. Matheson, *Collected Works*, p. 99.

14. *Luther's Works*, vol. 40, pp. 48–49.

15. Hans-Jürgen Goertz, *Thomas Müntzer: Apocalyptic Mystic and Revolutionary* (Edinburgh, 1993), p. 138.

16. Baylor, *Radical Reformation*, pp. 75, 80, 89–90.

17. Baylor, *Radical Reformation*, p. 230.

18. Scott, *Müntzer*, p. 144.

19. Baylor, *Radical Reformation*, p. 237.

20. Oberman, *Luther*, p. 289.

21. *Luther's Works*, vol. 36, p. 72.

22. Harro Höpfl (ed.), *Luther and Calvin on Secular Authority* (Cambridge, 1991), p. 30.

23. Marius, *Luther*, p. 345.

24. Marius, *Luther*, p. 428.

25. *Luther's Works*, vol. 46, pp. 20–23.

26. *Luther's Works*, vol. 46, pp. 32–33.

27. *Luther's Works*, vol. 46, p. 42.

28. *Luther's Works*, vol. 46, pp. 50–53.

29. Marius, *Luther*, p. 433.

30. Matheson, *Collected Works*, pp. 141–42.

31. *Luther's Works*, vol. 46, p. 49.

32. Matheson, *Collected Works*, p. 144.

33. Matheson, *Collected Works*, p. 148.

34. Matheson, *Collected Works*, p. 158.

35. Matheson, *Collected Works*, pp. 155–56.

36. Matheson, *Collected Works*, p. 157.

37. Matheson, *Collected Works*, p. 159.

38. *Luther's Works*, vol. 48, p. 40.

39. *Luther's Works*, vol. 48, pp. 53–54.

40. Oberman, *Luther*, p. 300.

41. *Luther's Works*, vol. 48, pp. 53, 306.

42. *Collected Works of Erasmus*, vol. 6, pp. 391–92.

43. *Collected Works of Erasmus*, vol. 7, pp. 111–12.

44. *Collected Works of Erasmus*, vol. 8, p. 117.

45. Gordon Rupp, *The Righteousness of God: Luther Studies* (London, 1953), p. 267.

46. *Collected Works of Erasmus*, vol. 8, p. 171.

47. Rupp and Drewery, *Luther*, p. 128.

48. Gordon Rupp and Philip Watson (eds.), *Luther and Erasmus: Free Will and Salvation* (London, 1969), p. 333.

49. Rupp and Watson, *Luther and Erasmus*, p. 102.

50. Johan Huizinga, *Erasmus and the Age of Reformation* (London, 2002), p. 165.

51. *Luther's Works*, vol. 54, pp. 19, 77, 84, 189; A. G. Dickens, *Martin Luther and the Reformation* (London, 1967), p. 86.

52. A. G. Dickens and W. R. D. Jones, *Erasmus the Reformer* (London, 1994), p. 138.

CHAPTER 4

1. G. R. Potter (ed.), *Huldrych Zwingli* (London, 1978), p. 94.

2. Ulrich Gäbler, *Huldrych Zwingli: His Life and Work* (Edinburgh, 1987), p. 31.

3. Gäbler, *Zwingli*, pp. 53–54.

4. Gäbler, *Zwingli*, p. 56.

5. Gäbler, *Zwingli*, p. 61.

6. Potter, *Huldrych Zwingli*, p. 18.

7. G. R. Potter, *Zwingli* (Cambridge, 1976), p. 81.

8. Potter, *Huldrych Zwingli*, pp. 21–25.

9. Potter, *Zwingli*, p. 102.

10. Potter, *Huldrych Zwingli*, p. 26.

11. Potter, *Zwingli*, p. 106.

12. Potter, *Huldrych Zwingli*, p. 26.

13. Potter, *Zwingli*, p. 130.

14. Gäbler, *Zwingli*, p. 80.

15. Potter, *Huldrych Zwingli*, p. 54.

16. Potter, *Zwingli*, p. 186.

17. Leland Harder (ed.), *The Sources of Swiss Anabaptism: The Grebel Letters and Related Documents* (Scottdale, PA, 1985), p. 276.

18. Hans-Jürgen Goertz, *The Anabaptists* (London, 1996), p. 10.

19. Harder, *Sources of Swiss Anabaptism*, p. 290.

20. Potter, *Huldrych Zwingli*, p. 41.

21. Potter, *Zwingli*, p. 185.

22. Potter, *Huldrych Zwingli*, p. 44.

23. Potter, *Huldrych Zwingli*, p. 55.

24. Potter, *Huldrych Zwingli*, p. 87.

25. Potter, *Huldrych Zwingli*, p. 113.

26. Potter, *Huldrych Zwingli*, p. 120.

27. Potter, *Huldrych Zwingli*, p. 83.

28. Oberman, *Luther*, p. 237.

29. *Luther's Works*, vol. 37, p. 231.

30. *Luther's Works*, vol. 36, pp. 31–33.

31. Potter, *Huldrych Zwingli*, p. 106.

32. Rupp and Drewery, *Luther*, pp. 138–39.

33. *Luther's Works*, vol. 49, p. 237.

34. Rupp and Drewery, *Luther*, p. 137.

35. *Luther's Works*, vol. 54, pp. 11, 152.

CHAPTER 5

1. Baylor, *Radical Reformation*, pp. 176–77.

2. Thieleman J. van Braght, *Martyrs Mirror* (Scottdale, PA, 2006), p. 419.

3. William R. Estep, *The Anabaptist Story: An Introduction to Sixteenth-Century Anabaptism* (third edition, Grand Rapids, 1996), p. 67.

4. Gustav Bossert, "Michael Sattler's Trial and Martyrdom in 1527", *Mennonite Quarterly Review* vol. 25 (1951), p. 214.

5. Bossert, "Michael Sattler's Trial", p. 216.

6. Bossert, "Michael Sattler's Trial", p. 217.

7. Henry C. Vedder, *Balthasar Hübmaier: The Leader of the Anabaptists* (London, 1905), p. 78.

8. Goertz, *Anabaptists*, p. 40.

9. Wayne Pipkin and John Yoder, *Balthasar Hubmaier: Theologian of Anabaptism* (Scottdale, PA, 1989), p. 49.

10. Pipkin and Yoder, *Hubmaier*, p. 66.

11. Estep, *Anabaptist Story*, p. 92.

12. Pipkin and Yoder, *Hubmaier*, p. 240.

13. Pipkin and Yoder, *Hubmaier*, p. 526.

14. Vedder, *Hübmaier*, pp. 242–44.

15. Goertz, *Anabaptists*, p. 121.

16. Marius, *Luther*, pp. 255–56.

17. Goertz, *Anabaptists*, p. 125.

18. Goertz, *Anabaptists*, p. 21.

19. Goertz, *Anabaptists*, p. 122.

20. Van Braght, *Martyrs Mirror*, p. 437.

21. Goertz, *Anabaptists*, p. 162.

22. James M. Stayer, *Anabaptists and the Sword* (second edition, Lawrence, Kansas, 1976), p. 211.

23. Goertz, *Anabaptists*, p. 31.

24. Stayer, *Anabaptists and the Sword*, pp. 251–52.

25. Stayer, *Anabaptists and the Sword*, p. 258.

26. Stayer, *Anabaptists and the Sword*, p. 262.

27. Stayer, *Anabaptists and the Sword*, p. 276.

28. Stayer, *Anabaptists and the Sword*, p. 272.

29. John C. Wenger (ed.), *The Complete Writings of Menno Simons* (Scottdale, PA, 1956), p. 668.

30. Wenger, *Menno Simons*, p. 669.

31. Wenger, *Menno Simons*, p. 670.

32. Wenger, *Menno Simons*, p. 670.

33. Goertz, *Anabaptists*, p. 153.

34. Wenger, *Menno Simons*, p. 674.

CHAPTER 6

1. Henry VIII, *His Defence of the Faith and its Seven Sacraments* (London, 2008), pp. xxxiv, 148–49.

2. John Foxe, *Acts and Monuments*, edited by Josiah Pratt (8 vols, London, 1877), vol. 4, p. 635.

3. Foxe, *Acts and Monuments*, vol. 4, p. 642.

4. David Daniell, *William Tyndale: A Biography* (New Haven, 1994), p. 79.

5. Charles Sturge, *Cuthbert Tunstal* (London, 1938), p. 132.

6. William Tyndale, *Doctrinal Treatises and Introductions to Different Portions of the Holy Scriptures* (Cambridge, 1848), p. 48.

7. Tyndale, *Doctrinal Treatises*, pp. 43–44.

8. *The Complete Works of St Thomas More* (15 vols, New Haven, 1963–97), vol. 6, part 1, p. 291.

9. William Tyndale, *The Obedience of a Christian Man*, edited by David Daniell (London, 2000), pp. 103–104.

10. Tyndale, *Obedience*, p. 82.

11. Tyndale, *Obedience*, p. 126.

12. Tyndale, *Obedience*, p. 41.

13. Daniell, *William Tyndale*, p. 277.

14. Foxe, *Acts and Monuments*, vol. 4, pp. 659–64.

15. *Complete Works of St Thomas More*, vol. 8, part 1, pp. 16–17.

16. G. E. Corrie (ed.), *Sermons by Hugh Latimer* (Cambridge, 1844), p. 222.

17. Foxe, *Acts and Monuments*, vol. 4, p. 655.

18. *Complete Works of St Thomas More*, vol. 8, part 1, p. 17.

19. Foxe, *Acts and Monuments*, vol. 5, p. 23.

20. Richard Marius, *Thomas More: A Biography* (London, 1985), p. 406.

21. Foxe, *Acts and Monuments*, vol. 4, p. 705.

22. Foxe, *Acts and Monuments*, vol. 5, p. 31.

23. Foxe, *Acts and Monuments*, vol. 5, pp. 131–32.

24. Foxe, *Acts and Monuments*, vol. 5, p. 15.

25. G. W. Bernard, *The King's Reformation: Henry VIII and the Remaking of the English Church* (Yale, 2005), p. 65.

26. Gerald Bray (ed.), *Documents of the English Reformation* (Cambridge, 2004), p. 114.

27. Christopher Haigh, *English Reformations: Religion, Politics and Society Under the Tudors* (Oxford, 1993), p. 141.

28. Richard Rex, *Henry VIII and the English Reformation* (second edition, Basingstoke, 2006), p. 18.

29. Haigh, *English Reformations*, p. 138.

30. Haigh, *English Reformations*, p. 118.

31. William Roper and Nicholas Harpsfield, *Lives of Saint Thomas More* (London, 1963), pp. 161–62.

32. Bray, *Documents*, p. 163.

33. Bray, *Documents*, p. 180.

34. Bray, *Documents*, p. 180.

35. J. E Cox (ed.), *Miscellaneous Writings and Letters of Thomas Cranmer* (Cambridge, 1846), p. 120.

36. Foxe, *Acts and Monuments*, vol. 5, p. 127.

37. Foxe, *Acts and Monuments*, vol. 5, p. 236.

38. Foxe, *Acts and Monuments*, vol. 5, p. 262.

39. Hastings Robinson (ed.), *Original Letters Relative to the English Reformation* (2 vols, Cambridge, 1846–47), vol. 1, pp. 36, 41.

CHAPTER 7

1. Mack P. Holt, *The French Wars of Religion, 1562–1629* (second edition, Cambridge, 2005), p. 17.

2. Bernard Cottret, *Calvin: A Biography* (Edinburgh, 2000), p. 85.

3. Holt, *French Wars of Religion*, p. 18.

4. R. J. Knecht, *Renaissance Warrior and Patron: The Reign of Francis I* (Cambridge, 1994), pp. 316–17.

5. *Calvin: Commentaries*, edited by Joseph Haroutunian and Louise Pettibone Smith (London, 1958), p. 52.

6. *Calvin: Institutes of the Christian Religion*, edited by John T. McNeill and translated by Ford Lewis Battles (2 vols, Philadelphia, 1960), vol. 1, p. 31.

7. *Institutes*, vol. 1, p. 11.

8. *Institutes*, vol. 1, p. 27.

9. *Institutes*, vol. 1, p. 14.

10. Alister McGrath, *A Life of John Calvin: A Study in the Shaping of Western Culture* (Oxford, 1990), pp. 94–95.

11. *Calvin: Commentaries*, p. 53.

12. Cottret, *Calvin*, pp. 130–31.

13. Cottret, *Calvin*, p. 146.

14. Cottret, *Calvin*, p. 149.

15. *John Calvin: Tracts and Letters* (7 vols, Edinburgh, 2009), vol. 4, p. 72.

16. *John Calvin: Tracts and Letters*, vol. 4, p. 187.

17. G. R. Potter and Mark Greengrass, *John Calvin* (London, 1983), p. 55.

18. Steven Ozment, *The Age of Reform 1250–1550* (London, 1980), p. 366.

19. Cottret, *Calvin*, pp. 174–78.

20. Potter and Greengrass, *John Calvin*, pp. 79–80.

21. Cottret, *Calvin*, p. 189.

22. Potter and Greengrass, *John Calvin*, p. 98.

23. Cottret, *Calvin*, p. 5.

24. Potter and Greengrass, *John Calvin*, p. 105.

25. Roland Bainton, *Hunted Heretic: The Life and Death of Michael Servetus, 1511–1553* (revised edition, Providence, Rhode Island, 2005), p. 105.

26. Potter and Greengrass, *John Calvin*, p. 107.

27. Bainton, *Hunted Heretic*, pp. 139–40.

28. Bainton, *Hunted Heretic*, p. 142.

29. Bainton, *Hunted Heretic*, p. 152.

30. Cottret, *Calvin*, p. 226.

31. Potter and Greengrass, *John Calvin*, p. 101.

32. Cottret, *Calvin*, p. 232.

33. Cottret, *Calvin*, p. 232.

34. Cottret, *Calvin*, p. 225.

35. Potter and Greengrass, *John Calvin*, p. 101.

36. *Institutes* II.xiv.8.

37. Cottret, *Calvin*, p. 196.

38. David Laing (ed.), *The Works of John Knox* (6 vols, Edinburgh, 1846–64), vol. 4, p. 240.

CHAPTER 8

1. Olin, *Catholic Reformation*, p. 119.

2. Olin, *Catholic Reformation*, p. 122.

3. Olin, *Catholic Reformation*, p. 125.

4. Olin, *Catholic Reformation*, p. 126.

5. Olin, *Catholic Reformation*, p. 121.

6. *Luther's Works*, vol. 49, p. 169.

7. Martin D. W. Jones, *The Counter Reformation: Religion and Society in Early Modern England* (Cambridge, 1995), p. 45.

8. Jones, *Counter Reformation*, p. 66.

9. Olin, *Catholic Reformation*, pp. 191, 193, 196.

10. Olin, *Catholic Reformation*, p. 197.

11. *Luther's Works*, vol. 34, p. 239.

12. Joseph Munitiz and Philip Endean (eds.), *Saint Ignatius of Loyola: Personal Writings* (London, 1996), p. 16.

13. Munitiz and Endean, *Saint Ignatius of Loyola*, p. 23.

14. Michael A. Mullet, *The Catholic Reformation* (London, 1999), p. 87.

15. Olin, *Catholic Reformation*, p. 204.

16. Munitiz and Endean, *Saint Ignatius of Loyola*, p. 358.

17. J. K. S. Reid (ed.), *Calvin: Theological Treatises* (London, 1954), p. 185.

18. *John Calvin: Tracts and Letters*, vol. 1, pp. 260, 276.

19. *Luther's Works*, vol. 41, pp. 263–64.

20. *Luther's Works*, vol. 41, pp. 263, 352.

21. *Luther's Works*, vol. 41, pp. 257–58.

22. Tanner, *Decrees*, vol. 2, p. 661.

23. Tanner, *Decrees*, vol. 2, p. 663.

24. Mullett, *Catholic Reformation*, p. 40.

25. Tanner, *Decrees*, vol. 2, pp. 664–65.

26. Tanner, *Decrees*, vol. 2, p. 679.

27. Tanner, *Decrees*, vol. 2, p. 722.

28. MacCulloch, *Reformation*, p. 231.

29. Robert Bireley, *The Refashioning of Catholicism, 1450–1700: A Reassessment of the Counter Reformation* (Basingstoke, 1999), p. 52.

30. Mullett, *Catholic Reformation*, p. 68.

31. Oberman, *Luther*, p. 150.

32. Jones, *Counter Reformation*, p. 4.

CHAPTER 9

1. Cox, *Miscellaneous Writings of Thomas Cranmer*, p. 127.

2. Bruce Gordon, *Calvin* (London, 2009), p. 254.

3. Bray, *Documents*, p. 255.

4. Bray, *Documents*, p. 255.

5. *The Two Books of Homilies Appointed to be Read in Churches* (Oxford, 1859), pp. 7, 9.

6. Dickens and Carr, *Reformation in England*, p. 128.

7. Patrick Collinson, *From Cranmer to Sancroft: English Religion in the Age of Reformation* (London, 2006), p. 76.

8. Robinson, *Original Letters*, vol. 1, p. 69.

9. *The First and Second Prayer Books of Edward VI* (London, 1957), pp. 3–4.

10. *First and Second Prayer Books*, pp. 286–88.

11. Anthony Fletcher and Diarmaid MacCulloch, *Tudor Rebellions* (fifth edition, 2004), pp. 151–52.

12. Fletcher and MacCulloch, *Tudor Rebellions*, pp. 64–65.

13. Robinson, *Original Letters*, vol. 1, p. 79.

14. Bray, *Documents*, pp. 281–82.

15. *First and Second Prayer Books*, pp. 388–89.

16. *First and Second Prayer Books*, pp. 225, 389.

17. Diarmaid MacCulloch, *Thomas Cranmer: A Life* (London, 1996), p. 526; David Loades, *John Dudley, Duke of Northumberland, 1504–1553* (Oxford, 1996), p. 198.

18. Bray, *Documents*, p. 291.

19. Bray, *Documents*, p. 287.

20. Bray, *Documents*, p. 297.

21. Bray, *Documents*, pp. 301–303.

22. Haigh, *English Reformations*, p. 205.

23. Haigh, *English Reformations*, p. 206.

24. Alec Ryrie, *The Age of Reformation: The Tudor and Stewart Realms 1485–1603* (Harlow, 2009), p. 178.

25. Robinson, *Original Letters*, vol. 2, p. 515.

26. Foxe, *Acts and Monuments*, vol. 7, p. 573.

27. Foxe, *Acts and Monuments*, vol. 6, p. 536.

28. Foxe, *Acts and Monuments*, vol. 6, p. 572.

29. Robinson, *Original Letters*, vol. 1, p. 105.

30. Foxe, *Acts and Monuments*, vol. 6, p. 611.

31. Aubrey Townsend (ed.), *The Writings of John Bradford* (2 vols, Cambridge, 1848–53), vol. 2, p. 190.

32. Foxe, *Acts and Monuments*, vol. 6, p. 628.

33. Foxe, *Acts and Monuments*, vol. 7, p. 53.

34. Foxe, *Acts and Monuments*, vol. 8, p. 502.

35. Eamon Duffy, *Fires of Faith: Catholic England under Mary Tudor* (London, 2009), p. 186.

36. Foxe, *Acts and Monuments*, vol. 7, p. 550.

37. Foxe, *Acts and Monuments*, vol. 8, p. 88.

38. MacCulloch, *Thomas Cranmer*, p. 603.

39. Foxe, *Acts and Monuments*, vol. 6, p. 645.

40. John Knox, *On Rebellion*, edited by Roger A. Mason (Cambridge, 1994), pp. 46–47.

41. Bray, *Documents*, p. 323.

CHAPTER 10

1. Laing, *Works of John Knox*, vol. 1, p. 177.

2. Foxe, *Acts and Monuments*, vol. 5, p. 636.

3. Gordon Donaldson, *Scottish Historical Documents* (Edinburgh, 1970), p. 116.

4. Foxe, *Acts and Monuments*, vol. 5, p. 647.

5. Laing, *Works of John Knox*, vol. 1, p. 260.

6. Knox, *On Rebellion*, pp. 49, 53, 66.

7. Knox, *On Rebellion*, p. 86.

8. Laing, *Works of John Knox*, vol. 1, p. 316.

9. Alec Ryrie, *The Origins of the Scottish Reformation* (Manchester, 2006), p. 187.

10. Hastings Robinson (ed.), *The Zurich Letters* (2 vols, Cambridge, 1842–45), vol. 1, pp. 39–40.

11. Laing, *Works of John Knox*, vol. 2, p. 24.

12. Donaldson, *Scottish Historical Documents*, p. 119.

13. Laing, *Works of John Knox*, vol. 2, p. 86.

14. Laing, *Works of John Knox*, vol. 2, p. 276.

15. Laing, *Works of John Knox*, vol. 2, pp. 278, 283–86.

16. Laing, *Works of John Knox*, vol. 2, p. 428.

17. Rosalind K. Marshall, *John Knox* (Edinburgh, 2008), p. 193.

18. *John Calvin: Tracts and Letters*, vol. 5, p. 321.

19. *John Calvin: Tracts and Letters*, vol. 6, p. 360.

20. *John Calvin: Tracts and Letters*, vol. 7, p. 52.

21. *John Calvin: Tracts and Letters*, vol. 7, p. 86.

22. Mark Greengrass, *The French Reformation* (Oxford, 1987), p. 40.

23. Holt, *French Wars of Religion*, p. 38.

24. William Naphy (ed.), *Documents on the Continental Reformation* (Basingstoke, 1996), p. 128.

25. *John Calvin: Tracts and Letters*, vol. 7, p. 67.

26. *John Calvin: Tracts and Letters*, vol. 7, p. 176.

27. Holt, *French Wars of Religion*, p. 48.

28. Greengrass, *French Reformation*, p. 63.

29. Greengrass, *French Reformation*, p. 67.

30. Holt, *French Wars of Religion*, p. 74.

31. Greengrass, *French Reformation*, p. 78.

32. Jonathan Israel, *The Dutch Republic: Its Rise, Greatness and Fall, 1477–1806* (Oxford, 1995), p. 148.

33. Israel, *Dutch Republic*, p. 162.

34. C. V. Wedgwood, *William the Silent* (new edition, London, 1956), p. 213.

35. Wedgwood, *William the Silent*, p. 250.

36. Haigh, *English Reformations*, p. 248.

37. Fletcher and MacCulloch, *Tudor Rebellions*, p. 163.

38. Fletcher and MacCulloch, *Tudor Rebellions*, p. 163.

39. Fletcher and MacCulloch, *Tudor Rebellions*, p. 114.

40. Geoffrey Elton (ed.), *The Tudor Constitution: Documents and Commentary* (second edition, Cambridge, 1982), pp. 425–27.

41. Ryrie, *Age of Reformation*, p. 235.

42. Laing, *Works of John Knox*, vol. 6, p. 568.

43. Elton, *Tudor Constitution*, p. 430.

44. W. H. Frere and C. E. Douglas (eds), *Puritan Manifestoes* (new edition, London, 1954), pp. 9, 19, 21.

45. William Nicholson (ed.), *The Remains of Edmund Grindal* (Cambridge, 1843), pp. 379, 387.

46. Haigh, *English Reformations*, p. 254.

47. *The History of the University of Oxford*, vol. 3, *The Collegiate University*, edited by James McConica (Oxford, 1986), p. 389.

48. Haigh, *English Reformations*, p. 263.

49. Evelyn Waugh, *Two Lives: Edmund Campion – Ronald Knox* (London, 2001), p. 80.

50. Waugh, *Two Lives*, pp. 123–25.

51. E. E. Reynolds, *Campion and Parsons: The Jesuit Mission of 1580–1* (London, 1980), p. 104.

52. Waugh, *Two Lives*, pp. 119–20.

53. Katharine Longley, *Saint Margaret Clitherow* (Wheathampstead, 1986), p. 160.

54. Roland Connelly, *The Women of the Catholic Resistance in England, 1540–1680* (Edinburgh, 1997), p. 73.

55. Christine Kelly, *Blessed Thomas Belson: His Life and Times, 1563–1589* (Gerrards Cross, 1987), p. 3.

EPILOGUE

1. James McConica, *Erasmus* (Oxford, 1991), p. 77.

2. Brad S. Gregory, *Salvation at Stake: Christian Martyrdom in Early Modern Europe* (London, 1999), p. 315.

Index

V

Valla, Lorenzo 7
Vallière, Jean 129
Van Batenburg, Jan 106
Van Brederode, Hendrik 206–207
Van Dorp, Maarten 19
Vatable, Françoise 129
Vermigli, Pietro Martire 174, 177, 182, 194, 203
Viret, Pierre 136–37, 140
Virgin Mary 3, 7, 15, 18, 20, 26, 29, 44, 63, 65, 89, 117, 130, 141, 158–59
Von Bora, Katherine 57
Von der Ecken, Johann 36
Von Mansfeld, Albrecht 56
Von Mansfeld, Ernst 44
Von Staupitz, Johannes 22, 24
Von Watt, Joachim 75
Von Zimmern, Katharina 73
Vulgate 7, 9, 11–12, 22, 73, 111, 167

W

Walpole, Henry 219
Ward, Margaret 219
Warham, William 119
Western Rebellion 175
White, Rawlins 185
Whitgift, John 214
Wiedemann, Jakob 96–97
Wilcox, Thomas 213
Willem of Orange 207–208
William of Ockham 6, 16
Wishart, George 191–92
Wolsey, Thomas 111–12, 115, 118
Wriothesley, Thomas 128
Wyatt, Thomas 182
Wycliffe, John 11, 112

X

Xavier, Francisco 162
Ximenes, Francisco 8

Z

Zwilling, Gabriel 39
Zwingli, Huldrych 62–76, 78–88, 92–93, 95, 98, 100, 112, 125, 127, 173, 186